"At this moment of housing crisis in large cities, Liz Falletta's impressively researched and illustrated case studies provide much-needed historical context, illuminating how choices made collaboratively by real estate developers, architects, and urban planners can create long-term economic value and an enduring design legacy in our communities."

—Ken Bernstein, Manager and Principal City Planner, Los Angeles Department of City Planning, Office of Historic Resources

"Through analysis and illustration – including vintage images – Falletta successfully uses past precedent to raise the plane of current discussions in the contested field where partisans are currently battling over the future of California housing policy. Her nuanced examination of form, product and design amenity is a must-read for those hoping to better understand how housing is developed, and how decisions made in the design and development processes can yield quantifiably different results."

—Steve Preston, FAICP, Vice President, Los Angeles Regional Planning History Group

By-Right, By-Design

Housing is an essential, but complex, product, so complex that professionals involved in its production, namely, architects, real estate developers and urban planners, have difficulty agreeing on "good" housing outcomes. Less-than-optimal solutions that have resulted from a too narrow focus on one discipline over others are familiar: high design that is costly to build that makes little contribution to the public realm, highly profitable but seemingly identical "cookie-cutter" dwellings with no sense of place and well-planned neighborhoods full of generically designed, unmarketable product types.

Differing roles, languages and criteria for success shape these perspectives, which, in turn, influence attitudes about housing regulation. Real estate developers, for example, prefer projects that can be built "as-of-right" or "by-right," meaning that they can be approved quickly because they meet all current planning, zoning and building code requirements. Design-focused projects, heretofore "by-design," by contrast, often require time to challenge existing regulatory codes, pursuing discretionary modifications meant to maximize design innovation and development potential. Meanwhile, urban planners work to establish and mediate the threshold between by-right and by-design processes by setting housing standards and determining appropriate housing policy. But just what is the right line between "by-right" and "by-design"?

By-Right, By-Design provides historical perspectives, conceptual frameworks and practical strategies that cross and connect the diverse professions involved in housing production. The heart of the book is a set of six cross-disciplinary comparative case studies, each examining a significant Los Angeles housing design precedent approved by-variance and its associated development type approved as of right. Each comparison tells a different story about the often-hidden relationships among the three primary disciplines shaping the built environment, some of which uphold, and others of which transgress, conventional disciplinary stereotypes.

Liz Falletta (Master of Architecture, Southern California Institute of Architecture; Master of Real Estate Development, University of Southern California [USC]) teaches architectural and urban design at USC's Price School of Public Policy. Her courses focus on design as an interdisciplinary activity and explore how the intersecting values of architecture, urban planning and real estate development can inform the design process and improve design outcomes. She is a licensed architect in the State of California, a member of the California Planning Roundtable and the developer of one of Los Angeles' first Small Lot Subdivisions.

Routledge Research in Planning and Urban Design

Routledge Research in Planning and Urban Design is a series of academic monographs for scholars working in these disciplines and the overlaps between them. Building on Routledge's history of academic rigor and cutting-edge research, the series contributes to the rapidly expanding literature in all areas of planning and urban design.

Post Socialist Urban Infrastructures
Edited by Tauri Tuvikene, Wladimir Sgibnev, Carola S. Neugebauer

The Metaphysical City
Six Ways of Understanding the Urban Milieu
Rob Sullivan

The City in Geography
Renaturing the Built Environment
Benedict Anderson

Public Infrastructure, Private Finance
Developer Obligations and Responsibilities
Edited by Demetrio Muñoz Gielen and Erwin van der Krabben

Planning Australia's Healthy Built Environments
Jennifer Kent, Susan Thompson

By-Right, By-Design
Housing Development Versus Housing Design in Los Angeles
Liz Falletta

Rebuilding Afghanistan in Times of Crisis
A Global Response
Adenrele Awotona

For more information about this series, please visit www.routledge.com/Routledge-Research-in-Planning-and-Urban-Design/book-series/RRPUD

By-Right, By-Design

Housing Development Versus Housing Design in Los Angeles

Liz Falletta

New York London

First published 2020
by Routledge
52 Vanderbilt Avenue, New York, NY 10017

and by Routledge
2 Park Square, Milton Park, Abingdon, Oxon, OX14 4RN

First issued in paperback 2020

Routledge is an imprint of the Taylor & Francis Group, an informa business

Library of Congress Cataloging-in-Publication Data
Names: Falletta, Liz, author.
Title: By-right, by-design : housing development versus housing design in Los Angeles / Liz Falletta.
Description: New York : Routledge, 2019. | Series: Routledge research in planning and urban design
Identifiers: LCCN 2019003449 (print) | LCCN 2019004073 (ebook) | ISBN 9781351202510 (e-book) | ISBN 9780815385059 (hardback)
Subjects: LCSH: Architecture, Domestic—California—Los Angeles. | Housing development—California—Los Angeles. | Architecture and society—California—Los Angeles.
Classification: LCC NA7238.L6 (ebook) | LCC NA7238.L6 F35 2019 (print) | DDC 728.09794/94—dc23
LC record available at https://lccn.loc.gov/2019003449

ISBN 13: 978-0-367-67062-7 (pbk)
ISBN 13: 978-0-8153-8505-9 (hbk)

Typeset in Sabon
by Apex CoVantage, LLC

With much love to:
Carolyn and John Falletta
David Sloane

Contents

List of Figures x
Acknowledgments xv

Introduction: Housing Values 1

PART 1
Housing Perspectives 17

1 Type in Transition, Proto-Dingbats:
Cheviot Manor Apartments vs. National Apartments 19

2 Value Out of Balance, Single-Family House Tracts:
Hirsh Tract vs. Modernique Homes 52

3 Lost in Translation, Garden Apartments:
Chesapeake Rodeo Apartments vs. Baldwin Hills Village 89

PART 2
Collaborative Models 127

4 Proliferating a Product Type, House Courts:
Clark Court vs. Horatio West Court 129

5 Design Well Timed, Four-Flats:
1060 S. Cochran Avenue vs. Mackey Apartments 164

6 Crafting Cost Benefit, Stucco Box/Podium Apartments:
1411 N. Hayworth Avenue vs.
Hollywood Riviera Apartments 197

Conclusion: Collaborative Prospects 227

Index 234

Figures

All figures not credited in the text are by Liz Falletta, the author.

0.1 Professional housing relationships: Typical disciplinary relationships and roles in housing production 7
0.2 Case study project map: Case study projects are located in the City of Los Angeles in the Mar Vista, Palms, Mid-City West and Baldwin Hills neighborhoods, as well as the Cities of Santa Monica and West Hollywood 11
1.1 Case Study 1: Proto-dingbats, the Cheviot Manor Apartments (left) vs. the National Apartments (right) 19
1.2 A selection of dingbats located in the Palms neighborhood of Los Angeles 21
1.3 The National Apartments and Palms neighborhood dingbats, including the Chevitot Manor (1), mapped 23
1.4 By-right case study project: The Cheviot Manor Apartments located at 10560 National Boulevard in Los Angeles built by Samuel Sheff 23
1.5 By-design case study project: The National Boulevard Apartments located at 10565 National Boulevard in Los Angeles, designed and built by architect Ray Kappe 25
1.6 Ray Kappe, perspective drawing: Apartment Building for Mr. and Mrs. P. Kappe, 1954 25
1.7 Annual construction of apartment house dwelling units surpassed that of single-family homes in 1957 for the first time since the 1920s (LACPC, 1959, p. 10) 28
1.8 Knotty pine kitchens were in vogue in the late 1950s and early 1960s. Here, actress Shirley Ann Chandler poses in one example in her newly built apartment, the Colfax Palms, located at 4300 Colfax Avenue in Studio City 31
1.9 Advertisements for the construction of "Income Units" in the *Los Angeles Times* (Display Ad 134, 1955, F24) 32
1.10 Pedestrian circulation diagrams: The Cheviot Manor Apartments (left) vs. The National Apartments (right) 40

1.11 Common open space diagrams: The Cheviot Manor Apartments (left) vs. The National Apartments (right) 41
1.12 Private open space diagrams: The Cheviot Manor Apartments (left) vs. The National Apartments (right) 42
1.13 Photo collage included in the 1958 Los Angeles City Planning Commission Annual Report illustrating how long curb cuts reduce on-street parking space (LACPC, 1959, p. 37) 46
2.1 Case Study 2: Single-family house tracts, Hirsh Tract (left) vs. the Modernique Homes (right) 52
2.2 A selection of houses in the Hirsh Tract 54
2.3 Modernique Home at 3550 Meier Street and Hirsh Tract houses, including 3559 May Street (1), mapped 55
2.4 Original Modernique Homes site plan with Hirsh Tract overlay by the author, showing the difference between the initially planned gridiron organization and the Hirsh Tract as built with houses organized around cul-de-sacs 57
2.5 By-right case study project: 3559 May Street in the Mar Vista neighborhood of Los Angeles 58
2.6 By-design case study project: Modernique Home at 3550 Meier Street in the Mar Vista neighborhood of Los Angeles 58
2.7 Axonometric drawing of a Modernique Home showing its flexible interior layout which can expand from one up to three bedrooms 59
2.8 Application of the 1930 Los Angeles zoning code to the City's recommended subdivision layout (LACPC, 1932, p. 12). Note that areas for single-family homes are protected by areas for multifamily and commercial on primary and secondary streets 63
2.9 Los Angeles City Planning Department recommended subdivision design strategies in lieu of the gridiron (top), which included alleys, lots backing up to major streets, local service roads and cul-de-sacs (LACPC, 1950, p. 36) 64
2.10 A sample subdivision map as submitted (gridiron) and as revised (cul-de-sacs) by the Los Angeles City Planning Department (LACPC, 1951, p. 33) 65
2.11 Both the Hirsh Tract (right) and the Modernique Homes (left) are disconnected from their surrounding urban context by jogging streets and a service road as well as cul-de-sacs (Hirsh) and an alley (Modernique) 67
2.12 Yards and landscape diagram: The Hirsh Tract (right) contributes less space and planting to the public realm than the Modernique Homes (left) which were articulately landscaped 74
2.13 Advertisement for the Modernique Homes published in the *Los Angeles Times* (Display Ad 74, 1948, p. E5) 81

3.1 Case Study 3: Garden Apartments, Chesapeake Rodeo Apartments (left) vs. Baldwin Hills Village (right) 89
3.2 Garden apartments in the Baldwin Hills neighborhood 91
3.3 Baldwin Hills Village and Garden Apartments in the Baldwin Hills neighborhood, mapped, including The Chesapeake Rodeo Apartments (1) 91
3.4 By-right case study project: The Chesapeake Rodeo Apartments, located at 4616 Rodeo Road in the Baldwin Hills neighborhood of Los Angeles 92
3.5 By-design case study project: Baldwin Hills Village, located at 5300 Rodeo Road in the Baldwin Hills neighborhood of Los Angeles 94
3.6 Detailed site plan of the design of two garden courts and one interlocking garage court at Baldwin Hills Village 94
3.7 Pedestrian circulation diagrams: The Chesapeake Rodeo Apartments (top) vs. Baldwin Hills Village (bottom) 99
3.8 Vehicular circulation diagrams: The Chesapeake Rodeo Apartments (top) vs. Baldwin Hills Village (bottom) 100
3.9 Common open space diagrams: The Chesapeake Rodeo Apartments (top) vs. Baldwin Hills Village (bottom) 101
3.10 Advertisement for Baldwin Hills Village that appeared in the *Los Angeles Times* on January 2, 1942 (Display Ad 29, 1942, B2) 109
3.11 Advertisement for the model apartment at the Chesapeake Rodeo Apartments that appeared in the *Los Angeles Times* on June 28, 1951 (Display Ad 6, 1951, p. 8) 110
3.12 Price range of tenant occupied dwelling units 1940: Most of the rental housing in Los Angeles rented for much less than Baldwin Hills Village at the time it was being planned and built (LACPC, 1943, n.p.). Median monthly rent in Los Angeles in 1940 was $27.83 111
3.13 Automobile registrations rose dramatically between the time Baldwin Hills Village and the Chesapeake Rodeo Apartments were built (LACPC, 1952, p. 13) 117
4.1 Case Study 4: House courts, Clark Court (left) vs. Horatio West Court (right) 129
4.2 House courts in the Ocean Park neighborhood of Santa Monica 130
4.3 Horatio West Court and house courts in the Ocean Park neighborhood of Santa Monica, mapped, including Clark Court (1) 131
4.4 An example of deteriorated court conditions documented by the Housing Commission of the City of Los Angeles in 1908 (Los Angeles Housing Commission, 1908, p. 5) 134

4.5 By-right case study project: Clark Court, located at 2411 Third Street in the Ocean Park neighborhood of Santa Monica 135
4.6 By-design case study project: Horatio West Court, located at 140 Hollister Avenue in the Ocean Park neighborhood of Santa Monica 136
4.7 Axonometric drawing of Horatio West Court, documented in 1968 137
4.8 Unit aggregation diagrams: Clark Court (left) vs. Horatio West Court (right) 140
4.9 Common open space diagrams: Clark Court (left) vs. Horatio West Court (right) 142
4.10 Private open space diagrams: Clark Court (left) vs. Horatio West Court (right) 143
4.11 Commercial development on Third Street in Ocean Park in 1905, around the time the parcels for the case study projects were subdivided 145
4.12 A crowded beach in Ocean Park on July 4, 1919, close to the time Horatio West Court was built 146
4.13 The Housing Commission of the City of Los Angeles considered courts built out of concrete to be ideal (Los Angeles Housing Commission, 1913, p. 30) 153
5.1 Case Study 5: Four-flats, 1060 S. Cochran Avenue (left) vs. Mackey Apartments (right) 164
5.2 A selection of four-flats in the Mid-Wilshire neighborhood of Los Angeles 166
5.3 The Mackey Apartments and four-flats in the Mid-Wilshire neighborhood of Los Angeles, mapped, including 1060 S. Cochran Avenue (1) 167
5.4 By-right case study project: 1060 South Cochran Avenue in the Mid-Wilshire neighborhood of Los Angeles 168
5.5 By-design case study project: Mackey Apartments, located at 1137 South Cochran Avenue in the Mid-Wilshire neighborhood of Los Angeles 169
5.6 The proforma for the Mackey Apartments prepared by architect R. M. Schindler estimated a 15% cash-on-cash return 171
5.7 Mackey Apartments floor plans, with overlay by author showing variable unit configuration 172
5.8 Vehicular access and parking diagrams: 1060 S. Cochran Avenue (left) vs. The Mackey Apartments (right) 176
5.9 Common open space diagrams: 1060 S. Cochran Avenue (left) vs. The Mackey Apartments (right) 177

5.10 Private open space diagrams: 1060 S. Cochran Avenue (left) vs. The Mackey Apartments (right) 178
5.11 A David Barry & Company advertisement for subdivisions in the new Wilshire District (Display Ad 204, 1922, p. V3) 182
5.12 Relative land and building values at the time the case study projects were built. Construction costs returned to pre-depression levels more quickly than Los Angeles land values (Trend Study, 1939, p. E2) 183
5.13 Ratio of lots to population: Los Angeles needed only 109,117 lots to house six people per parcel in 1930 but had a total of 188,532 lots, an excess of nearly 80,000 (LACPC, 1930, p. 51) 188
6.1 Case Study 6: Stucco Box/Podium, 1411 N. Hayworth Avenue vs. Hollywood Riviera Apartments 197
6.2 A selection of stucco box/podium apartment buildings in West Hollywood 199
6.3 The Hollywood Riviera Apartments and stucco box/podium buildings in West Hollywood, mapped, including 1411 N. Hayworth Avenue (1) 200
6.4 By-right case study project: 1411 North Hayworth Avenue in West Hollywood 201
6.5 By-design case study project: The Hollywood Riviera Apartments located at 1400 North Hayworth Avenue in West Hollywood 202
6.6 Rendering of the Hollywood Riviera Apartments early in the design process before Fickett decided to use a butterfly roof on the front volume of the building 203
6.7 Vehicular access and parking diagrams: 1411 North Hayworth Avenue (left) vs. The Hollywood Riviera Apartments (right) 206
6.8 Pedestrian circulation diagrams: 1411 North Hayworth Avenue (left) vs. The Hollywood Riviera Apartments (right) 208
6.9 Common open space diagrams: 1411 North Hayworth Avenue (left) vs. The Hollywood Riviera Apartments (right) 209
6.10 The pool lifestyle was attractive to young apartment dwellers in the 1950s 213
6.11 The Hollywood Riviera Apartment's irregularly shaped courtyard pool 214

Acknowledgments

Many people helped make this project a reality, and I am grateful for love and support from many directions. First, though, thank you to the Los Angeles Forum for Architecture and Urban Design (L.A. Forum) for publishing the article that I realize now, almost 20 years later, eventually became this book. “Same Difference” evaluated Baldwin Hills Village, which had just been named a National Historic Landmark, and Aliso Village, a public housing project slated for imminent demolition. “These projects were built in the same year, shared architects and architectural styles; their budgets, landscaping and planning strategies were similar, yet, after 60 years, one was valorized and the other razed,” I wrote. “How could projects so strikingly alike at their inception follow such radically divergent paths and what can their histories tell us about the value of ‘good design’?” (Falletta, 2001). I understand now that I have been trying to answer this question ever since, propelling me to graduate school in real estate development, trying my hand at small-scale housing development and ultimately teaching design across disciplines to future real estate developers and urban planners at the University of Southern California (USC). The idea of comparing works of “architecture” to their vernacular counterparts, which came from Catherine Bauer’s comparison of Baldwin Hills Village and Los Angeles’s mid-century public housing projects, became a lecture, a housing class and eventually an exhibition, also supported by the L.A. Forum, at the Woodbury University Hollywood Outpost (WUHO) Gallery (Bauer, 1944). I’m sure I haven’t totally figured out the answer to this question, but I still believe it is an important one, and I know I am closer with this book than I was with that first article back in 2001. Thank you to everyone who got me from there to here.

Once I finally got serious about making this material into a book, I benefited from thoughtful feedback and support from many generous colleagues. The four-flat case study was presented at a Lusk Research seminar, the AIA Urban Design Committee and Femmes Fatales VII Pecha Kucha Night sponsored by the Association for Women in Architecture and Design. Colleagues Lise Bornstein, Richard Green, Trudi

Sandmeier, Will Wright and Ed Woll all provided helpful comments in these forums. Three case studies were presented at Lisa Schweitzer's Rebel Planning Seminar, with useful feedback from Lisa, Tridib Banerjee and Sarah Mawhorter. Case studies were also presented at several Association of Collegiate Schools of Planning annual conferences, as well as a Society for American City and Regional Planning History conference at which Margaret Crawford, Bryce Lowery and Rick Willson all had good insights. Kate Diamond and Anthony Guida both had excellent advice during the WUHO Gallery exhibition, which was then exhibited at the USC School of Architecture and the Price School of Public Policy. Overall research outcomes were presented as part of the ACSA/AIA Housing Research Lecture Series and the Woodbury University School of Architecture Real Estate Development Seminars. I also received a Clarence S. Stein Institute for Urban and Landscape Studies Research Fellowship and gained assistance from the USC Price School Student Undergraduate Research Experience program.

Many had a hand in making this book a reality. Thank you to all the students who helped gather source materials, search for sales comps and diagram projects, especially Nick Ayers, Taylor Coyne, Matt Keipper and Jon Ocon. I'm grateful also for my faculty colleagues who have been encouraging, especially Dean Jack Knott, Marlon Boarnet, Raphael Bostic, Siobhan Burke, Chava Danielson, Richard Green, Eric Haas, Annette Kim, Bryce Lowery, Chris Redfearn, Jenny Schuetz, Lisa Schweitzer, Takako Tajima and Ingalill Wahlroos-Ritter. Thanks to Mimi Zeiger for her thoughtful advice about getting books published, and to Thurman Grant for sharing his experiences with book promotion. Important assistance with images came from Todd Gaydowski and Michael Holland at the Los Angeles City Archive and Records Center, Sherri Giles and Jerri Allyn of the Village Green Homeowners Association and Kathy Lo at the Santa Monica Public Library, as well as the staff at the Architecture and Design Collection at UCSB, the Getty Research Institute, and the Rare Book and Manuscript Collections at Cornell. Many thanks also to Kate Schell at Routledge, as well as Krystal LaDuc and Alexis O'Brien. You demystified the publishing process and made it as straightforward as possible.

Support from great friends got me through the long book-writing process. So much thanks to Todd Gish, whose excellent dissertation and insightful housing articles laid some of the groundwork for this book, and to Brettany Shannon for being my co-working buddy and a reader of book proposals. Thanks to Arianne Groth for reflective walks in the arroyo and to Aleks Jaeschke for her steadfast support and always well-timed advice; to Rebecca Lowry for thinking good thoughts and Donnajean Ward for her last-minute research help. And to Anne Bray and Sara Daleiden for their hard questions I usually didn't have good answers to. I am grateful to count you all among my Los Angeles family. I hope you call upon me in the future in all the ways I have called upon you.

Most important, none of this would have happened without the support of my colleague, mentor and friend David Sloane. Thank you for thinking this was a good idea from the very beginning and making the process a whole lot more fun. For believing it was important and being there whenever I needed you. And for giving me all the right advice at the right time. What's good here is largely thanks to you.

A special thank you, also, to my parents, Carolyn and John Falletta, who supported the book in more ways than one. Love you always.

And, finally, this wouldn't be complete without acknowledging puppy Eli, my main book-writing distraction. We can go on that dog hike now.

References

Bauer, C. (1944). Description and Appraisal . . . Baldwin Hills Village. *Pencil Points*, 25(9), 46–60.

Falletta, L. (2001). *Same Difference: Baldwin Hills and Aliso Villages*. Retrieved from www.laforum.org

Introduction
Housing Values

Housing is an essential, but extremely complex, product, so complex that professionals involved in its production, namely, architects, real estate developers and urban planners, have difficulty agreeing on "good" housing outcomes. Less-than-optimal solutions that have resulted from a too-narrow focus on one discipline over others are familiar: high design that is costly to build that makes little contribution to the public realm, highly profitable but seemingly identical "cookie-cutter" dwellings with no sense of place and well-planned neighborhoods full of generically designed, unmarketable product types. Housing makes up the majority of our urban landscape, yet those who create it are often at odds. This professional push-and-pull resonates through our housing stock, ensuring that few projects are considered "good" from all three points of view.

Differing roles, languages and criteria for success shape these perspectives, which, in turn, influence attitudes about housing regulation. Real estate developers, for example, prefer projects that can be built "as-of-right" or "by-right," meaning that they meet all current planning, zoning and building code requirements and can be approved quickly. Design-focused projects, heretofore "by-design," by contrast, often require time to challenge existing regulatory codes, pursuing discretionary modifications meant to maximize design innovation and development potential. Meanwhile, urban planners work to establish and mediate the threshold between by-right and by-design processes by setting housing standards and determining appropriate housing policy. But just what is the right line between "by-right" and "by-design"? How has this boundary shifted over time as the quality and desirability of housing outcomes are evaluated? Do zoning, development standards and other housing regulations facilitate or inhibit the production of "good" housing?

These questions are being debated nationally as cities work to adapt to higher densities, address new housing types and make housing more equitable. Local housing regulations in many high-growth cities intended to shape broadly good outcomes have made it more difficult to respond to housing needs from all three disciplinary perspectives, creating barriers to improved design quality, overall housing supply and affordability (Monkkonen, 2016; The White House, 2016). Los Angeles is no exception, with high barriers to entry and legendarily complex approvals processes. But Los Angeles also offers an ideal environment in which to study the often-siloed work of housing professionals through the lens of housing regulation. In Los Angeles, one finds an internationally recognized history of design innovation in single and multifamily housing types, set against a backdrop of speculative building in pursuit of the "American Dream," all propelled by a pro-development planning regime. Throughout the 20th century, Los Angeles architects, real estate developers and urban planners all experimented with tools to enhance housing production from their own point of view, with one's success often viewed as another's failure.

Although architects, real estate developers and urban planners must all work together to build housing, few tools exist to identify points of congruence that can increase capacity for collaboration. *By-Right, By-Design* seeks to fill this void by comparing projects that are physically and locationally similar, yet which clearly value some results over others. The goal is not to merge paradigms or find common ground but, rather, to tutor each field's participants in the languages, mind-sets and values of the others so that they can work together more effectively to improve housing outcomes from multiple points of view. Essentially, the book aims to help current and future professionals "code-switch," that is, shift between two or more languages in the context of a single conversation, learning how each field's decisions make it harder or easier for the other disciplines involved in housing to meet their goals (Gardner-Chloros, 2009). Are there strategies, mind-sets and frameworks that could amplify the ability to make mutually beneficial decisions, helping students and practitioners better balance competing design, planning and development goals in individual projects? Could these improve housing outcomes as professionals respond to changing design expectations, market conditions and housing needs? This is what the case studies in this book aim to reveal.

Some caveats before proceeding. First, architects, real estate developers, and urban planners are discussed as broad professional categories throughout the book, invoking their most typical values and, at times, their stereotypes. These stereotypes are used to help a diverse housing audience see their own attitudes, positive and negative, in the analysis and provide a basis from which to expand their point of view.

Second, the professionals involved in the housing projects examined worked in a U.S./American context during the first half of the 20th century with all that implies regarding issues of race, gender and social class. Los Angeles' history of housing inequity is embedded in the fabric of these typological models and noted exemplars. All were built well before the advent of participatory urban planning methods. Though this important conversation is not a part of this book, this bias underlies the design, real estate development and urban planning structures that enabled the case study projects to be built.

Third, in the case studies, "by-design" projects are not presumed to represent better housing outcomes, nor are projects in the "by-right" category by default inferior. These categories are used to sort projects based on the values they exemplify, allowing the consequences of differing priorities to be evaluated. The resulting analysis reveals both benefits and shortcomings in either approach. Also, "by-right" is not static. By-right projects reflect a specific set of rules in force when the projects were built, rules that have necessarily evolved over time in response to the outcomes of both by-right and by-variance approaches.

Finally, many other actors work in the housing arena: citizens, tenants, neighborhood organizations, owners, building contractors, heritage conservationists, investors, policymakers and lenders, to name just a few. All these players can and do influence housing production in any given situation. These case studies analyze only the work of architects, real estate developers and urban planners in order to isolate the primary complexities inherent in the housing production process and build a straightforward comparative framework. Likewise, the studies also recognize that these housing professions can be practiced in diverse ways and have been practiced differently over time. By focusing on fundamental values, mind-sets and languages, the work hopes to build perspective-taking capacity that can operate in a variety of scales, settings and future conditions.

Housing Values

Architects, real estate developers and urban planners all agree that housing matters, but their differing goals and values make producing housing defined as "good" from more than one perspective difficult. Everyone involved in housing production has experience with:

- architects who believe clients are patrons, not partners, and prioritize personal expression over responses to building type, urban context or sense of place;
- real estate developers who believe markets are always right and prioritize short-term deals over long-term city making; and
- urban planners who believe housing is foremost a public good and fail to recognize benefits from market-driven housing production, profits and preferences.

Biased Outcomes

These disciplinary attitudes, though stereotypical, are operative. The professions involved in housing production too often uphold biased outcomes, believing better design costs more, good planning means less yield and profitable development requires relentless repetition and sameness. By managing the differing, and difficult, goals of design innovation, profitability and social equity as trade-offs, rather than synergies, housing professionals ensure that their work is valued by their peers but is unremarkable, or even unpalatable, to other professionals in the housing field. Good results are clearly not obtained by valuing one or even two of these disciplines over the third. Yet, both in the field and in academia, these attitudes are real barriers to collaboration, making it difficult to agree on housing goals, on specific housing policy and on the quality of individual housing projects.

That this would be the case is understandable. Housing is challenging to produce. Given the risks involved, having experts focused exclusively on maximizing image and function, financial feasibility and profitability or equitable access and neighborhood character is desirable. The image and identity of home are important cultural concerns, housing would not get built if it were not profitable to do so and neighborhoods would be unaffordable and isolating if access to shelter was not prioritized. But the tensions among these priorities make producing housing broadly understood as "good" incredibly difficult. Few theories exist that examine the optimum relationships among housing disciplines, and they, more often than not, are adversarial (Peiser, 1990). Matthew Carmona, for example, has theorized these disciplines as "tyrannies," proposing design coding as a way to turn their "zones of conflict" into more productive "compromise" and "negotiation" (Carmona, 2009, pp. 2643–2644). The differing goals and values of architects, real estate developers and urban planners are crucial to the production of housing that meets societal needs but make it difficult to play well with others throughout the process.

"Good" Housing per Discipline

So, just what is "good" housing from each of these points of view? And how do the roles played by architects, real estate developers and urban planners conflict?

Architects recognize their role as the envisioners of the community whose decisions about the form and space of housing impact our way of life, visual environment and urban landscape. Designers value originality and innovation, personal design interests and the cultivation of a coherent body of work. Architects typically prefer projects that are more singular and inventive and therefore must be built "by-variance" (or "by-design" for the purposes of these case studies) since they typically transgress existing regulations or meet them in new ways. By their definition, "good" housing creates new shapes, configurations and images

(American Institute of Architects (AIA), 2018; Davis, 1977; Levitt, 2009; Sherwood, 1978).

Real estate developers understand themselves as the builders of the community whose decisions help determine the quality, type and price of housing available in any given neighborhood. Developers value profitability, speed to market and the cultivation of a track record or legacy. Developers typically prefer by-right projects since they are less risky and more repeatable. By their definition, "good" housing is financially feasible, approvable, efficient, buildable, marketable and easy to manage (Schmitz, 2000; Miles, Berens, Eppli, & Weiss, 2007; Urban Land Institute, 2018).

Urban planners identify as the caretakers or stewards of the community whose procedures and guidelines work to ensure that housing is equitable, affordable and accessible. Urban planners partner with architects and real estate developers to ensure that decisions about housing take social and spatial justice, public participation, identity and sense of place into account. Planners determine where a project falls on the spectrum between by-right and by-design. By their definition, "good" housing is livable, contextual, connected, adaptable and racially and economically diverse (American Institute of Certified Planners, 2016; Barnett, 1974; Chandler et al., 2005; Schneider, 1994; Schwartz, 2015; Taylor, 1982).[1]

All three professions too often play the blame game, claiming that one discipline's requirements detract from better outcomes in their own field, maintaining that:

- the project would have been more innovatively designed with a more reasonable budget and fewer code requirements,
- the project would have been more profitable if there weren't so many conditions of approval and if it was cheaper to build, or
- the project would have better met affordable housing goals with more exacting form-based codes and inclusionary housing requirements.

Often housing professionals are not wrong in these complaints. But these attitudes, while occasionally therapeutic, are a real obstacle to better housing outcomes. Luckily, Los Angeles's housing history is full of practitioners who understood housing production as more of a three-legged stool than a zero-sum game.[2] Architect Robert Alexander appreciated how planning for housing has more impact on our way of life than designing houses:

> But you know the form of the house is absolutely unimportant. In the field of form, the community plan is the only important thing. It must have size and shape, a center, a head, a heart, a soul, and a purpose.
> (Perkins, 1944, p. 62)

Developer Ray Hommes understood that "good design" underwrites project revenues as well as project costs:

> A clever architect working closely with a merchant builder make an unbeatable combination. An architect with vision, ability and training can create something unique, functional and appealing, and through research add new ideas in materials and equipment. A builder who doesn't use an architect is out of date and won't be able to compete.
>
> (The Fickett Formula, 1953, p. 132)

And Los Angeles zoning engineer Huber Smutz recognized the profound effect planning regulation can have on property values:

> A notable movement was evidenced in the "defrosting" of frozen business property; land which had been previously reserved as business property in over-anticipation of the demand that was never manifested, [which] was reclassified for residential use. In many cases this resulted in the immediate utilization of heretofore dormant real estate, with property owners securing a welcome return on their investment.
>
> (L.A. City Planning Commission, 1936, p. 22)

Looking closely at more balanced projects built by these broad-minded professionals and others like them can help us develop resources that bring the perspectives of design, real estate and planning into more productive relation.

Fostering More Balanced Outcomes

So how to create a set of tools that could help students and practitioners move from a biased to a balanced approach to housing production? This task is immediately made more complicated by the fact that each profession looks to different projects as exemplary. The set of reference examples that communicate and instill disciplinary values is different from field to field. And these works are never evaluated side-by-side across disciplines rather than within their silos. Although these exemplars are often perceived by those in the industry to be maximally different (i.e., it is assumed that if they excel from the point of view of one field, they necessarily fail from the perspective of others), is this actually the case? What more could we understand if we looked at these works alongside one another? This book examines whether this perceived divergence is upheld in actual fact and asks what can be learned from looking at these works comparatively rather than in isolation: (1) Do these examples support disciplinary expectations or contradict them? (2) Do the qualities that make these projects worthy of study in one discipline necessarily detract from the project's ability to address the values of the other disciplines involved in housing production? and, (3) Do these projects employ strategies that are valuable from more than one disciplinary perspective?

By-Right, By-Design Framework

The concepts of "by-right" and "by-design" can facilitate this type of cross-disciplinary comparison. Used together, these categories create a continuum upon which to sort housing outcomes and estimate the distribution of value allotted to each discipline's participation in a project (Figure 0.1). From there, we can begin to surmise how these projects addressed the tensions among housing fields. In other words, how the values of architecture, real estate development and urban planning were poised in relation to one another to actually get these projects built. *By-right* (or, alternately, *as-of-right*) is a term used by real estate development professionals to describe projects that can be approved ministerially; that is, the project cannot be denied approval if it meets certain criteria. By-right projects are built to current planning, building and zoning codes and do not require any exceptions to these rules. By-right projects take less time, are more certain and are, therefore, more repeatable. *By-design* (or, alternately, *by-variance* or *by-negotiation*) is a term being used in this book to describe corollary projects that are approved discretionarily; that is, even if the project meets all the current requirements in an alternate manner, approval can still be denied. Projects built by-design push

DEVELOPERS

BUILDERS OF THE COMMUNITY
Typically prefer BY-RIGHT projects since they are less risky and more repeatable.

TOOLS
Market Analyses & Proformas

VALUES
Financial Feasibility / Profitability
Speed to Market
Track Record / Legacy
Management of overall vision and development opportunities.

PLANNERS

CARETAKERS OF THE COMMUNITY
Planners determine where a project sits on the BY-RIGHT, BY-DESIGN spectrum.

TOOLS
Regulatory Plans & Codes

VALUES
Social & Spatial Justice
Public Participation
Community Identity / Sense of Place
Management of Long-Range Impacts

ARCHITECTS

ENVISIONERS OF THE COMMUNITY
Typically prefer BY-DESIGN projects since they are more innovative and unique.

TOOLS
Models, Drawings & Diagrams

VALUES
Design Innovation / Originality
Design Identity / Body of Work
Form, Space, Program & Materials
Management of Image & Function

BY-RIGHT | BY-DESIGN
Ministerial — Discretionary

Figure 0.1 Professional housing relationships: Typical disciplinary relationships and roles in housing production.

for the evolution of codes, restrictions and standards, adjusting them to maximize design and development opportunities. By-design projects are riskier and harder to replicate because they depend on an urban planner saying "yes," when he or she could have also said "no."

That urban planner who says "yes," or "no," determines whether a project can be built by-right because they:

- establish and update development standards using regulatory plans and codes that set the ministerial baseline applicable to all projects; and
- either are the decision-makers in discretionary cases, or make recommendations to those elected or appointed to do so, deciding whether to bend these rules in response to a hardship inherent to the property or greater purpose given the intent of those rules (Curtin & Talbert, 2007; Fulton & Shigley, 2005).

Developers prefer by-right projects since they reduce risk. Architects prefer by-design projects since they allow for the maximization of design opportunities and innovations. Planners are the referees who also work to set the rules of the game. A cross-disciplinary analysis of real estate development models built to regulatory requirements (by-right), versus innovative architecture built by variance (by-design), all approved by urban planners at the time they were built, reveals points of similarity among disciplines that could increase capacity for collaboration and identifies more judicious projects that take a balanced approach to rule following, rule breaking and rule making that can begin to be held up as exemplary by multiple housing professions.

Methodology

The studies contained in this book use a cross-disciplinary comparative case method to examine common real estate development models built as-of-right versus innovative architecture built by variance. By-design projects were selected from the canon of significant housing precedents accepted as exemplars by the design profession (Gebhard & Winter, 2003). Related by-right projects represent building types built in large numbers by landlords and developers (Chandler, 2005; Schmitz, 2000). All are located in Southern California and were approved, either by-right or by-design, by urban planners. Six comparisons examining a range of housing types and densities were studied. Projects had to be privately built and remain in existence to be included. They are presumed to span the length of "good" housing in the sense that they had to be deemed "good enough" from at least two out of three perspectives to be built.

To create each By-Right, By-Design comparative case pairing, I began with an innovative design precedent (i.e., a well-documented project by a well-known architect accepted as notable by other designers and architectural historians) and expanded out from its location until I found an example of its related development type (i.e., a common, basic type produced as best practice by builders and real estate developers). In most cases, relatable projects were located across the street, within the same block or around the corner from one another. With one exception, all by-design projects sought some sort of discretionary government approval to be built, and all have been protected under local, state, national or international preservation mechanisms.[3] All by-right development types were built by lesser known architects or with stock plans without discretionary variances or modifications. These represent the range of responses considered to be "good" or "good enough" by planners since they all gained approval one way or the other.

Once projects were paired, physical similarities were confirmed through site visits and compared via analyses of basic design and planning documents (original plans and specifications when available, planning applications and determinations, building permits and certificates of occupancy, etc.), evaluating commonalities in massing, unit aggregation and type, circulation, pedestrian access, vehicular access, provision of common and private open space and parking. Thorough cross-disciplinary project histories were then collected using archival documents from the Los Angeles City Planning, Building and Safety and Public Works Departments, the Los Angeles City Archives and the Los Angeles County Assessor's Archives, as well as relevant architect's archives. Additional information was gathered from the Historic American Building Survey, the National Register of Historic Places, the California State Historic Preservation Office, the Los Angeles Office of Historic Resources, magazine and newspaper publications contemporary to the projects and published secondary sources. Short, in-person interviews of architects and current building owners were conducted when possible. Extended interviews of key players cataloged in the University of California, Los Angeles Center for Oral History Research were also used.

Comparative cases were then documented and analyzed from design, real estate development and urban planning perspectives using the tools appropriate to each profession. These tools are used to evaluate whether the projects are more similar, or more different, from each disciplinary perspective and to assess whether they uphold or transgress disciplinary stereotypes. Project design was documented with original plans, sections and photographs when available, as well as those redrawn and retaken by the author. Design performance was analyzed via analytical drawings and diagrams comparing the projects' approach to massing, spatial organization, unit type, unit aggregation, pedestrian and vehicular circulation, parking, common and private open space and context. A content analysis of published assessments of significance was also conducted.

Real estate development performance was studied via market analyses, static proformas and a general understanding of the quality and character of the Los Angeles real estate market at the time projects were built. Market comparables were gathered from the *Los Angeles Times* and other newspaper advertisements. Building cost and value data were gathered from building permits, local construction cost publications and title reports. Metrics such as capitalization rates, absorption rates and average rental rates were gathered from the *Los Angeles Times*, City Planning Commission annual reports and trade publications. Financing mechanisms were also compared if information was available (Federal Housing Administration loan guarantees, Section 608, etc.).

Urban planning performance was studied via the regulatory plans and codes in force at the time the projects were built and the variances sought from them. Zoning atlases, zoning maps, subdivision maps, Los Angeles zoning codes, California state housing policies, planning applications and determinations were all used to evaluate project's approach to urban planning regulation. City Planning Commission meeting minutes and annual reports and documentation of land-use debates in the *Los Angeles Times* were used to evaluate the success of these policies going forward, noting the need for overlays, moratoria and revisions in response to unintended consequences.

A cross-disciplinary comparative analysis of projects that are physically and geographically similar, but which clearly value one set of interests over others—"by-right" development types built in large numbers versus singular exemplars built "by-design," which together span the range of outcomes acceptable to the urban planners who approved them at the time they were built—illuminates the actual relationships among the professionals who created these projects and brings the trade-offs that were made between disciplines to get them built, positive or negative, into relief.

Overview of Comparative Cases

Six comparative case studies form the heart of the book (Figure 0.2). Each cross-disciplinary case tells a different story about the often hidden relationships among the three primary disciplines shaping housing production, an understanding that is largely missed if our perspective is limited to a single lens (Carmona, 2009). The first three demonstrate the consequences of focusing on one housing discipline over others, showing how design, development and urban planning matter in the housing production process.

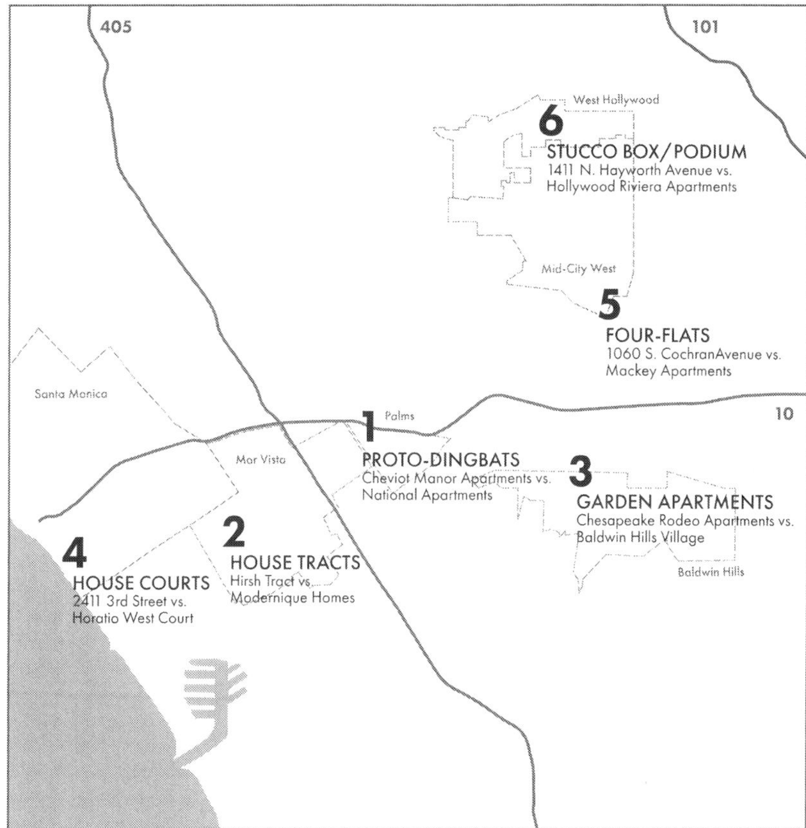

Figure 0.2 Case study project map: Case study projects are located in the City of Los Angeles in the Mar Vista, Palms, Mid-City West and Baldwin Hills neighborhoods, as well as the Cities of Santa Monica and West Hollywood.

Case Study 1: "Type in Transition" examines how regulatory and financial constraints can eclipse design opportunities. Both case study projects, the National Boulevard Apartments (1954), designed and developed by architect Raymond Kappe, and the developer-built apartment building directly across the street (1955), struggled to adapt existing housing models to the increased allowable density and stricter development standards contained in the city's still-new 1946 zoning code. Because of their generous hillside sites, both are able to preserve the access to outdoor space that characterized the courtyard and garden apartments that precede them while prefiguring the higher unit counts, open front garages and wide curb cuts that characterize the dingbat apartments that followed them. Although architects and designers are trained to innovate and adapt existing housing types to reflect changing cultural values, tastes and standards, dingbats' tight infill sites and high lot coverage limited design innovation to scripted font signage and other outlandish surface decoration. Consequently, dingbats addressed significant housing demand from the mid-1950s through the 1970s but without the character, amenity and intimate scale of the earlier housing types. Design matters. This case shows how thoughtful design, either vernacular or avant-garde, can turn the constraints inherent in urban planning and real estate development into opportunities, but only to a certain point.

Case Study 2: "Value Out of Balance" illustrates how design innovation can outpace financial and market capacity. Although the Modernique Homes (1948), designed by architect Gregory Ain and developed by B. M. Edelman, represented an "enlightened" approach to development that valued innovative design and planning strategies, the surrounding market, including the adjacent single-family tract to the east (1950), did not translate the higher cost of these innovations into increased sales prices. The Modernique Homes was a real estate development failure in the short term but an eventual real estate investment success in the long term once a Historic Preservation Overlay Zone was implemented in the early 21st century, demonstrating both the limits of planning and design innovation in market-rate development and the important role such innovations play in shaping future housing preferences. Development matters. This case shows how good design and good planning cannot be implemented unless they are sensitive to the issues impacting financial performance and are employed in projects that are financially feasible.

Case Study 3: "Lost in Translation" examines a situation where planning regulation failed to translate an innovative "design precedent" into a viable "product type." Baldwin Hills Village (1942), now called the Village Green, is renowned for its large acreage devoted to landscape, absence of through streets and clever spatial organization that manages cars and pedestrians. These features were innovative and helped define garden apartments as a type, but gaining permission to implement them required years of discretionary government approvals. Although the Chesapeake Rodeo Apartments (1954) is located less than 1,000 feet from Baldwin Hills Village, it takes no lessons from the precedent-setting project next door, primarily because the elements that made Baldwin Hills Village so successful were not incorporated into the planning and zoning code so that they could be implemented by-right. Today, the Village Green is a desirable, well-maintained project that contains units that outperform the local market. The Chesapeake Rodeo has struggled with management issues as well as high turnover and vacancy rates. Urban planning matters. This case shows how good housing often comes down to good physical planning since planning's domains—density, unit type, parking, open space and development pattern—arguably determine a basic quality of life.

The second three case studies suggest collaborative models, mind-sets and mutually beneficial strategies to improve housing outcomes from all three perspectives.

Case Study 4: "Proliferating a Product Type" addresses how good planning policy can support positive and wide-ranging development outcomes. State and local housing regulations evolved quickly in the early part of the 20th century to discourage lot packing, tenement housing and other housing practices believed to be unsanitary. However, far from dampening production, these rules both prompted more responsible development and supported a range of interpretations, seen in Irving Gill's Horatio West Court (1919) and a more typical bungalow court three blocks east (1921). Most bungalow courts, like the by-right case example, gather small, detached units around a common central landscaped courtyard opening to the street with either a pedestrian path or a driveway, down the center. Horatio West Court elaborates upon this type by creating larger, more luxurious two-story units built in a modern style out of concrete rather than wood. State and local regulation shaped the open space, unit size and ventilation requirements for house courts, ensuring that they were habitable, but did not create so many requirements that the buildings' design could not respond to a range of market, social and class conditions. This case shows how good planning and policy can encode flexibility and encourage typological innovation.

Case Study 5: "Design Well-Timed" illustrates how good market timing can support design innovation. Four-flats, like the case example (1926), were often built to look like large, Spanish-style single-family homes and typically stacked units two up, two down in a single volume with private entries on the ground level for each unit. The Mackey Apartments (1939), designed by architect Rudolph Schindler for owner/occupant Pearl Mackey, clearly builds on the type, but its modern architecture obscures its four-flat configuration. However, since the by-right case example was built near the peak of the market cycle before the Great Depression, and The Mackey Apartment's construction coincided with the real estate market's initial recovery from that downturn, the rents generated by the two projects when they were first brought to market were approximately the same. But Mrs. Mackey had to spend much less on land and construction than the four-flat built in 1926. Sealing the deal was a convertible studio apartment that could be rented independently of the owner's unit. In this case, awareness of the market cycle and the use of known development types all worked to hedge the risks associated with design innovation.

Case Study 6: "Crafting Cost Benefit" underscores how targeted design innovation can be used to shape profitable development models. Most apartments in Los Angeles built during the first half of the 20th century were surface parked. Beginning in the 1950s, however, both parking code and parking demand made tucking the parking under the building financially feasible for the first time. The Hollywood Riviera Apartments (1954), designed by architect Edward H. Fickett for owner Julian Weinstock and Associates, and a developer-built podium apartment building (1958) directly across the street exemplify this time of transition. The Hollywood Rivera locates parking under the southern half of the building in an open court. By the time the second case was built, it was profitable to park fully underground with an enclosed courtyard above. Fickett's apartments built from the late 1940s to the late 1950s incrementally evolve the podium strategy, creating buildings that were profitable for developers and desirable to tenants while maintaining their architectural significance.

These case studies echo the words of Edward Fickett when he spoke to his fellow architects:

> Members of the building industry must work together to create a better understanding and relationship between the professional planning groups and the contractors, builders and developers. This is a basic requirement if we intend to establish successfully a better environment in which to live and work, as well as to provide improved housing for Americans.
>
> (Fickett, 1961, p. 27)

Through careful study of the examples included in this book, students and professionals involved in housing production can learn to:

1. speak one another's language and begin to appreciate their differing methods, tools and values;
2. understand how decisions made from their own professional perspective can impact the ability of other professions to meet their project goals; and
3. recognize opportunities for mutually beneficial decision-making.

Notes

1. Tellingly, when I ran these "typical" professional roles and values by friends and colleagues in all three professions, many responded by saying that I had accurately captured the two other housing disciplines but had mischaracterized their own.
2. I borrowed the "three-legged-stool" analogy from my good friend Nick Saponara, a fellow architect-developer-planner.
3. Horatio West Court by architect Irving Gill did not require any discretionary approvals because the city of Santa Monica had yet to institute any zoning laws at the time it was built from which it would need relief.

References

American Institute of Architects (AIA). (2018). *AIA 2018 Code of Ethics and Professional Conduct*. Retrieved from http://aiad8.prod.acquia-sites.com/sites/default/files/2018-09/2018_Code_of_Ethics.pdf

American Institute of Certified Planners. (2016). *AICP Code of Ethics and Professional Conduct*. Retrieved from https://planning-org-uploaded-media.s3.amazonaws.com/document/AICP-Ethics-Revised-AICP-Code-Professional-Conduct-2016–04–01.pdf

Barnett, J. (1974). *Urban Design as Public Policy, Practical Methods for Improving Cities*. New York, NY: Architectural Record Books.

Carmona, M. (2009). Design Coding and the Creative, Market and Regulatory Tyrannies of Practice. *Urban Studies*, *46*(12), 2643–2667.

Chandler, R., Clancy, J., Dixon, D., Goody, J., Wooding, G., & Lawrence, J. (2005). *Building Type Basics for Housing*. Hoboken, NJ: John Wiley & Sons.
Curtin, D. J., & Talbert, C. T. (2007). Curtin's California Land Use and Planning Law. Point Arena, CA: Solano Press.
Davis, S. (1977). *The Form of Housing*. New York, NY: Reinhold.
Fickett, E. H. (1961). Frankly Speaking. *AIA Journal*, *36*(9), 25–29.
The Fickett Formula: Good Design Works Both Ways. (1953, March). *House and Home*, 132–139.
Fulton, W., & Shigley, P. (2005). *Guide to California Planning* (3rd ed.). Point Arena, CA: Solano Press Books.
Gardner-Chloros, P. (2009). *Code-Switching*. Cambridge, UK: Cambridge University Press.
Gebhard, D., & Winter, R. (2003). *An Architectural Guidebook to Los Angeles*. Salt Lake City, UT: Gibbs Smith.
L.A. City Planning Commission. (1936). *Annual Report*. Los Angeles, CA: L.A. City Archive.
Levitt, D. (2009). *The Housing Design Handbook: A Guide to Good Practice*. New York, NY: Routledge.
Miles, M. E., Berens, G. L., Eppli, M., & Weiss, M. A. (2007). *Real Estate Development, Principles & Process*. Washington, DC: The Urban Land Institute.
Monkkonen, P. (2016). *Understanding and Challenging Opposition to Housing Construction in California's Urban Areas. UC Center Sacramento White Paper*. Retrieved from https://docplayer.net/41479424-Housing-land-use-and-development-lectureship-white-paper-december-1-2016.html
Peiser, R. (1990). Who Plans America? Planners or Developers? *Journal of the American Planning Association*, *56*(4), 496–503.
Perkins, L. (1944). Perspectives, a Head, a Heart, a Soul, and a Purpose: Robert Evans Alexander. *Pencil Points*, *25*(9), 61–62.
Schmitz, A. (2000). *Multifamily Housing Development Handbook*. Washington, DC: ULI-The Urban Land Institute.
Schneider, F. (Ed.). (1994). Floor Plan Atlas, Housing. Basel, Switzerland: Birkhäuser Verlag.
Schwartz, A. F. (2015). *Housing Policy in the United States*. New York, NY: Routledge.
Sherwood, R. (1978). *Modern Housing Prototypes*. Cambridge, MA: Harvard University Press.
Taylor, L. (1982). *Housing, Symbol, Structure, Site*. New York, NY: Rizzoli.
Urban Land Institute. (2018). *ULI Code of Ethics*. Retrieved from https://americas.uli.org/membership/code-of-ethics/
The White House. (2016). *Housing Development Toolkit*. Retrieved from www.whitehouse.gov/sites/whitehouse.gov/files/images/Housing_Development_Toolkit%20f.2.pdf

Part 1

Housing Perspectives

1 Type in Transition, Proto-Dingbats

Cheviot Manor Apartments vs. National Apartments

Figure 1.1 Case Study 1: Proto-dingbats, the Cheviot Manor Apartments (left) vs. the National Apartments (right).

Introduction

A New Zoning Code Shapes Housing for Better and for Worse

The dingbat apartment, a low-rise, medium-density housing type that emerged in Los Angeles during the late 1950s, has been both maligned and valorized throughout its existence. Early on, architecture critics and urban planners vilified dingbats as flimsy, cheap, tawdry buildings with only a thin "veneer of 'architecture' tacked onto their street sides" (Pastier, 1972, F7). They had "not one inch of outdoor space," and although they usually came with aspirational names like "The Riviera Palms," the "Cheviot Lanai" and "Wilton Manor," they were believed to be a "space-optimizing method of squeezing cash from the landscape while blighting it aesthetically" (Indiana, 2004, n.p.; Pastier, 1972, F7; Piercy, 2003). Later, dingbats were valued for their role as a "remarkably successful transitional [housing] solution" as Los Angeles densified in the 1960s, commended for their provision of "clean, well-lighted space at a human scale, for a reasonable price and with the popular approval to which high-art Modernism aspired, but too seldom achieved" (Chase, 2000, p. 29; Rubin, 1977, p. 535). More recently, dingbats have been appreciated for their mid-century design, and many examples are now eligible for preservation.[1] The Los Angeles Forum for Architecture and Urban Design even held the Dingbat 2.0 competition in 2010, asking designers to redefine and reform the dingbat for the 21st century (Grant & Stein, 2016). As architecture critic Mimi Zeiger writes, "[a]lmost every Angeleno has a dingbat story" (Zeiger, 2016, n.p.).

Though there are many variations, pure dingbats are characterized by their low-rise, boxy form, typically no more than two stories in height; parking that is "tucked under" the building at grade in open carports; and a flat facade facing the street embellished with scripted signage, ornamental lighting and stylistic references ranging from "Tacoburger Aztec to Wavy-Line Modern, from Cod Cape Cod to unsupported Jaoul vaults, . . . and even—in extremity—Modern Architecture" (Banham, 1971, p. 177) (Figures 1.2 and 1.3). Behind the facade, these stucco-over-wood-frame buildings are straightforward and pragmatic, exhibiting a "primitive modern" style, with flat roofs, smooth facades, surface-mounted metal-frame windows and slender metal columns supporting soft-story overhangs (Banham, 1971, p. 175). Circulation is typically exterior and single-loaded (i.e., motel style, with direct access from the exterior into the apartment), with outdoor walkways connecting units to parking areas at the front, side and rear. Buildings typically house 5 to 12 units on a single lot with high lot coverage and long curb cuts.[2]

Dingbat apartments were built throughout Southern California and the southwest in the 1950s, 1960s and into the 1970s, emerging during a time of significant transition for Los Angeles residential development. By the mid-1950s, real estate developers were responding to higher land costs as the city was increasingly built out, unsold inventory as the postwar single-family housing boom addressed shortfalls in supply and an increase in rental demand due to a decline in the population of

Figure 1.2 A selection of dingbats located in the Palms neighborhood of Los Angeles.

home-buying age (Smith, 1964; Treffers, 2012). Urban planners were not only managing suburban-style growth in the San Fernando Valley but also beginning to shift their focus to the regulation of infill apartment development in the Los Angeles Basin (L.A. City Planning Commission [LACPC], 1955). And architects, whose large-scale experiments in super-block planned garden apartments had waned in response to a backlash against both public housing and fraudulent private investment, were concentrating on custom single-family homes and one-off medium-density, low-rise multifamily projects on infill sites (Brackman, 2007; Parson, 2005).[3]

Accelerating change in this context was the introduction of Los Angeles's first comprehensive zoning plan in 1946, which consolidated, coordinated and expanded the City's existing zoning regulations. These changes added residential zoning capacity while increasing development standards, making tested housing types more challenging to profitably design and build. Known types, including bungalow courts, four-flats, courtyard housing and garden apartments, contained high ratios of outdoor to indoor space and were therefore inherently low density.[4] An increase in required parking to one space per family unit in all residential zones, for example, put pressure on the common open space that characterized the courtyard type, eventually encouraging its elimination. Greater underlying allowable density promoted taller, boxier buildings with smaller units, made even boxier due to increased required setbacks that reduced building footprint (L.A. City Planning Department, 1946; Land Use Survey Co., 1952). New formal and spatial design strategies would clearly be required if development opportunities were to be maximized.

Consequently, new housing types like the dingbat arose, which were mass-produced across large swaths of Los Angeles, addressing significant housing demand but without the character, amenity and intimate scale of earlier housing types. Was this outcome inevitable given the economic and regulatory forces at the time and, as architect Raymond Kappe has noted, the "power the professionals affiliated with architecture but not architects themselves [had] over the process" (Smith, 1995, n.p.)? A case study of two "proto-dingbats," one a vernacular example and the other by a noted architect, suggests that in the early to mid-1950s, the dingbat as we know it now wasn't the only housing future in sight. Both the developer-built Cheviot Manor Apartments and the National Apartments, designed and developed by Kappe, imply alternate paths and illuminate essential negotiations among real estate development, urban planning and design and their impact on housing outcomes.

Proto-Dingbats

The Cheviot Manor Apartments and the National Apartments are both hybrid types in which past and future development patterns are equally visible (Figure 1.1). Neither building fits clearly into the garden or courtyard apartment typologies, characterized by two-story, walk-up buildings in traditional styles organized around landscaped courtyards and patios, that precede them or the dingbat apartment typology, characterized by low-rise, low-modern "stucco box" structures organized around parking and car access, that proliferated a few years after they were constructed. Both are built on generous hillside sites, allowing parking to be tucked under in front while preserving open space uphill, facilitating their backward-yet-forward-looking forms. Because their physical configurations and development histories capture this transition, both projects suggest avenues untaken worthy of study relative to the optimization of professional housing relationships.

Owner Samuel Sheff built the Cheviot Manor Apartments at 10560 National Boulevard in the Palms neighborhood of Los Angeles in 1955 with Theo W. Berg acting as general contractor (Figure 1.4). No

Figure 1.3 The National Apartments and Palms neighborhood dingbats, including the Chevitot Manor (1), mapped.

Figure 1.4 By-right case study project: The Cheviot Manor Apartments located at 10560 National Boulevard in Los Angeles built by Samuel Sheff.

architect is listed on the building permit (L.A. Department of Building & Safety [LADBS], 1955a, 1955b). Sheff constructed a companion building at 10554 National Boulevard at the same time, mirroring 10560 to create a narrow, shared courtyard between the two hillside properties. Each I-shaped building houses eight units, an even mix of one-bedroom, one-baths and two-bedroom, one-baths. A central stairway between the two structures leads up from the parking area at the street with seven spaces per building, which are tucked under the two-story building volume in open carports. The central courtyard area is relatively flat and landscaped with grass and palm trees. Concrete paths on either side lead to each building, each with two interior yet open-access stairways to four units. Units average 1,050 square feet. The building's style is somewhat indeterminate but leans toward a Vernacular Modern mixed with Spanish (details that were very likely a later addition). The common entry court and the open yet covered common entry stairs make the Cheviot Manor Apartments look more like a garden apartment, but the project's name, use of scripted font signage, vertical wood siding facade and tuck-under parking are associated with the dingbat typology. The building was built by-right and required no discretionary approvals.[5]

The National Apartments, directly across the street at 10565 National Boulevard, was designed and built by Ray Kappe in 1954, his first independent project as a newly licensed 26-year-old architect (Figures 1.5 and 1.6). His father, Phineas Kappe, is listed as both the owner of the property and the building's contractor on the building permit (LADBS, 1954). It was constructed alongside an apartment building designed and built by architect Carl Maston (10555 National Boulevard), Kappe's former employer and mentor. Kappe's building steps six one-bedroom, one-bath units up a steep hillside site with parking for five cars tucked underneath at grade, plus one uncovered space adjacent. Kappe used a pinwheel organization to improve on the more typical courtyard/garden apartment type prevalent at the time, allowing units up the hill to use the roofs of lower units as outdoor rooms (Falletta, 2012). His goal was to make the units feel as individual as possible while maximizing privacy and private outdoor space (Smith, 1995, n.p.). The pinwheel scheme generates a winding pedestrian path through the building, creating small areas of common open space and community, as well as identity and difference among the units themselves. Units are compact but feel spacious since they have open floor plans and large floor-to-ceiling windows connecting to generous outdoor patios and decks. Most units have almost as much outdoor square footage as they do indoor, both averaging about 650 square feet. The project's architecture is characterized by flat roofs, post-and-beam wood construction, horizontal windows, floor-to-ceiling glass windows and vertical wood siding. Carports

Figure 1.5 By-design case study project: The National Boulevard Apartments located at 10565 National Boulevard in Los Angeles, designed and built by architect Ray Kappe.

Figure 1.6 Ray Kappe, perspective drawing: Apartment Building for Mr. and Mrs. P. Kappe, 1954.

Credit: The Getty Research Institute, Los Angeles (2008.M.36).

defined by slender metal columns with no garage doors make the project float and look more Modern. This also makes the building look more like a dingbat apartment, with a blank facade over the rear ends of cars, while the focus on outdoor space relates more clearly to the garden apartment typology.[6] The project was published in *Arts & Architecture* magazine and received an AIA Design Award (Two Income-Unit Structures, 1955).

The National Apartments was built "by-design" from the perspective of this study because its design innovations required discretionary approval to be built. These were necessary given the odd shape and approximate 20% upslope topography of the lot but also allowed Kappe to reduce the impact of parking, giving him room to shift, stack and rotate units to define significant private outdoor space. Kappe obtained a yard variance to allow the building to encroach 7 feet into the required 15-foot setback as well as a reduction in the 10-foot passageway requirement that mandated an accessway to the rear of the property (LACPD, 1954). As built, the building setback ranges 2.5 feet to 12 feet from the triangulated front property line. Kappe was required to build the public sidewalk, curb and gutter as a condition of approval. An adjacent owner had applied for a similar variance the year before, which was denied (LACPD, 1953).

In these two cases, good real estate fundamentals, coupled with large hillside sites, generated design solutions that accommodated changing markets, regulations and lifestyles.[7] Although the National Apartments is clearly more architecturally innovative, both buildings were able to accommodate the car while preserving important connections to outdoor space that had characterized Los Angeles housing to date. Most sites in the Los Angeles basin are flat, however, so, as development continued, desirable qualities exhibited in both projects were eliminated due to regulatory constraints and a focus on yield. What can these proto-dingbats tell us about the relationship between real estate development, urban planning and design and the impact of real estate and urban planning practices and policies on design outcomes?

Real Estate Development

Context

During the mid-1950s, the fundamentals for multifamily housing development were favorable throughout the nation and investors were optimistic about the future. Americans' personal savings had increased steadily since World War II and financial institutions had money to lend (Smith, 1964). These funds were available on increasingly generous terms, often at 90% to even 100% loan-to-value (Smith, 1964, p. 33). Demographic shifts favoring those of renter ages and the positive promotion of a renter lifestyle in the media both increased demand for apartments (Treffers, 2012). And multifamily development was treated favorably by the Internal Revenue Service, offering accelerated depreciation for "first time" users of a property and advantageous capital gains treatment (Smith, 1964, p. 31). The stage was set for the dingbat as the "primary agent of medium-density sprawl" (Grant & Stein, 2016, p. 10).

Most dingbats were built speculatively on standard 50-foot-wide lots by contractors and small developers, many for onetime, owner-user investors who lived on the property (Chase, 2000, p. 13). Projects represented a relatively small financial outlay and typically had 5 to 12 units composed of a mix of 650- to 700-square-foot one-bedroom and 900-square-foot two-bedroom units (Chase, 2000, p. 13). The use of new technologies developed in wartime and converted to domestic use, including the nail gun, prefabricated aluminum windows and wall-to-wall carpeting, sped projects to market in 6 to 8 months (Treffers, 2012). Dingbats were built in large numbers in the Palms, Westlake and Sherman Oaks neighborhoods of Los Angeles, as well as in Santa Monica and West Hollywood, but there are specimens to be found in every part of the city. By 1957, the first year multifamily building permits outpaced those for single-family housing since the 1920s, the dingbat's formation was complete (Treffers, 2012, p. 54) (Figure 1.7). Given such a favorable environment, it is not hard to understand how the dingbat came to populate vast swaths of Los Angeles in neighborhoods as disparate as Venice Beach and Highland Park, all tarted up just "enough to get [tenants] in, not more" (Nero, 1972, W24).

Samuel Sheff

Samuel Sheff, builder of the Cheviot Manor Apartments, was a real estate developer and contractor active in Los Angeles in the 1950s and early 1960s. In addition to building the Cheviot Manor, Sheff was the contractor for a 24-unit, two-story apartment house at 239 Commonwealth Avenue in Los Angeles in 1959 (Photo Standalone 15, 1959). In 1961 Sheff was the contractor for a three-story apartment building at 423 S. Rexford Drive in Beverly Hills, said to cost $500,000, with a roof garden, 30-foot interior waterfall, "built-in hi-fi and wet bar" and underground parking for 30 cars (Beverly Hills, 1961, P6). Also in 1961, Sheff was denied a variance to reduce a 25-foot front setback to 15 feet for an apartment building on Greenfield Avenue in Westwood (Planners Refuse, 1961). Sheff died in early 1962 (Obituary 1, 1962).

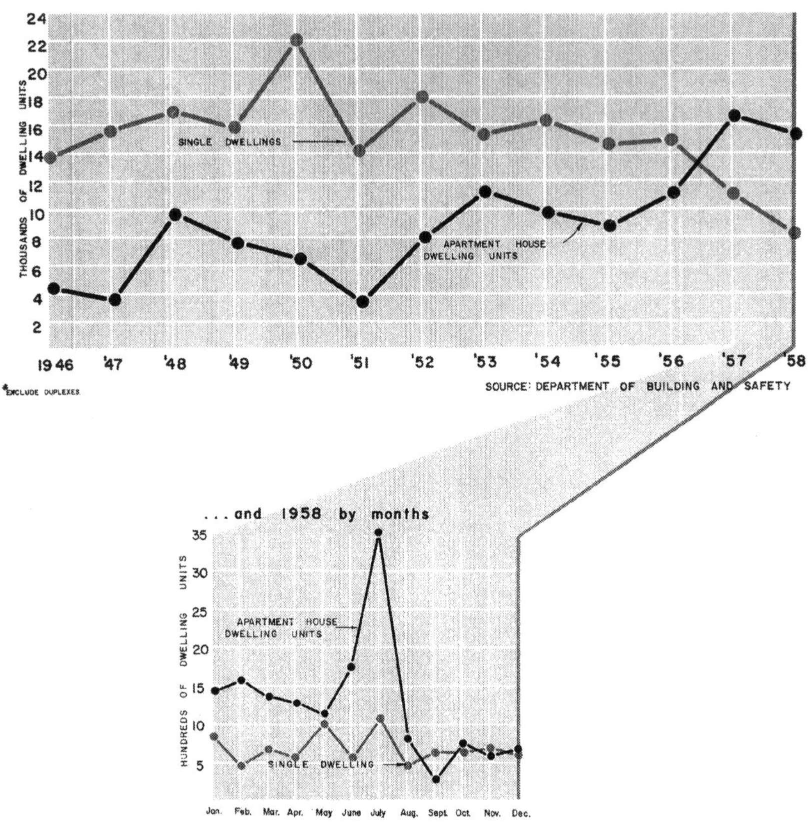

Figure 1.7 Annual construction of apartment house dwelling units surpassed that of single-family homes in 1957 for the first time since the 1920s (LACPC, 1959, p. 10).

Credit: Los Angeles City Archives and Records Center.

Ray and Phineas Kappe

The Kappes developed the National Apartments as a learning opportunity for Ray and an investment venture for Phineas, who was a hairdresser and women's clothing retailer by trade but who had some real estate investment experience ($320,000 Volume, 1950; Smith, 1995).[8] At the time the building was built, Ray had just completed two years in the office of his mentor Carl Maston, an expert in the garden apartment typology (Smith, 1995). Maston often invested in his own development projects and encouraged Kappe to do the same as a way to launch his own architectural practice (Falletta, 2012). In early 1954, Maston identified two parcels on National Boulevard and suggested that he buy one and Kappe the other so that they could do side-by-side design–build projects. Kappe bought the land for $5,000, which he borrowed from his father. Both architects agreed to use similar materials so that the two projects would communicate, but followed their own design interests (Falletta, 2012).[9] The buildings were built in tandem using the same subcontractors, who would simply come over to Kappe's project once they finished at Maston's (Falletta, 2012). Ray used his own housing preferences in lieu of an actual market analysis, planning to market the units to young, newly married couples like himself and his wife Shelly (Falletta, 2012; Marriage Announcement 3, 1950).[10] Kappe and his family retain ownership and management of the property today.

How do the Cheviot Manor Apartments and National Apartments compare from a real estate development perspective? Does the Cheviot Manor's status as a by-right project mean that it was more profitable? Does the National Apartments noted design mean that it was a poor investment?

Subdivision *8,750-Square-Foot Rectangular Lot vs. 6,670-Square-Foot Trapezoidal Lot*

Land for both case study projects was first parcelized into large hillside lots during the late 1800s as a part of "The Palms" subdivision. The area was originally part of Rancho La Ballona which was used as grazing land for cattle and sheep during the Spanish and Mexican eras. In 1886, Joseph Curtis and Edward H. Sweetser bought 560 acres and subdivided the flat land on either side of the Los Angeles and Independence Railroad's "grasshopper station" in 1887 (Ingersoll, 1908, p. 352; L.A. County Department of Public Works, 1887). Platted around the station just east of the case study sites (National Boulevard between Motor Avenue and Woodbine Street) were 50-foot by 150-foot homesites, with 8 miles of paved streets and imported palm trees (Ingersoll, 1908, p. 353).[11] The town was built up quickly and had a schoolhouse, a hotel, churches of various denominations and even some industry in the form of eucalyptus oil manufacturing by the early 1900s (Ingersoll, 1908, p. 355). Land for the Cheviot Manor Apartments was further subdivided in 1907 by the Palms Land, Light and Water Co. into rectangular lots approximately 60 feet by 166 feet (L.A. County Department of Public Works, 1907). Land for the National Apartments was further subdivided by a lot-cut process, creating its approximately 100-foot-deep trapezoidal lot that ranged from 64 feet wide at the street to 80 feet at the rear property line. Palms was annexed into the City of Los Angeles in 1915. The case study lots were considered unbuildable until most of the flat lots in the city were built out in the 1950s.

Market Timing *Built Pre-1957 (1955) vs. Built Pre-1957 (1954)*

Both the Cheviot Manor Apartments and the National Apartments were built and leased up in time to capture all the benefits of the apartment housing boom that began in 1957. In the early to mid-1950s, a strong rental market that would last over ten years was just starting to take shape. Land costs were rising since most of the open land in the city proper was built out, making single-family housing development less economical. Automobile ownership was also rising, along with commute times, spurring a "back-to-the-city movement" and a market for close-in housing (Apartment House Building Boom, 1957). And new jobs were drawing many young people to the westside area of Los Angeles with the post–World War II expansion of the aircraft manufacturing and entertainment industries. Later, in the late 1950s and early 1960s, record numbers of young people would come of age, as war babies and baby boomers became young adults, while the silent generation aged into early retirement, all demographics that typically rented apartments. And the apartment lifestyle would become increasingly acceptable and even desirable in Los Angeles, the "City of Homes" (Figure 1.8). Apartments offered "sophisticated city living" for singles and couples in their 20s and 30s, confirmed bachelors and "matron[s] with a young point of view" (A Bachelor's Apartment, 1963; Lenox, 1959):

> For gone are the dark, drab, shabbily carpeted hallways and stiff-lipped neighbors. In their place are balconies, courtyards, swimming pools and a young, friendly country club set. Only, of course, these people don't belong to a country club—they just act and live like they do. Their country club is the apartment house.
>
> (Alpert, 1959, J12)

Construction Costs *$4,562 per Unit vs. $4,166 per Unit*

The Cheviot Manor Apartments and the National Apartments are comparable on a cost per unit basis but diverge sharply on a cost per square foot basis.[12] Mr. Sheff listed $73,000 as the cost for both Cheviot Manor buildings on a combined building permit, $36,500 per building, or $4,562 per unit (LADBS, 1955b). A building cost of $25,000, or $4,166 per unit, was listed by Ray Kappe on the National Apartments building permit (LADBS, 1954). By this measure, units at the National Apartments were 8.7% less expensive to build than those at the Cheviot Manor. Per unit costs for both case study projects were on par with

Figure 1.8 Knotty pine kitchens were in vogue in the late 1950s and early 1960s. Here, actress Shirley Ann Chandler poses in one example in her newly built apartment, the Colfax Palms, located at 4300 Colfax Avenue in Studio City.

Credit: Dean Gordon, Valley Times Photo Collection. Los Angeles Public Library.

those of contractors who advertised income units in the *Los Angeles Times* in 1954 and 1955 (Figure 1.9). Van M., Inc Building Contractors advertised a "4 Unit Deluxe" for $15,900, or $3,975 per unit (Display Ad 142, 1954, F18). Wernette & King General Contractors advertised building eight units for $33,450, or $4,181 per unit (Display Ad 109, 1954, E14). And Westkett Homes, Inc advertised a four-unit apartment building with

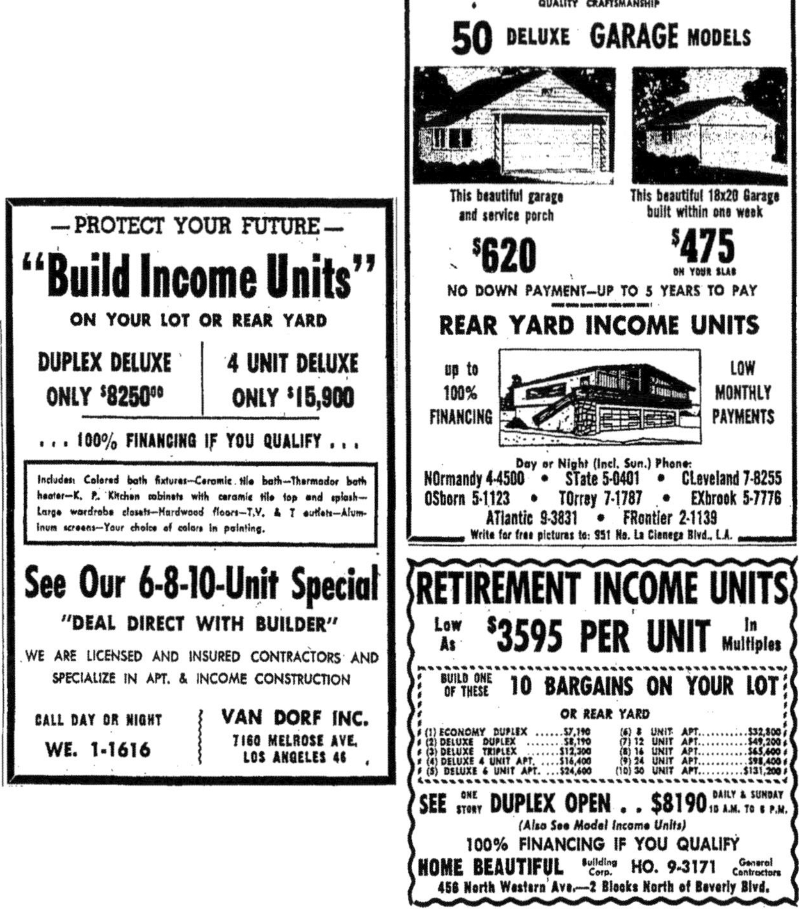

Figure 1.9 Advertisements for the construction of "Income Units" in the *Los Angeles Times* (Display Ad 134, 1955, F24).

two-bedroom units for $18,900, or $4,725 per unit (Display Ad 134, 1955, F24).

On a cost per square foot basis, however, the National Apartments was 48% more expensive to build than the Cheviot Manor Apartments. Cheviot Manor's units cost $4.34 per square foot, while those at the National Apartments cost $6.41. This small difference in unit cost yet large difference in per square foot cost results from the National Apartments' small unit size and minimal yet flexible apartments that maximized private outdoor space.

Funding *Private Financing vs. Private Financing*

Funding for apartments was relatively easy to obtain during the mid-1950s, and both case study projects were privately financed without government insurance or guarantee (Smith, 1964). By this time, wartime rent controls had finally been lifted, and sales of single-family homes, which were becoming more and more expensive, were declining. Lenders turned away from tract development because of unsold inventory but were happy to lend to apartment developers, which allowed them to diversify but stay in Los Angeles's still-growing residential market (Apartment House Building Spurts, 1957). Apartment developers targeted their rental rates above controlled rent but less than the higher monthly payments now required to buy a home (Apartment House Building Boom, 1957). By 1955 there was "more money now available for real estate investment than there are offerings for sale at a fair market price," said William A. Walters, national president of the Institute of Real Estate Management of the National Association of Real Estate Boards ('55 Held Boom Year, 1955). Increasingly, savings-and-loan institutions and insurance companies provided this money rather than conventional banks (Doti & Schweikart, 1989). Samuel Sheff likely obtained a commercial loan of this type for Cheviot Manor. Kappe and his father secured a private construction loan to build the National Apartments (Falletta, 2012).

Marketing and Absorption *Minimal and Quick vs. Minimal and Quick*

The case study projects were marketed minimally and probably leased up quickly. The Cheviot Manor Apartments was promoted with advertisements in the *Los Angeles Times* and, presumably, signage on site. Sheff built the project purely as an investment and offered both buildings for sale in August 1955 as a 16-unit complex while it was still being leased:

> New deluxe bldg. Every deluxe feature plus w. to w. carpets, garb. disps., sep. stall showers, sep. forced air units ea. apt., venetian blinds, eating space in kitchen + sep. dining room, patio for each apt.
> (Classified Ad 25, 1955, A17)

Asking rent was $100 for one-bedroom and $130 for two-bedroom units, among the higher asking rents for apartments in the Westwood area of Los Angeles, which ranged from about $60 up to $225 at the time (Classified Ad 17, 1955, A21). Other unfurnished apartments on the same block of National Boulevard were asking $100 to $125 (Classified Ad 15, 1957). The Cheviot Manor's units would have been desirable for their larger-than-typical size, outdoor patios, separate dining rooms and eat-in kitchens. No more advertisements appeared in the *Times* until 1957 and then 1966.

Ray Kappe marketed his building to young singles and couples by word of mouth and signage at the property (Falletta, 2012). No advertisements for the property appeared in the *Los Angeles Times*, but asking rents for apartments in the neighborhood ranged from $70 to $265 during the last 3 months of 1954. If the National Apartment's units rented for the same rate per square foot as one-bedroom units in the Cheviot Manor, asking rent would have been $62. Given the level of privacy and amount of outdoor space at the National Apartments, and the fact that no apartment in the area was advertised for less than $70, this is likely low. Its units probably rented at close to $100, what other apartments on the 10500 block of National Boulevard were asking. The units would have been desirable for their large amount of private open space, open plan, flexible interiors and built-in storage.[13]

Outcomes *Investment Performance*

As real estate investments the case study projects are more similar than they are different. The projects required a similar amount of capital and were built in a growing multifamily area with strong rents. Most important, both were built before the mid-century apartment boom and would have been able to earn back their construction costs in gross rent quickly.[14]

Urban Planning

Context

All the factors that made apartments a good investment in the mid- to late 1950s put pressure on urban planners, then working hard to shape the "Los Angeles of tomorrow" (LACPC, 1953, p. 2). By the early 1950s, Los Angeles planners were very focused on tract development in the Valley but were also looking seriously at citywide needs, including allocating land for parks and schools, gleaning best practices in the form and location of shopping centers and studying off-street parking needs. Planning for movement was also critical at this time as use of the rail lines declined and car ownership surged, opening opportunities for development in locations not served by rail. Los Angeles County had 1,545,351 passenger car registrations by 1950, the most in the nation, equal to 2.7 Angelenos per vehicle (LACPC, 1952, p. 10). By the end of 1956, almost 35 miles of freeway had opened to traffic and 22.4 miles were under construction out of a total of 165 miles planned for the Los Angeles metropolitan area (LACPC, 1957, p. 13).

By the mid-1950s, Los Angeles was also beginning to see significant infill and redevelopment in close-in neighborhoods. Raw land was increasingly distant from the city center, the cost of land in the city proper was rising every year and the population in older, close-in neighborhoods was declining. By 1954, planners were actively encouraging multifamily development near existing and expanding urbanized communities in the Los Angeles Basin, and 40% of the total building permits issued that year were for multiple units (LACPC, 1955, p. 10). This made the reconversion of sites originally developed from the 1880s through the 1920s viable, along with the development of sites of a size, shape or topography that had made them previously uneconomical to improve (Mulcahy, 1960). Height, area and yard variances were increasing by double digits, reflecting "the tremendous building activity especially in residential construction and the endeavor of the architects or designers to try out unique designs or to conform the design of the dwelling to the topographical problems of the particular lot" (LACPC, 1955, p. 42). Hillside lots, like those of the case study buildings, were definitely the "last frontier" (LACPC, 1961, p. 10).

To what degree are the National Apartments and the Cheviot Manor Apartments similar or different from an urban planning perspective? Does the fact that the Cheviot Manor was developed as of right while the design innovations of the National Apartments required discretionary approval mean one met planning goals better than the other?

Needed Housing Types Rental Housing vs. Rental Housing

Both case study projects provided much-needed multifamily rental housing suitable for singles, couples and roommates in an increasingly desirable area. The Palms neighborhood had been growing rapidly since the 1920s. Its population doubled between 1930 and 1940 and again between 1940 and 1950 to 36,348. Palms grew an additional 15% between 1950 and 1954, to a population of 41,860 (LACPC, 1955, p. 8).

Zoning and Development Standards R3 in R4 vs. R3 in R4

Land for both case study projects was zoned R4 at the time they were built but both were effectively built to the standards of the R3 zone. This is likely because apartment demand was not yet booming in the mid-1950s and because the projects' steeply upsloping sites would require too much costly excavation to develop to the higher limits of the R4 zone (Land Use Surveys Co., 1952).

Use

Both case study projects conformed to their zone in terms of use. In the early 1950s the R4 zone allowed apartments, house courts and churches, along with all uses allowable in the more restrictive residential zones, which included boarding houses, multiple dwellings, duplexes and single-family homes (Land Use Surveys Co., 1952).

Height and Setbacks

Neither case study building came anywhere near the maximum height limit for the R4 zone, which allowed for buildings up to six stories, or 75 feet, in height (Land Use Surveys Co., 1952). Both case study projects are two stories over parking and no taller than 35 feet, meeting the lower height standard of the R3 zone. Required front setbacks in the R4 and R3 zone were 15 feet. (Land Use Surveys Co., 1952).

Density

Buildings in the R4 zone were allowed to have 400 square feet to 800 square feet of lot area per dwelling unit, about 54 to 108 dwelling units per acre, depending on how many rooms in each apartment (Land Use Surveys Co., 1952). Both case study projects' densities align with the R3 zone (36 to 54 dwelling units per acre) and are equally as dense as one another, 40 dwelling units per acre for Cheviot Manor Apartments and 39 dwelling units per acres for the National Apartments. The minimum lot size was 5,000 square feet, which the projects also easily exceeded.

Parking

The Cheviot Manor Apartments meets the parking requirement for the R4 zone while the National Apartments exceeds it. At the time the case study projects were built, the zone required one space for most dwelling units but allowed two spaces per three smaller units (under three rooms). The Cheviot Manor Apartments provides seven spaces, four for the four two-bedroom units and three for the four one-bedroom units. The National Apartments is parked at one space per unit, meeting the higher standard required in the R3 zone, though its smaller units would have qualified for the two spaces for three-unit calculation, for a total of four required spaces.

Public Realm

The quality of the public realm in both case study projects is severely limited by their parking strategy. Tuck-under parking requires long curb cuts and driveway aprons that cut through sidewalks and limit protective street parking. Curb cuts for both buildings are nearly as long as their front property lines, almost 60 feet. This also means that most of the front yard setback is paved and not landscaped. The backsides of cars dominate the public-facing facades of the buildings.

***Outcomes** Planning Performance*

Both the Cheviot Apartments and the National Apartments perform reasonably well and are almost equivalent from a planning perspective. Neither pushes against the maximums in the zoning code (height and density) and both meet or exceed some code minimums (parking). Building less densely than the underlying zoning allows both case study buildings more space to provide benefits planners value but did not yet regulate, generously sized units with ample private and common outdoor space.

Design

Context

The 1950s saw Modernism going more mainstream as Los Angeles became a "suburban metropolis." Los Angeles's residential architects and architecture gained national attention in journals like *Architectural Forum* and *Arts + Architecture*, as well as decorating and design magazines like *Sunset* and *House Beautiful* (Smiley, 2001, p. 42). As argued by architect David Smiley, the early 1950s had really seen the development of two Modernisms, one a pure or high Modern based on "production aesthetics" and the other a lower Modern "frictionless inhabitation" promoted by the domestic culture industry (Smiley, 2001, p. 42). High Modern envisioned a pure architecture for a technologically advanced future, innovative, prefabricated, clean-lined and efficient, in image, structure and space. Well-known architects including Charles and Ray Eames, Craig Ellwood, Pierre Koenig, Richard Neutra and Sumner Spaulding were all designing high Modern single and multifamily housing at this time. Lower Modern houses and apartments offered living spaces that were modern in function if not design, with flexible features and built-in furniture like high Modern homes, but with a more traditional image (Smiley, 2001, p. 42). The dingbat's accidental Modernism exhibits both these extremes at once—its rear-facing abstraction the result of ruthless cost-cutting rather than aesthetic conviction and it's "façade architecture" providing token style, be it Colonial, Tudor or Polynesian (Rubin, 1977, p. 535).

Jack Chernoff

The foremost dingbat designer in Los Angeles was undoubtedly Jack Chernoff, a high-volume architect for apartment developers who was known as "'Packin' Jack' because he [could] get more units on a lot than anybody else in the field" (Nero, 1972, W24). From the mid-1950s to the early 1970s, Chernoff designed more than 2,000 apartment buildings for small developers, many not unlike the Cheviot Manor Apartments

(Chase, 2000). "We'll push the law to its ultimate. Sometimes the apartments aren't the keenest looking buildings, but they're the best moneymakers," he said (Nero, 1972, W24). In 1956 Chernoff designed Maple Manor, a 25-unit apartment building in Glendale with "Hawaiian Modern styling" (Article 30, 1956, E5). He designed the Diplomat in 1962, a 57-unit apartment building in Koreatown/Mid-City with a roof garden, pool and putting greens (Photo Standalone 18, 1962, I20). As well as two dingbats in Highland Park in 1965, the Highland-Riviera East and the Highland-Riviera West, both employing a Postmodern style with large mansard roofs and inset windows, with units that incorporated "Greek traditional décor" (Two Highland Park Apartments Opening, 1965, H26). Real estate developers loved him because he "turn[ed] out a lot of volume at a moderate price." And his units rented "better than their neighbors, even though they are smaller by some 150 square feet" (Nero, 1972, W24). "We give them the illusion of space," Chernoff said (Nero, 1972, W24). Although Chernoff professed all his buildings to be individual and unique, the dingbat as a building type quickly became formulaic. When designing dingbats, architects would work backward from parking requirements, rather than being inspired by potential improvements to unit type or open space, making these building literally driven by the automobile.

Ray Kappe

Ray Kappe opened his architectural practice in 1954, after graduating from Berkeley in 1951 and working for Anshen + Allen in San Francisco and then Carl Maston in Los Angeles.[15] Kappe is best known for his custom single-family homes, but he designed numerous small apartment buildings during the first decade of his career, including the Berkus–Kappe Apartments, 1958; the Paul Hammond Apartments, 1960; the Vedanta Society Apartments, 1961; the C & C Development-Moorpark Apartments, 1963; the Fredonia Apartments, 1964; the Kling Street Apartments, 1964; and the Gale Drive Associates Apartments, 1964. These buildings could all be described as Mid-Century Modern, but Kappe experimented with style throughout his career, focusing on spatial experimentation, relationships to the natural environment, modular construction and spatial fluidity (Falletta, 2012). He went on to design more than 100 single-family homes as well as commercial, institutional and educational buildings, most recently experimenting with prefab construction.[16] Kappe was also a longtime design educator who taught at the University of Southern California, was the founding department chair of Cal Poly Pomona's architecture school in 1968 and, with a few like-minded colleagues, established the Southern California Institute of Architects (SCI-Arc) in 1972, which he directed until 1987. Kappe is still in practice today.

To what degree are the National Apartments and the Cheviot Manor Apartments similar or different from a design perspective? Does the National Apartments status as an award-winning design project mean that it is better designed than Cheviot Manor? Does the fact that Cheviot Manor was built purely as a short-term investment mean that it lacks architectural value?

Site Strategy *Cut and Fill vs. Terraced*

By now most of the easily developable land in Los Angeles had already been improved, creating design challenges for architects. As a result, both case study projects are built on upsloping hillside sites with parking tucked under the volume of the building at the street. The Cheviot Manor Apartments cuts a flat pad into its 8,516-square-foot site for an elevated two-story building block. The National Apartment tiers building volumes up the hill on its 6,670-square-foot site.

Building Organization and Massing *Two-Story "I"-Shaped vs. One-Story Stepped*

The Cheviot Manor Apartments uses a single building volume while the National Apartments is designed to make one building read as several. The Cheviot Manor's building is two-story (three if the parking below is counted) and slightly "I"-shaped. The stem of the "I" has a low-pitch hipped roof while the arms have overhanging flat roofs. The National Apartments steps its flat-roofed units up the hill with the upper units using the roofs of the lower units as outdoor space. The building is split from front to back with a pedestrian pathway, making its form look more irregular and individualized.

Unit Types and Amenities *Spacious yet Compartmentalized vs. Compact yet Open*

Cheviot Manor's units are on average 400 square feet larger than the National Apartment's, with a greater diversity of types. Cheviot Manor contains eight units, an even mix of one-bedroom, one-baths and two-bedroom, one-baths. Units average 1,050 square feet. Rooms are compartmentalized as was typical in the 1950s.

The National Apartments contains six units, all one-bedroom, one-bath. Units average 650 square feet. They are compact but feel more spacious due to their open plan and large windows connecting to generous outdoor patios and decks. Units originally had wardrobes that were movable so that space between the living area and private sleeping area could be exchanged at will. These failed often and eventually had to be fixed in one position with glazing above (Falletta, 2012).

Pedestrian Access and Entry *Grouped vs. Individualized*

The Cheviot Manor gathers apartment entries together into two groups of four while the National Apartments provides separate exterior entries for each unit (Figure 1.10). A stairway to the left of 10560 National Boulevard, shared with 10554, leads up from the parking area at the street to a narrow courtyard between the two buildings. From here a concrete path leads to two covered yet open-access stairways, each leading to four units, two on either side.

The National Apartments are accessed by a stair to the left of the building leading up from the parking area to a common courtyard on the second level. Three units have individual, covered entries to their units from this level from a stepped "L"-shaped pathway. Opposing "L"-shaped stairs lead to the entries for the other three units, one from the first stair landing and the other two from an open corridor. All are shaded by a pergola. The resulting pinwheel organization creates a winding pedestrian path

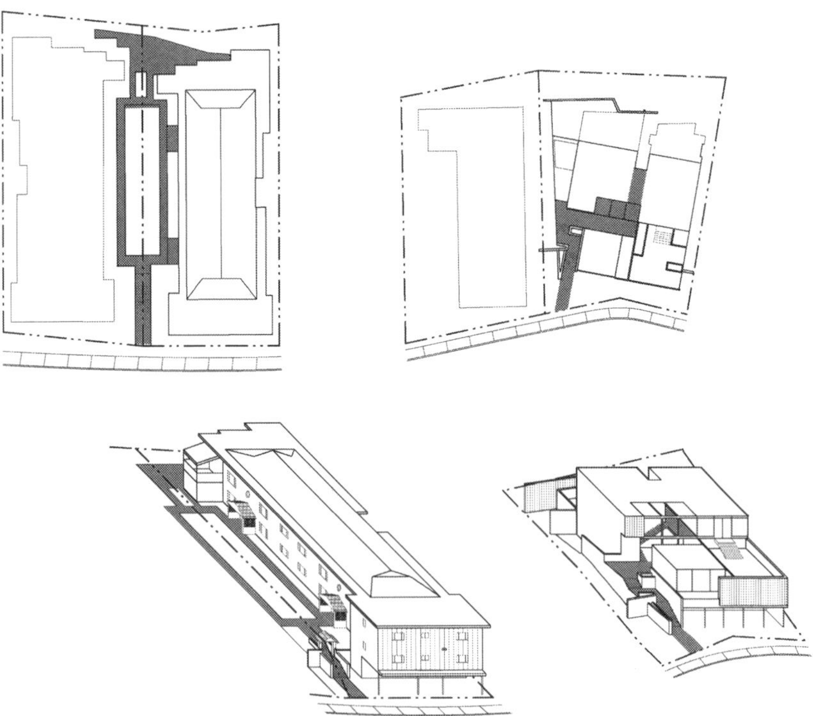

Figure 1.10 Pedestrian circulation diagrams: The Cheviot Manor Apartments (left) vs. The National Apartments (right).

through the building, generating small areas of common open space and community, as well as identity and difference among the units themselves.

Vehicular Access and Parking *Seven Spaces vs. Six Spaces*

Parking for both projects is located at the front of their sites at grade in open carports requiring long curb cuts. Spaces are "tucked under" the volumes of the buildings which are held up by slender metal posts. Cheviot Manor provides five covered and two uncovered spaces. The National Apartments provides five covered and one uncovered space. The lack of garage doors (one less thing to pay for) not only makes the projects float and look more Modern but also makes the buildings look more like dingbat apartments, with the rear ends of cars as part of the facade.

Common Open Space *Centralized Pass-Through vs. Linear Pass-Through*

The Cheviot Manor Apartments has nearly five times the common open space of the National Apartments, but it is much less useable than the smaller spaces provided at Kappe's building (Figure 1.11). The Cheviot

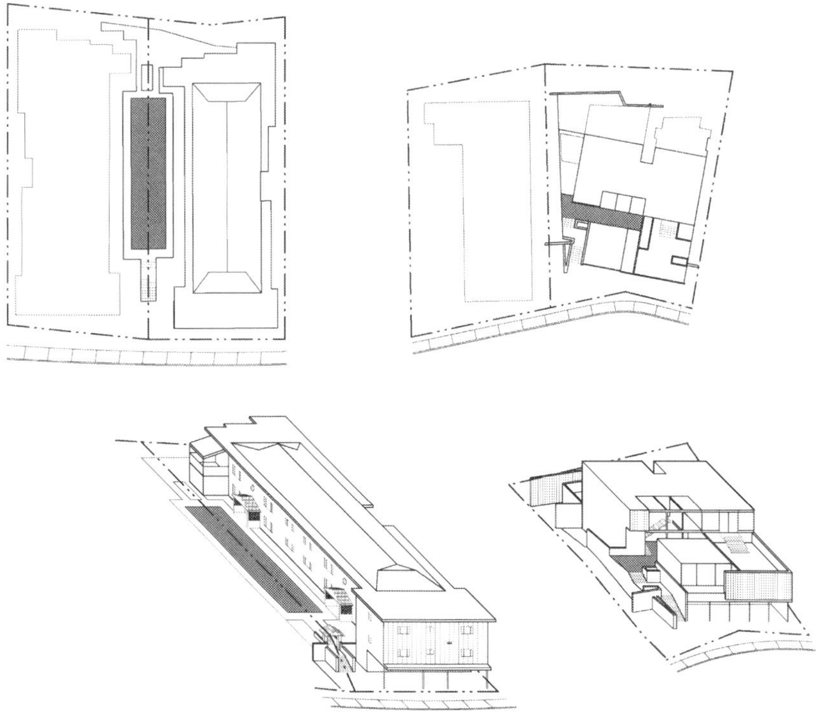

Figure 1.11 Common open space diagrams: The Cheviot Manor Apartments (left) vs. The National Apartments (right).

Manor shares a narrow central courtyard area with its companion building at 10554. This is approximately 30 feet by 100 feet, or 3,000 square feet; relatively flat; and minimally landscaped. The National Apartments has a small common courtyard at the center front of the building, approximately 22 feet by 16 feet, or 352 square feet. This is landscaped with planters and shaded by pergolas, providing many places for residents to sit and gather.

Private Open Space *Standard vs. Substantial*

Private outdoor space is limited at the Cheviot Manor Apartments and generous at the National Apartments (Figure 1.12). The Cheviot Manor has small inset patios and balconies on the west side of the building, approximately 20 to 30 square feet. Units at the National Apartments have almost as much outdoor square footage as they do indoor, averaging about 650 square feet. These outdoor patios and decks are connected to the living space of the units with floor-to-ceiling glass windows and sliding doors. These

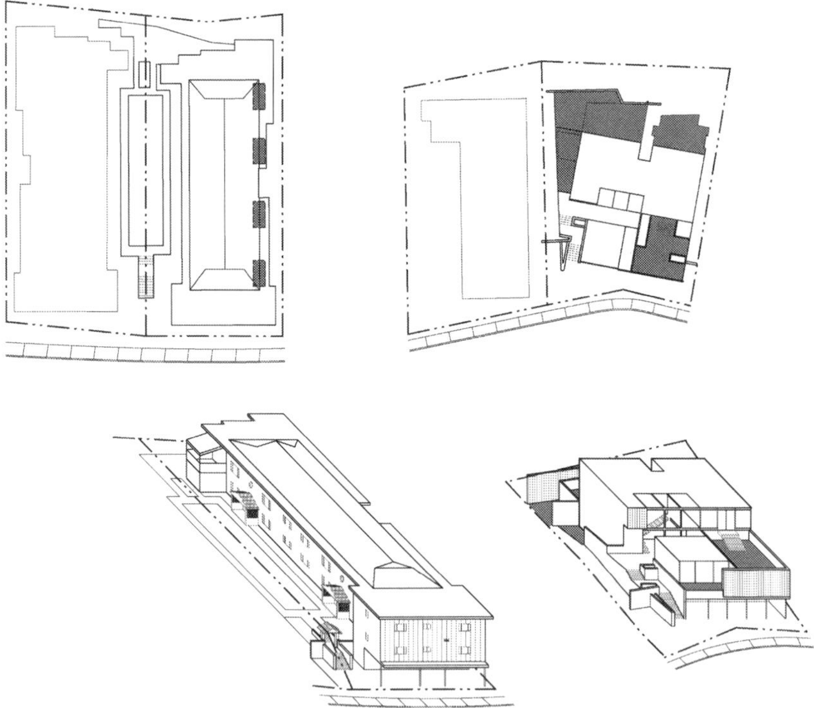

Figure 1.12 Private open space diagrams: The Cheviot Manor Apartments (left) vs. The National Apartments (right).

spaces are wholly private, enclosed by planting, fencing and retaining walls, extending the living space outdoors.

Structure and Materials *Wood Frame vs. Post-and-Beam*

Both case study projects use slim metal posts to hold up the building over onsite parking spaces, round for the Cheviot Manor Apartments and I-shaped for the National Apartments, but use different structural systems for the buildings themselves. The Cheviot Manor uses traditional wood-frame construction sheathed in wood siding at the front and stucco elsewhere. The National Apartments uses wood post and post-beam construction, leaving the 4-inch by 6-inch wood columns and 4-inch by 12-inch beams exposed. This approach allows for a more open plan, blending the kitchen, dining and living spaces together.

Architectural Style *Vernacular Modern vs. Mid-Century Modern*

Both case study buildings use Modern architectural styles, though the National Apartments has much more formal and material character. The Cheviot Manor Apartments is built in "Minimal Modern" or "Vernacular Modern" style characterized by low-pitch overhanging roofs, clean rectilinear volumes, aluminum sliding windows and wood siding on the front facade. The National Apartments is built in a Mid-Century Modern style, characterized by the project's flat roofs, post-and-beam wood construction, horizontal windows, floating steps, floor-to-ceiling glazing and the use of vertical wood siding.

Outcomes *Design Performance*

The National Apartments is clearly the better work of architecture, but that does not mean that the Cheviot Manor Apartments is without merit. It made trade-offs that were acceptable at the time it was built that can be improved upon today:

- Units are generously sized and adaptable to different household types.
- Common open space exists and could be better articulated in terms of image and use.
- Private open space exists.
- Circulation breaks the units into "quad" neighborhoods for social interaction.
- The building's style could be contemporized.

Both buildings, however, were better designed than the "pure" dingbats that came after them, which had less interior and exterior space, less architectural detail and often exterior corridors that comprised the buildings' only outdoor space.

Conclusion

A New Zoning Code Shapes Housing for Better and For Worse

For better or for worse, regulatory changes in the late 1950s killed off hybrid experiments like the case study projects, crystalizing the dingbat apartment into an expression of pure real estate development rationale. Three significant shifts in planning policy fostered a sharp rise in dingbat development in the late 1950s yet heralded the type's quick demise by the late 1960s and early 1970s.

Rezoning of Close-In Neighborhoods Like Palms

First, by the 1950s, many close-in neighborhoods of Los Angeles had deteriorating housing stock that was 50-plus years old. In 1956, the City's "Blight Study Committee" found that 9% of the dwelling units in Los Angeles were substandard and 400 out of 1,000 neighborhoods were at risk of decline, including Palms, which had been identified by the 1950 census as containing deteriorated dwellings (LACPC, 1957, pp. 20, 21). Under an urban renewal program called "New Neighborhoods for Old," the original Palms area subdivided for single-family homes in 1887 was rezoned to R3, raising their potential development value and prompting a second wave of development in an increasingly desirable westside location (LACPC, 1957, p. 24). All the area's historic houses were razed, and the neighborhood is now dense with dingbat apartments built from the late 1950s to the 1970s, mostly on 50-foot by 150-foot lots that yielded six to nine units (34 to 52 dwelling units per acre).

Quickly Evolving Zoning Requirements and Development Standards

Second, zoning requirements, development standards and planning processes were all evolving quickly during the 1940s and 1950s, creating uncertainty for housing developers. This discouraged experimentation and encouraged the practice of "packing" the maximum number of units on a site to hedge against a changing regulatory environment. Before 1946, for example, no residential zones limited density, but in the 1946 code, R3 required 1,650 square feet of lot area per dwelling unit, changing by 1948 to a range of 1,200 square feet for units with more than three rooms to 1,000 square feet per dwelling units with three rooms and 800 square feet for fewer than three rooms (36 to 54 dwelling units per acre). In addition, the only required open spaces in the zoning code at this time were front, side and rear setbacks, allowing buildings to fill their lots to the setback lines. Requiring open space hadn't been necessary before since outdoor open spaces were inherent in earlier Los Angeles housing types, but not so with the dingbat, which maximized its building footprint. And finally, requests that had earlier required variances were adjusted so that they could be allowed by-right. Many buildings with tuck-under parking, for example, especially those in hillside areas with semi-subterranean garages, were over the two-and-a-half-story limit for the R3 zone but still under its 35-foot-height limit, requiring a discretionary approval. By 1956, city planners had adjusted the definition of "story" to allow for a ministerial approval of two-story apartments over "semi-basement" garages (LACPC, 1957, p. 42).

Incrementally Increasing Parking Regulations and Driveway Standards

And third, the lack of street parking in neighborhoods experiencing multifamily housing development became a pressing issue by the late 1950s. "The growing number of two-car households and the drop in patronage of transit lines combined to create a parking tangle that cannot be unraveled as things stand now," reported the *Los Angeles Times* (Easing Street-Parking Problem, 1957, B4). In response, the City increased its off-street parking requirements for multifamily zones in 1957. For most of the 1950s, the requirements had been one space per unit for dwellings in the R2 and R3 zones while parking requirements in the R4 and R5 zones varied from 1:1 for larger units to 2:3 for smaller ones (LACPC, 1958). The new regulations required one space per dwelling unit in all residential zones and 1.25 spaces for buildings with more than six dwelling units of more than three rooms per unit (LACPC, 1958, p. 38).

The practice of tuck-under parking at the front of a property was also compounding the parking problem. This strategy required long curb cuts, which left little length of full-height curb for on-street parallel parking (Figure 1.13). In 1958, Los Angeles passed the Driveway Approach and Curb Space Control Ordinance, stipulating minimum and maximum widths of driveways and minimum full-height-curb distances between driveways (LACPC, 1959, p. 37). These regulations limited front yard parking to one or two spaces per lot, so dingbat developers could no longer build garages the whole width of the street-facing facade. This pushed more onsite parking to the side and the rear, taking up more lot area with driveways and required back-up space.

Finally, in October 1964 the Planning Commission moved to a scheme that used habitable rooms to calculate required parking for multifamily

Figure 1.13 Photo collage included in the 1958 Los Angeles City Planning Commission annual report illustrating how long curb cuts reduce on-street parking space (LACPC, 1959, p. 37).

Credit: Los Angeles City Archives and Records Center.

units. This decision spelled the dingbat's demise. Excluding kitchens less than 150 square feet, bathrooms, hallways and closets, dwellings with two habitable rooms (i.e., studio and one-bedroom apartments) required one space per unit, those with three habitable rooms (i.e., two-bedroom apartments) required one-and-a-half spaces per unit, and units with four or more habitable rooms required two spaces per unit (Planners Will Consider, 1964). Some developers did build dingbats with all studio or one-bedroom units in response to this new regulation, but their lack of unit diversity made them less marketable. This was the beginning of the end for small-scale multifamily development in Los Angeles. Historian Barbara Rubin observed that by the late 1960s:

> the illusion of sub-urban scale could no longer be maintained; even the more peripheral satellite communities could no longer contain their expanding populations in dingbat neighborhoods.
>
> (Rubin, 1977, p. 535)

Denser housing types with higher parking ratios would be required as Los Angeles grew into the late 20th century, losing touch with its low-rise, medium-density housing roots.

Lessons Learned *Design Matters*

Design matters. Architects are trained to innovate and adapt existing housing types to reflect changing cultural values, tastes and standards. Good design can turn the constraints inherent in urban planning and real estate development into opportunities, but only to a point. When urban planning and real estate development environments aren't sensitive to design opportunities, housing residents lose.[17] The National Apartments and its neighbor across the street represent very good efforts but ones that ultimately couldn't push back against overwhelming forces maximizing dwelling units per acre. The subsequent outcome, the dingbat apartment, reduced design opportunities to the medallions and scripted fonts that graced its otherwise blank front facades and consequently provided less quality of life for their residents.

Notes

1. See the Los Angeles Conservancy: www.laconservancy.org/locations/hayworth-avenue-dingbats, retrieved 7/27/18.
2. Dingbats are a subset of the "stucco box" or "decorated box" apartment category, which also includes larger buildings constructed over two or more lots which share the dingbat's smooth stucco geometric abstraction but with interior courtyards and often pools (Chase, 2000; Treffers, 2012). For more about stucco box apartments see Chapter 6: Crafting Cost Benefit.
3. For more about garden apartments see Chapter 3: Lost in Translation.
4. Los Angeles also saw the development of medium- and high-rise multifamily buildings in the 1920s.
5. 10560 National Boulevard met the City's 15 foot front setback requirement when it was built. Later, the front portion of the property was dedicated to the city so that it could expand the public right of way on National Boulevard. This moved the front property line to a location just in front of and aligned with the front facade of the building.
6. Kappe, when interviewed, was adamant that the project is not a dingbat, but rather an improved courtyard/garden apartment (Falletta, 2012). The project's indoor/outdoor qualities do relate more closely to the garden apartment typology, though Kappe makes more of this space private than common.
7. Although both case study projects come in pairs, this investigation evaluates only the 10560 half of the Cheviot Manor and the National Apartments at

10565. The major design differences exhibited by the Maston/Kappe pair would confuse a case study that looked at the projects as double lots.

8. In 1950 Phineas Kappe bought a six-unit apartment at 1412 Kelton in Westwood for $65,000, where he was living when he and Ray built the National Apartments (40 Bixby Crest Homes, 1950). As Ray was growing up, the Kappes always lived in apartments, never a single-family home (Smith, 1995, n.p.).
9. Maston's project uses similar language and materials as Kappe's project but is spatially less innovative. Four one-bedroom, one-bath units step straight up the hill with little variation or spatial interplay, and a fifth unit is located on a second story at the rear. The small apartment units (smaller than Kappe's) are all accessed from a side pathway and entered through a fenced private patio. Covered parking is provided for three cars, tucked under the front unit with one additional uncovered space. Although the projects do communicate well from the street, forming an asymmetrical pair with similar facades and parking strategies, Kappe did not believe it to be one of Maston's better projects (Falletta, 2012).
10. At this point, Ray thought he would do one real estate development project a year with his father, who would be responsible for the leasing and management (Falletta, 2012). Sadly, Phineas died in 1957 on the day he and Ray's mother were to move into a new house built for them by their son (Smith, 1995). Ray did develop one more apartment building with his aunt and uncle, an eight unit in Baldwin Hills at 4150 Hillcrest Drive in 1958 (Photo Standalone 31, 1959). Called the Berkus–Kappe Apartments, Ray eventually sold the building to a resident of the neighborhood because it had become hard for him to rent (Falletta, 2012).
11. These homesites were later redeveloped into a whole enclave of dingbat apartments.
12. This analysis takes the cost listed on the case study buildings' permits at face value. However, owners are incentivized to undervalue construction costs on permit applications since these valuations are used as a basis for the calculation of required fees.
13. The building is very desirable to architects and architecture students, who Kappe had a lot of access to when he started teaching in the 1960s.
14. Using the building's asking rents, Cheviot Manor Apartments would gross $920 a month or $11,040 a year, making back its construction cost in 3.3 years. Assuming rents of $90, probably low, the National Apartments would gross $540 per month, or $6,480 per year, making back its construction cost in 3.9 years.
15. Kappe's work at Anshen + Allen involved post and beam Eichler Homes (Smith, 1995, n.p.).
16. See www.livinghomes.net/.
17. Architects should, likewise, be engaged with planning regulation and development practice, working to understand their perspectives and shape their outcomes.

References

40 Bixby Crest Homes Sold During Past Week. (1950, April 9). *Los Angeles Times*, D6. Retrieved from www.proquest.com

$320,000 Volume of Deals Reported. (1950, April 9). *Los Angeles Times*, D6. Retrieved from www.proquest.com

'55 Held Boom Year for Real Estate Activity. (1955, August 7). *Los Angeles Times*, F1. Retrieved from www.proquest.com

A Bachelor's Apartment. (1963, May 5). *Los Angeles Times*, K18. Retrieved from www.proquest.com

Alpert, D. (1959, June 7). This, Too, Is Apartment Living. *Los Angeles Times*, J12. Retrieved from www.proquest.com

Apartment House Building Boom. (1957, September 18). *Los Angeles Times*, B4. Retrieved from www.proquest.com

Apartment House Building Spurts. (1957, August 24). *Los Angeles Times*, A6. Retrieved from www.proquest.com

Article 30. (1956, March 25). *Los Angeles Times*, E5. Retrieved from www.proquest.com

Banham, R. (1971). *Los Angeles, The Architecture of Four Ecologies*. London, UK: Penguin Books.

Beverly Hills Apartment Building Rising. (1961, February 12). *Los Angeles Times*, P6. Retrieved from www.proquest.com.

Brackman, H. (2007). Making Room for Millions, Housing in Los Angeles. In Hynda L. Rudd and Tom Sitton et al. (Eds.), *The Development of Los Angeles City Government, An Institutional History 1850–2000* (pp. 371–413). Los Angeles, CA: Los Angeles City Historical Society.

Chase, J. (2000). *Glitter Stucco and Dumpster Diving, Reflections on Building Production in the Vernacular City*. New York, NY: Verso.

Classified Ad 15. (1957, September 23). *Los Angeles Times*, B25. Retrieved from www.proquest.com

Classified Ad 17. (1955, October 22). *Los Angeles Times*, A21. Retrieved from www.proquest.com

Classified Ad 25. (1955, August 24). *Los Angeles Times*, A17. Retrieved from www.proquest.com

Display Ad 109. (1954, October 3). *Los Angeles Times*, E14. Retrieved from www.proquest.com

Display Ad 134. (1955, September 11). *Los Angeles Times*, E26. Retrieved from www.proquest.com

Display Ad 142. (1954, November 27). *Los Angeles Times*, F18. Retrieved from www.proquest.com

Doti, L. P., & Schweikart, L. (1989, May). Financing the Postwar Housing Boom in Phoenix and Los Angeles, 1945–1960. *Pacific Historical Review*, *58*(2), 173–194.

Easing Street-Parking Problem. (1957, November 10). *Los Angeles Times*, B4. Retrieved from www.proquest.com

Falletta, L., Interviewer. (2012, June 15). Ray Kappe Interview.

Grant, T., & Stein, J. G. (Eds.). (2016). *Dingbat 2.0, The Iconic Los Angeles Apartments as Projection of a Metropolis*. Los Angeles, CA: Doppel House Press & Los Angeles Forum for Architecture and Urban Design.

Indiana, G. (2004, January 25). If you lived here, you'd be home by now. *Los Angeles Times*. Retrieved from http://articles.latimes.com/2004/jan/25/books/bk-indiana25

Ingersoll, L. A. (1908). *Ingersoll's Century History, Santa Monica Bay Cities*. Los Angeles, CA: Ingersoll.

L.A. City Planning Commission. (1952). *Accomplishments 1951*. Los Angeles, CA: L.A. City Archive.

L.A. City Planning Commission. (1953). *Accomplishments 1952*. Los Angeles, CA: L.A. City Archive.

L.A. City Planning Commission. (1955). *Accomplishments 1954*. Los Angeles, CA: L.A. City Archive.

L.A. City Planning Commission. (1957). *Accomplishments 1956*. Los Angeles, CA: L.A. City Archive.

L.A. City Planning Commission. (1958). *Accomplishments 1957*. Los Angeles, CA: L.A. City Archive.

L.A. City Planning Commission. (1959). *Accomplishments 1958*. Los Angeles, CA: L.A. City Archive.

L.A. City Planning Commission. (1961). *Accomplishments 1960*. Los Angeles, CA: L.A. City Archive.

L.A. City Planning Department. (1946). Zoning Ordinance No. 90,500.

L.A. City Planning Department. (1953). Yard Variance, Case YV6298, 10565 National Boulevard. L.A. City Archives.

L.A. City Planning Department. (1954). Yard Variance, Case YV7146, 10565 National Boulevard. L.A. City Archives.

L.A. County Department of Public Works. (1887). Miscellaneous Record (MR) 21–43–45, The Palms. Retrieved from http://dpw.lacounty.gov/sur/nas/landrecords/misc/MR021/MR021-043.pdf

L.A. County Department of Public Works. (1907). Map Book (MB) 13–1a, Tract No. 40. Retrieved from http://dpw.lacounty.gov/sur/nas/landrecords/tract/MB0013/TR0013-001a.pdf

L.A. Department of Building & Safety. (1954). Building Permit and Certificate of Occupancy, WLA12300, 10565 National Boulevard. Building Records Section.

L.A. Department of Building & Safety. (1955a). Building Permit and Certificate of Occupancy, WLA14095, 10554 National Boulevard. Building Records Section.

L.A. Department of Building & Safety. (1955b). Building Permit and Certificate of Occupancy, WLA14096, 10560 National Boulevard. Building Records Section.

Land Use Survey Co. (1952). *Property Zoning Atlas of Central and West Los Angeles*. Los Angeles, CA: Brewster Enterprise.

Lenox, B. (1959, June 7). Apartment Living—For a Matron with a Young Point of View. *Los Angeles Times*, J12. Retrieved from www.proquest.com

Marriage Announcement 3. (1950, January 3). *Los Angeles Times*, A12. Retrieved from www.proquest.com

Mulcahy, F. (1960, May 8). Older Buildings Razed: Reconversion Process Arrives in Young City of Los Angeles. *Los Angeles Times*, N1. Retrieved from www.proquest.com

Nero, B. (1972, February 13). The Blooming of the Plastic Hibiscus. *Los Angeles Times*, W24. Retrieved from www.proquest.com

Obituary 1. (1962, January 8). *Los Angeles Times*, C13. Retrieved from www.proquest.com

Parson, D. (2005). *Making a Better World: Public Housing, the Red Scare, and the Direction of Modern Los Angeles*. Minneapolis, MN: University of Minnesota Press.

Pastier, J. (1972. February 13). Blue-Light Districts Flourish and City Hall Doesn't Even Bat an Eye. *Los Angeles Times*, F7. Retrieved from www.proquest.com

Photo Standalone 15. (1959, June 14). *Los Angeles Times*, F7. Retrieved from www.proquest.com

Photo Standalone 18. (1962, September 30). *Los Angeles Times*, I20. Retrieved from www.proquest.com

Photo Standalone 31. (1959, January 11). *Los Angeles Times*, F12. Retrieved from www.proquest.com

Piercy, C. (2003). *Pretty Vacant, the Los Angeles Dingbat Observed*. San Francisco, CA: Chronicle Books.

Planners Refuse Setback Permit. (1961, October 29). *Los Angeles Times*, WS5. Retrieved from www.proquest.com

Planners Will Consider Parking Space Increase. (1964, February 7). *Los Angeles Times*, F8. Retrieved from www.proquest.com

Rubin, B. (1977). A Chronology of Architecture in Los Angeles. *Annals of the Association of American Geographers*, 67(4), 521–537.

Smiley, D. (2001). Making the Modified Modern. *Perspecta*, *32*, 38–54.

Smith, A. B., Interviewer. (1995). *Interview of Raymond Kappe*. Los Angeles, CA: UCLA Oral History Program. Retrieved from http://oralhistory.library.ucla.edu/viewItem.do?ark=21198/zz0008zs1t

Smith, W. F. (1964). *The Low-Rise Speculative Apartment Building*. Berkeley, CA: The Center for Real Estate and Urban Economics Institute of Urban and Regional Development.

Treffers, S. A. (2012). *The Dingbat Apartment: The Low-Rise Urbanization of Post World War II Los Angeles* (Master's Thesis), University of Southern California. Retrieved from www.proquest.com

Two Highland Park Apartments Opening. (1965, June 27). *Los Angeles Times*, H26. Retrieved from www.proquest.com

Two Income-Unit Structures. (1955). *Arts and Architecture*, 72(10), 16–17.

Zeiger, M. (2016, June 14). *Is Los Angeles a City of Houses*. Retrieved from http://mimizeiger.com/category/architecture/dingbats/

2 Value Out of Balance, Single-Family House Tracts

Hirsh Tract vs. Modernique Homes

Figure 2.1 Case Study 2: Single-family house tracts, Hirsh Tract (left) vs. the Modernique Homes (right).

Introduction

When Short-Term Costs Doom Further Development, but Ensure Greater Future Value

Subdivisions of single-family homes are the dominant form of housing development in Los Angeles and the individual house in its garden remains the enduring image and identity of the city. Housing tracts are typically organized as blocks of repetitive freestanding houses on individual lots with their own front, side and rear yards. Los Angeles has grown this way throughout its history, but most intensively right after World War II when growth spiked and large subdivisions became the norm: 128,882 dwelling units were built between 1946 and 1950, by which time 37.46% of the City's land area was zoned for single-family housing (LACPC), 1951, p. 36).[1] Prior to the war, housing tracts were usually organized around gridded blocks, sometimes with alleys and often with small-scale multifamily buildings mixed in. The land subdivider was usually not the builder in this era, a time when the city had an excess of lots, often in "undeveloped area[s]" with "uncertain future[s]" (Weiss, 1987, p. 2). When owners believed it was advantageous to build, they typically hired a contractor to build a house from stock plans, mail-order house kits or architectural plans provided by lenders. Postwar, as local, state and national subdivision standards evolved and the housing industry professionalized, curvilinear blocks and streets became preferred, often using cul-de-sacs and perimeter access roads to deflect through traffic and interiorize neighborhoods. Merchant builders emerged at this time, specialized firms that acquired and subdivided land upon which they built and sold homes in large numbers. Many of these organizations believed themselves to be more "community builders" than subdividers, contractors or agents, building Los Angeles neighborhood by neighborhood rather than tract by tract (Urban Land Institute (ULI), 1947; Weiss, 1987). How did this transition occur and what can it tell us about the role of real estate development in housing production relative to urban planning and design goals?

A comparison between two tracts of homes built at the height of the postwar boom addresses these questions: a tract built by the Hirsh-Edmunds Building Company and architect Hugh Gibbs in 1950 and the adjacent tract to the west, the Modernique Homes built by the Advance Development Company, Inc. and architect Gregory Ain in 1948 (Figure 2.1). By the late 1940s, the real estate industry had begun to meet the crushing demand for homes across the U.S. but was also beginning to be critiqued by both architects and urban planners for the perceived social homogeneity, visual uniformity and general ugliness of the suburbs they were building for returning servicemen and their families (Jackson, 1985). The Modernique Homes, also known as the Mar Vista Tract, sought to address these critiques by creating a community that was socially connected, inclusive and affordable via modern, flexible houses on large lots with shared landscaping (Denzer, 2005) (Figure 2.4). Though the Mar Vista Tract represented an "enlightened" approach to development that valued innovative design and site planning, its advancements were out of sync with the surrounding market and the project was a financial failure.

Home buyers were interested in the communal yards, convertible interior space and modern style of the Modernique Homes, but were unwilling or unable to pay a nearly 50% premium over comparable homes in the neighborhood to enjoy them. The project sold so poorly that an equivalently sized parcel of land to the east set aside for a planned second phase had to be sold to a conventional developer, Harold Hirsh, who quickly subdivided and improved the land in the more customary manner with small houses in traditional styles on independent lots grouped around cul-de-sacs (Figures 2.2 and 2.3). This tract, heretofore called the Hirsh Tract, though reflecting the best practices of the time, is, on the whole, more isolated and individualized with less in common to bring neighbors together. Hirsh was just building houses, but Edelman was clearly building a community.

Although the case study projects balance individuality and community differently in their site design, houses in both tracts are examples of the "post-war minimal house" that proliferated across Los Angeles from 1945 to 1953 (Caltrans, 2011, p. 67). These homes were engineered to be economical, since most postwar households were new, small and living on entry-level incomes without much savings. Their design maximized functionality and efficiency, providing "better living in fewer rooms" (Hise, 1997, p. 66). Houses were typically one to one-and-a-half stories

Figure 2.2 A selection of houses in the Hirsh Tract.

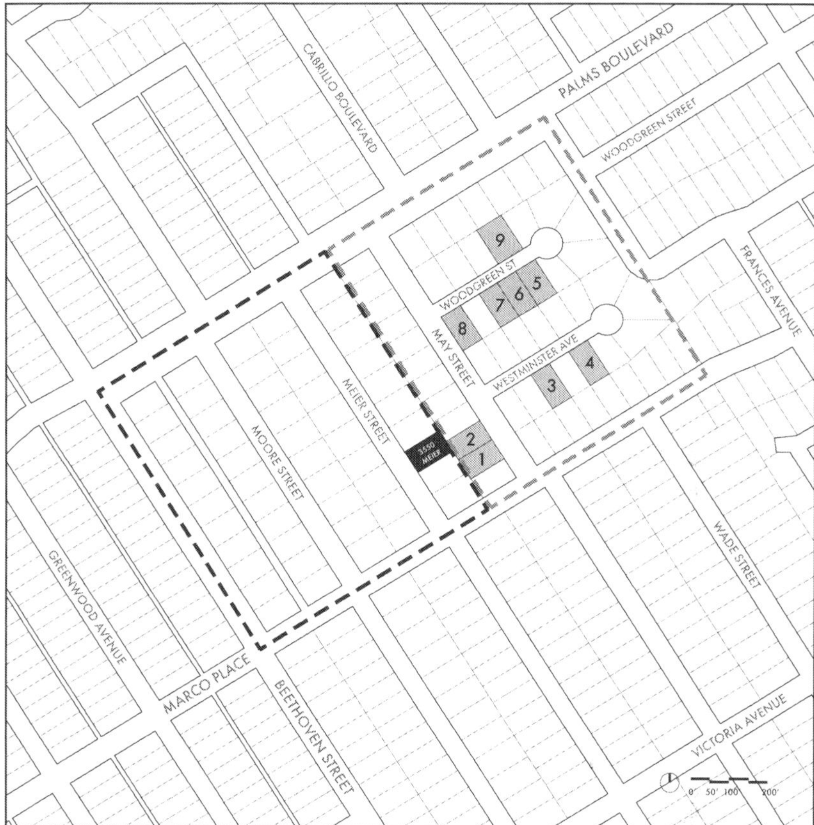

Figure 2.3 Modernique Home at 3550 Meier Street and Hirsh Tract houses, including 3559 May Street (1), mapped.

and 750 square feet to 1,020 square feet, with compact floor plans to reduce the linear footage of exterior wall (Caltrans, 2011, p. 68). A large tract of these homes would usually use a limited number of house plans, rotated, reversed and clad differently to provide variety, adding small covered porches on the front to define the entry. Houses were built with conventional wood framing and did not include basements. Most had garages with one-piece tilt-up garage doors, usually attached to the house by 1950. These homes were mainly built in the "Minimal Traditional" style like those in the Hirsh Tract, styles such as Colonial or Mission stripped of much of the detail these revival styles employed in the 1920s and 1930s. The Modernique Homes, unusually, was built in Mid-Century Modern, an inherently minimal style, including flat roofs, floor-to-ceiling windows and post-and-beam structure.

Tract Histories

The Hirsh Tract was subdivided by Harold and Sylvia Hirsh in October 1949 into 57 lots grouped around two cul-de-sacs with a perimeter of outward facing parcels (L.A. County Public Works [LACPW], 1949) (Figures 2.2 and 2.3). Mr. Hirsh was a partner in the Hirsh-Edmunds Building Company, a large-scale builder and developer of conventional tracts in Los Angeles throughout the 1950s, which acted as the contractor for the project (L.A. Department of Building & Safety [LADBS], 1949). After subdivision, ownership of the parcels was transferred to Associated Home Furnishers, Inc. which developed the tract with a collection of modest homes, all designed by architect Hugh Gibbs, a key player in the development of an "economy house" plan for the Home Builders Institute of Los Angeles in 1948 (Lower Cost, 1948) (Figure 2.5). The project is an example of a small, but typical, vernacular housing tract that uses five different two-bedroom, one-bath and three-bedroom, one-bath house plans, each with multiple variations and detached garages at the rear. All told, at least 28 different options were built, and no plan was used more than four times. The homes, which ranged from 904 to 1,250 square feet, on 5,460- square-foot to 11,120-square-foot lots were built in Minimal Traditional styles, including American Colonial, Spanish Colonial, Monterrey and Ranch. They were built quickly, with permits obtained in November 1949 and Certificates of Occupancy issued in July 1950, 8 to 9 months (LADBS, 1950). Building permit records show the homes being constructed for $7,500, which were likely then sold for $8,500 to $9,000 given comparable homes advertised for sale in the area. (LADBS, 1949b).[2] Given their experience, this team was well positioned to quickly deliver low-cost, marketable homes at a reasonable price and they did everything to speed the project to market, following all Los Angeles, California and Federal Housing Administration rules.

The Mar Vista Tract was subdivided by the Advance Development Company, Inc., Barney M. Edelman, president, in February 1948 into 52 lots on three rectilinear blocks (LACPW, 1948). Its "Modernique" houses, homes "Modern in Design and Unique in Livability," were designed in 1947 by architect Gregory Ain in association with Joseph Johnson and Alfred Day and built by contractor Barnett B. Poles (Display Ad 74, 1948; LADBS, 1948).[3] Lot sizes ranged from 6,500 square feet to 7,500 square feet. A standard 1,050-square-foot house plan was used to create construction efficiencies and economies of scale, which was rotated and mirrored across the site to provide variation, create different social conditions between neighbors and encourage engagement with the public realm (Figures 2.4 and 2.6).[4] The location of the garage was also shifted from lot to lot to create 16 different overall plans (Denzer, 2005, p. 277). Flexible interior planning allowed the homes to be configured as one-, two- or three-bedrooms, adapting to various lifestyles and stages (Figure 2.7). With the flexible space, homes could accommodate a young married couple in their "open" position,

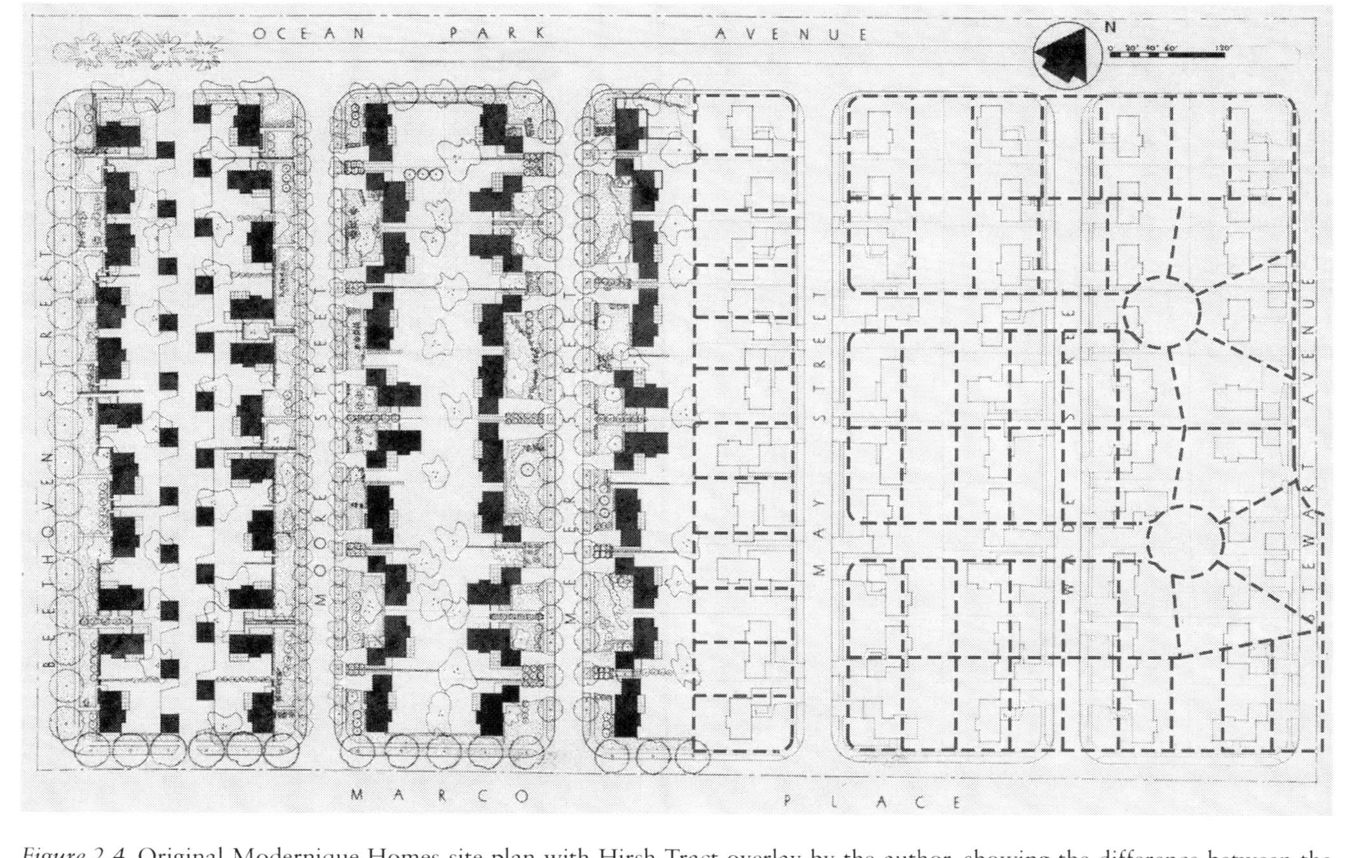

Figure 2.4 Original Modernique Homes site plan with Hirsh Tract overlay by the author, showing the difference between the initially planned gridiron organization and the Hirsh Tract as built with houses organized around cul-de-sacs.

Credit: Gregory Ain papers, Architecture and Design Collection. Art, Design & Architecture Museum, University of California, Santa Barbara.

Figure 2.5 By-right case study project: 3559 May Street in the Mar Vista neighborhood of Los Angeles.

Figure 2.6 By-design case study project: Modernique Home at 3550 Meier Street in the Mar Vista neighborhood of Los Angeles.

then "expand" by partitioning off additional rooms once the family grew and then opened again when the children moved out. Permits were obtained in February 1948 which show the houses being constructed for $7,000 (LADBS, 1948).[5] Certificates of Occupancy were issued in January and February 1949, 12 to 13 months, and the houses were offered for sale at $11,000 and then $12,950 (LADBS, 1949a). For both architect and developer, the goal of the Mar Vista project was to

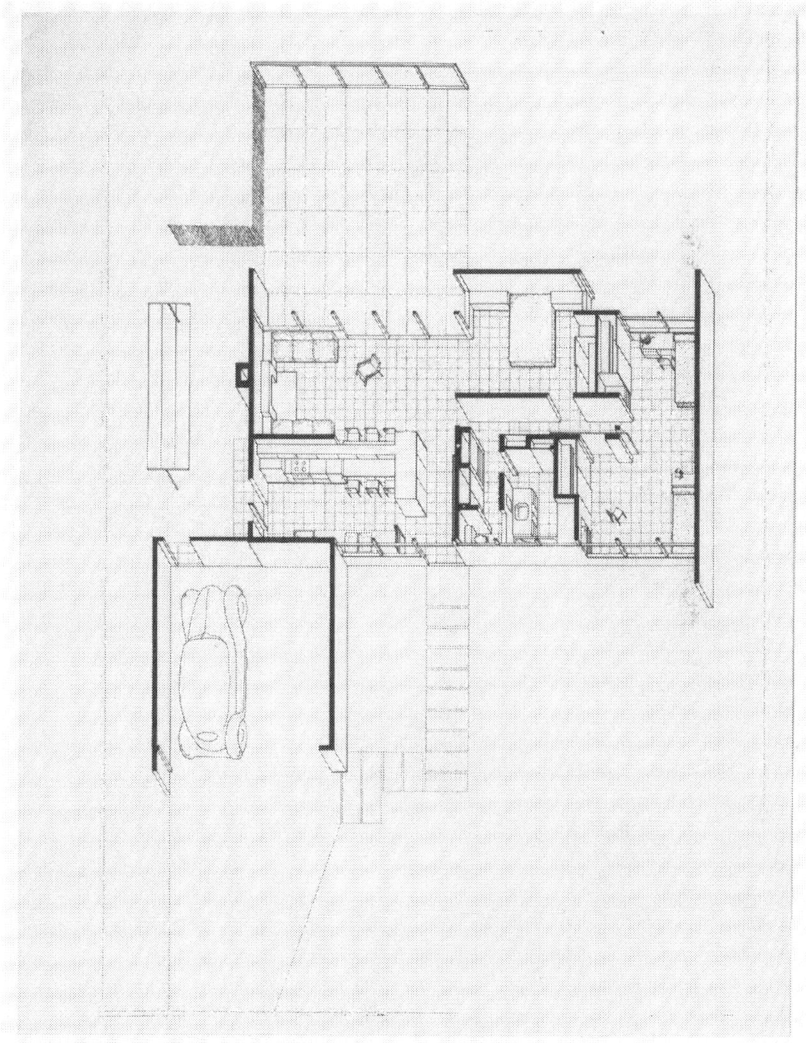

Figure 2.7 Axonometric drawing of a Modernique Home showing its flexible interior layout which can expand from one up to three bedrooms.

Credit: Gregory Ain papers, Architecture and Design Collection. Art, Design & Architecture Museum, University of California, Santa Barbara.

create an inclusive community with cost-efficient homes that supported modern lifestyles (Ain, 1951; McCoy, 1984). On the whole, the design of the tract favored difference, openness and inclusion rather than homogeneity, privacy and exclusion as seen in most typical subdivisions of the era (Denzer, 2005). The tract was designated as a Historic Preservation Overlay Zone in 2004.

The Mar Vista Tract's innovations, however, created regulatory hurdles for the project that the Hirsh Tract did not face. A sliding partition separating the living room from the master bedroom, for example, was originally prohibited by the Federal Housing Administration (FHA) because it would cover a heater when open. Ain replaced the sliding door with a hinged alternative (Denzer, 2005). The FHA was also concerned about the marketability of the tract's Modern architectural style and preferred that houses with more conventional styles be mixed in with the original modern design. Ain and Edelman could not agree to this, so the FHA decided it would only insure the project if the houses were built in stages to "test the [market] acceptance" (McCoy, 1984, p. 129). The tract's gridiron subdivision pattern was also considered to be undesirable by the Los Angeles City Planning Department, especially since its use required that some of the homes face Beethoven Street, a busy thoroughfare. The City required that the homes facing this street be alley-accessed, though they would have preferred that the tract use a "back-up design" orienting the rear of the lots to Beethoven or, better yet, abandon the gridiron for cul-de-sacs (LACPC, 1950). As a result of these negotiations, the original 102 house project was reduced to 52 houses on half of the site. The project's first phase became its only phase.

Urban Planning

Context

Local and national regulation both worked to shape the unprecedented growth of Los Angeles after World War II. Urban planners in LA were focused on subdivision standards as well as an overall master plan (i.e., general plan) to direct and structure the city's significant physical growth. These tasks entailed creating more specific spatial and dimensional standards as well as more detailed zoning requirements. At the same time, the FHA, established in 1934, was working to expand homeownership opportunities for Americans and ensure that those homes were a good investment. The agency accomplished this largely through the provision of loan guarantees to local banks, which lent the funds for families to purchase homes that met the FHA's strict underwriting criteria, which ranged from minimum standards for home construction to appropriate neighborhood location to the social status of its residents.[6] By the time the case study projects were built, both of these regulators were speaking in concert, on balance encouraging conformity and sameness, rather than originality and difference, as a better value for both homeowners and the community as a whole.

Los Angeles City *Planning Department Subdivision Regulation*

Subdivision in early Los Angeles was haphazard, piecemeal and excessive, often resulting in isolated, unbuildable lots. The City Planning Commission regulated land subdivision from its inception in 1920, working to simplify and standardize the process to ensure that lots were legal, accessible and buildable. To this end, the Commission adopted Standard Subdivision Guide in 1926 that described the "typical lot layout for varying degrees of land subdivision" (LACPC, 1928, p. 12). The accompanying diagram shows 40-acre quadrants that could ultimately be subdivided into eight residential blocks with a gridiron pattern using a hierarchy of streets to be dedicated to the City as public rights of way. Subdivision was the bulk of the commission's work at this time, yet activity fell off somewhat in 1929 and then considerably during the Great Depression. By 1930 the city had an excess of almost 80,000 parcels (L.A. City Planning Department [LADCP], 1930, p. 50).

After 10 years of subdivision oversight, Los Angeles city planners had begun to realize that "the value and character of an entire section is largely influenced by the original subdividers" (LADCP, 1930, p. 48). Subdivision practices in the 1920s, though regulated, had still resulted in many jogged streets, overscaled intersections, isolated development and a decided lack of dedicated open space. During the 1930s, planners began to think about subdivision more as the essential patterning of communities rather than simply the control of land speculation. Planners took advantage of the market downturn to both refine standards and educate subdividers, hoping to find a point at which the "advantages to the community and the [land]owner [would] be about equal" (LADCP, 1930, p. 48).

To accomplish this, however, property had to be properly zoned. Los Angeles planners believed a neighborhood composition of "53% single family homes, 5% apartments, 4% for business, 10% neighborhood parks and playgrounds, 28% streets and circles" to be optimal (LADCP, 1930, p. 49). By 1932, city planners had applied this formula to the recommended subdivision layout, still in a gridiron format (Figure 2.8). The case study projects' zone, R1, required "one family residence to one recorded lot," with 25-foot front, 7-foot side and 25-foot rear setbacks (LACPC, 1931, p. 18).

Subdivision activity picked up in the mid-1930s and then boomed after World War II, creating 2,893 lots in 1945, 10,880 in 1946, 6,317 in 1947, 8,346 in 1948 and 11,049 in 1949 (LACPC, 1949, p. 37; 1950, p. 36). A comprehensive zoning update in 1946 adjusted the requirements for the R1 zone slightly, adding a covered onsite parking requirement of one space per dwelling unit (LADCP, 1946, p. 14). Adjustments in 1948 changed the setback requirements, reducing the front setback from 25 feet to 20 feet (LADCP, 1946, p. 15; 1948, p. 10). But by this time the City Planning Department's recommendations and requirements for the physical design of subdivisions had begun to shift. Planners now believed that the traditional urban grid of the past created too many dangerous intersections and through streets, costly and redundant street infrastructure and less quality of life for those in homes fronting major streets. Planners offered four alternatives to correct these shortcomings:

Rear Alley Access—Parking for lots facing busy streets located on interior alleys.
Back-up Design—Lots back up to major streets and face local interior streets.
Local Service Road—Homes buffered by a local street parallel to a busy thoroughfare.
Cul-de-Sacs—Access lots using cul-de-sacs that end just short of a major street (LACPC, 1950, p. 36) (Figure 2.9).

By 1950, a year in which nearly 16,000 lots were recorded, Los Angeles planners had completed the transition from the traditional urban grid to the insular strategies of suburbia. Three example tracts documented in the 1950 LA City Planning Commission *Annual Report* were gridiron on submittal but, to be approved, were revised using curvilinear streets, long blocks, looping streets and cul-de-sacs to disconnect the neighborhood from its surrounding context and create an interiorized community (LACPC, 1951, pp. 30–31) (Figure 2.10).

FHA Underwriting Criteria

The FHA's underwriting and construction standards required to obtain mortgage insurance also significantly shaped the configuration of housing tracts in Los Angeles along the same suburban lines. Loan defaults and local bank failures experienced during the Great Depression spurred the creation of the FHA in 1934 to stabilize the mortgage market and create a home financing system that could expand homeownership. The agency quickly began guaranteeing low-cost mortgages made by local FHA-approved private banks, protecting local lenders in case of default. Prior to this time, home loans were typically short term (3 to 5 years) with no amortization and 50% or lower loan-to-value ratios. The FHA regulated interest rates and loan terms, amortizing loans over 20, 25 and then 30 years and increasing the loan-to-value ratios to 80%. These

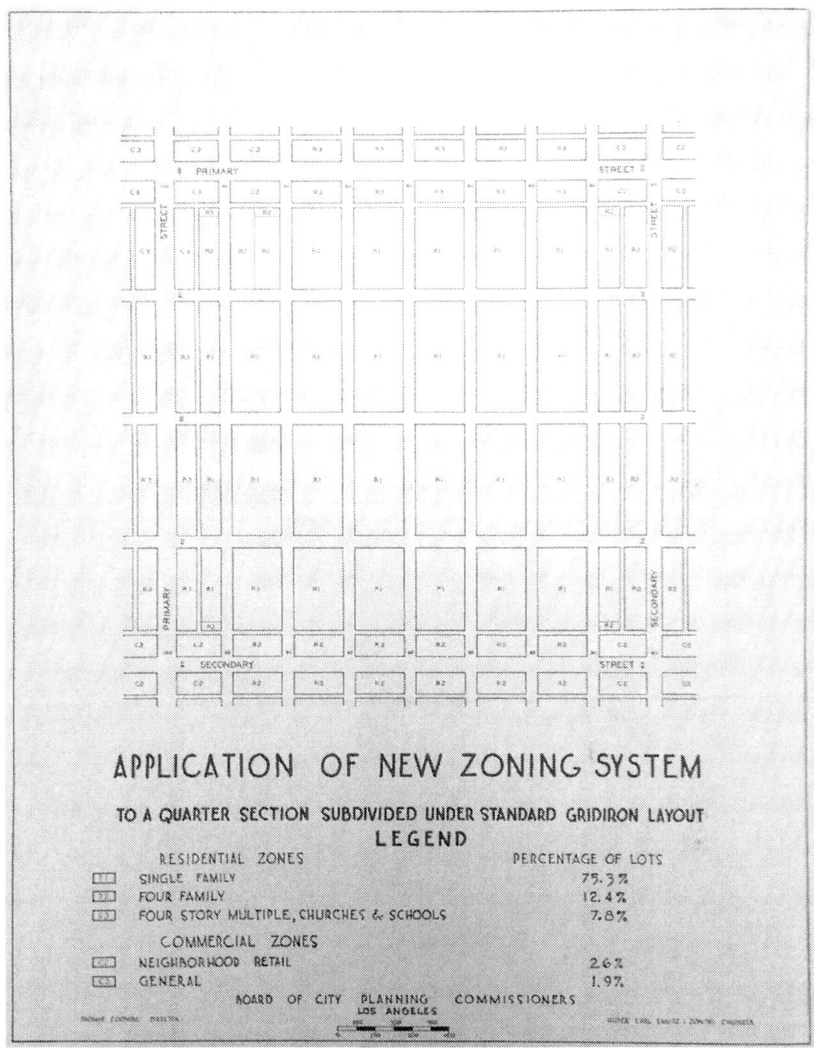

Figure 2.8 Application of the 1930 Los Angeles zoning code to the City's recommended subdivision layout (LACPC, 1932, p. 12). Note that areas for single-family homes are protected by areas for multifamily and commercial on primary and secondary streets.

Credit: Los Angeles City Archives and Records Center.

measures dramatically reduced the down payment necessary to purchase a home and reduced monthly debt service payments since the loan was extended over a longer period of time. These tools boosted homeownership rates in the US from 47.8% in 1930 to 55.0% in 1950 (US Census

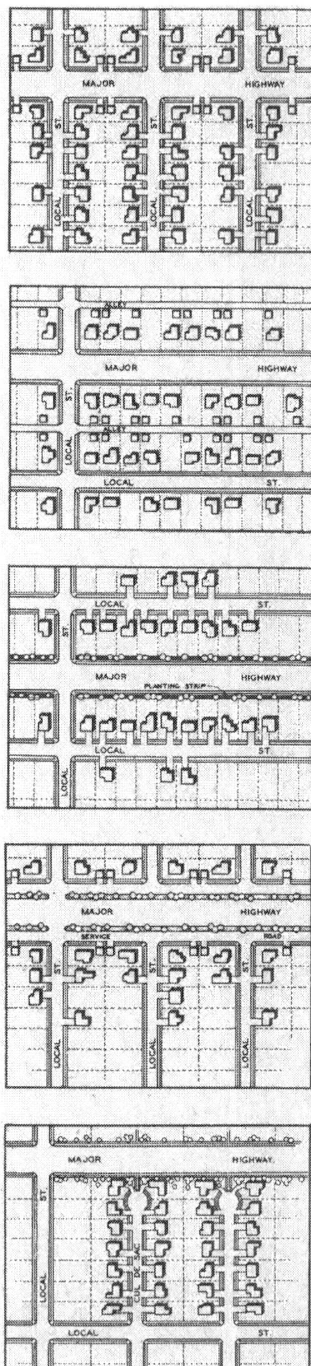

Figure 2.9 Los Angeles City Planning Department recommended subdivision design strategies in lieu of the gridiron (top), which included alleys, lots backing up to major streets, local service roads and cul-de-sacs (LACPC, 1950, p. 36).

Credit: Los Angeles City Archives and Records Center.

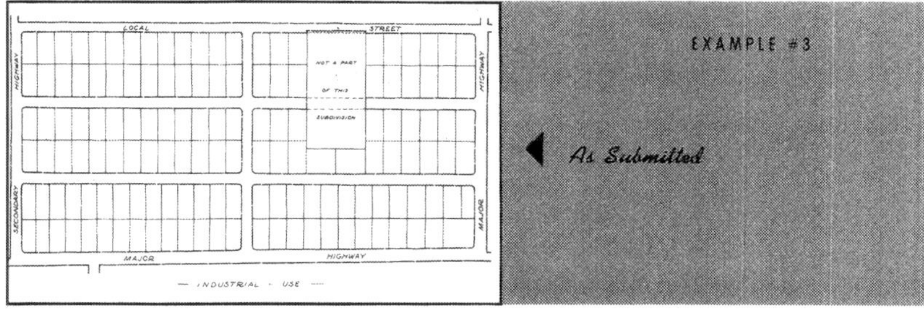

This plat, as revised, was accepted wholeheartedly by the subdivider despite the fact that additional expense would be involved in street construction. Cul-de-sac treatment was introduced to reorient lots facing industrial uses. Intersections along traffic streets were reduced to a minimum. The complete plan provides a physical pattern for better living.

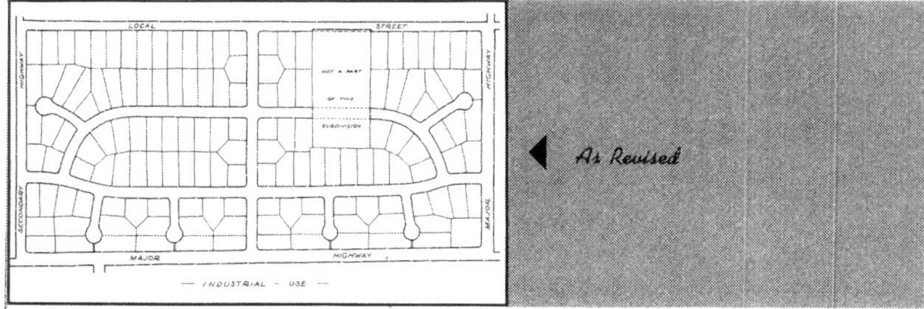

Figure 2.10 A sample subdivision map as submitted (gridiron) and as revised (cul-de-sacs) by the Los Angeles City Planning Department (LACPC, 1951, p. 33).

Credit: Los Angeles City Archives and Records Center.

Bureau, 2011). By the late 1940s, most house tracts for sale in Los Angeles were FHA insured.

One of the most important criteria for FHA approval was that homes have adequate "protection" using either zoning restrictions or long-term protective covenants. These needed to regulate use, lot size, setbacks, design, minimum cost and size of dwellings and the "prohibition of nuisances," which was interpreted widely and could mean noxious uses or "undesirable" neighbors, i.e., racial minorities and immigrants (FHA, 1940, p. 28). The Los Angeles Planning Department was supportive from the beginning:

> The splendid property standards set up by the Federal Housing Administration as requirements for mortgage insurance and their insistence that proper zoning protection be provided before the property is eligible for FHA loans, are materially benefiting the work of this Department. Their requirements have made property owners more zoning conscious than ever before, and the interest which

> property owners displayed in proper zoning and re-zoning is most encouraging.
>
> (LACPC, 1935, p. 19)

Once the FHA instituted this requirement, Los Angeles saw an uptick in zone-change requests to R1 almost immediately (LACPC, 1938, p. 17). From July 1937 through June 1938, representatives of the FHA checked the zoning for 31,610 individual mortgage insurance applications (LACPC, 1938, p. 24).

The FHA also supported the view of Los Angeles city planners that subdivisions should be designed as whole neighborhoods rather than isolated islands of single-family development facing uncontrolled land. The FHA disseminated these beliefs through its many *Land Planning* and *Technical Bulletins* that spelled out best practices from its perspective. In Land Planning Bulletin No. 1, *Successful Subdivisions, Principles of Planning for Economy and Protection Against Neighborhood Blight*, the FHA declared that there is "Profit in Planned Neighborhoods" at all price points and that the "successful developer is more than a subdivider of land or a builder of houses. He is a crafter of communities" (FHA, 1940, p. 2). In *Planning Profitable Neighborhoods*, Technical Bulletin No. 7, it argues that "Subdivisions planned as neighborhoods are more profitable to developers, better security for investors, more desirable for homeowners" (FHA, 1938, p. 6). To enhance community feel, it suggests planning for the extension of major streets, providing school and church sites, locating commercial areas conveniently, looking at parks as a neighborhood asset and preserving natural features for improved appearance (FHA, 1940, p. 13). The FHA also wholeheartedly approved of Los Angeles's transition from gridiron to curvilinear blocks. It thought the grid created "a monotonous, uninteresting architectural effect" that "fails to create a community aspect" since it was felt to have little character, unnecessary cross streets and dangerous through streets (FHA, 1936, pp. 10, 12).

How similar or different are the Hirsh Tract and the Mar Vista Tract from an urban planning perspective? Does the fact that one was built as-of-right and the other required discretionary approval mean that one met planning goals better than the other?

Spatial Organization *Hybrid Grid/Cul-de-Sac vs. Gridiron With Alley*

The site plans of the case study projects both capture the awkward transition from gridiron blocks with alleys to curvilinear blocks with cul-de-sacs (Figure 2.11). The Hirsh Tract is organized around a single rectilinear block on May Street that connects to two short cul-de-sacs

Figure 2.11 Both the Hirsh Tract (right) and the Modernique Homes (left) are disconnected from their surrounding urban context by jogging streets and a service road as well as cul-de-sacs (Hirsh) and an alley (Modernique).

(Woodgreen and Westminster Streets), creating a primarily inward-looking street pattern cut off from surrounding development. Houses face the street and are placed in the middle of their lots, set back 20 feet from the sidewalk. Unusually, houses on the north and south edges of the tract face out, addressing a frontage road paralleling Palms Boulevard to the north and Marco Place, a local through street, to the south.

The Mar Vista Tract, subdivided a year and a half earlier than the Hirsh Tract, is organized around two-and-a-half rectilinear urban blocks organized in a grid pattern connected to, but slightly off from, the street configuration of surrounding development. Houses face Beethoven, Moore and Meier Streets and are sited variably on their lots, set back from 20 feet to 40 feet from the sidewalk. The block between Beethoven and Moore Streets is alley-accessed to ensure that homeowners did not have to back out onto Beethoven, a busy through street. The side of the tract also connects to the frontage road running parallel to Palms Boulevard and Marco Place.

Despite their differences in spatial organization, the case study projects are very similar from the perspective of other important planning metrics.

Zoning *R1 vs. R1*

Both case study projects were zoned R1 allowing for one single-family home per 5,000-square foot lot (50 ft by 100 ft) at the time they were built. Lot sizes and dimensions in both projects exceed the requirements of the zone. Lots in the Hirsh Tract range from 5,460 to 11,120 square feet while lots in the Mar Vista Tract range from 6,500 to 7,500. The Hirsch Tract's lots are narrower, ranging from 56 to 58.5 feet for rectangular lots, while the Mar Vista Tract lots range from 65 to 73 feet in width. Lot depths in the two tracts are equivalent, at approximately 100 feet.

Density *6.72 Dwelling Units/Acre vs. 6.27 Dwelling Units/Acre*

Both the Hirsh Tract and the Mar Vista Tract are less dense than required by the R1 zone and about equally as dense as one another. One single-family dwelling unit per 5,000 square feet equals 8.72 dwelling units per acre, while the case study tracts are each about six dwelling units per acre.

Height and Setbacks *One Story vs. One Story*

The case study projects easily meet FHA's and Los Angeles's regulations for height and setbacks. Both originally built one-story houses. Setbacks in the Hirsh Tract are 20 feet while in the Mar Vista Tract they vary from 20 feet to 40 feet, allowing more room for a park-like public realm.

Parking *Two-Car Detached Garage at Rear vs. Two-Car Attached Garage at Front*

Both tracts provide two-car garages on site, doubling the zoning requirement of one covered parking space per dwelling unit. The Hirsch Tract's garages are detached from the house and placed in the rear with a driveway down the side. The Mar Vista Tract's garages are attached in the front with a short driveway (or detached in the rear off an alley). This was undoubtedly a response to market forces. By 1950 Los Angeles County had the most automobile registrations in the nation at 1,545,351, exceeding the next metropolitan area, the five boroughs of New York City, by nearly 500,000 cars (LACPC, 1952, pp. 10, 13).

Planning Outcomes *Letter of the Law vs. Spirit of the Law*

The case study projects seem very similar in terms of basic planning metrics but are actually quite different from one another when evaluated as whole neighborhoods. As expected given its by-right status, the Hirsh Tract plays by the rules and does exactly what is required so as to speed the project to market. Also as expected, the Mar Vista Tract pushes for the evolution of planning regulation in response to design innovation, but it does so in the name of community, i.e., that which the rules were purported to create in the first place. The Hirsch Tract's homes are marooned on small cul-de-sacs with a minimal public realm and little to bring neighbors together. Ironically, by breaking a few rules, Ain and Edelman's neighborhood met the spirit of planning regulation better than actual adherence to those rules. The Modernique Home's flexible houses meant that families could stay in the neighborhood as they grew. The development's expansive, park-like common front yards provided a place for children to play when parks were scarce. And its distinctive architecture gave the community a forward-thinking image and identity when many were identical and cookie-cutter.

Design

Context

Design became less formal and more abstract during the post–World War II era, when well-designed yet inexpensive homes and furnishings were in great demand. Leading designers broke free of tradition and were optimistic about a future where unpretentiousness, regeneration, modernization, mass production and adaptability were all common themes. "Modern" housing was being produced in a variety of manners. Postwar architects were racing to incorporate new materials and technologies from the war into housing and many were exploring prefabricated housing and minimal dwelling. But most houses were modern without being Modernist. Architect David Smiley has surmised that there were really two modernisms at work in the postwar era, one based on a "production aesthetic" that was modern in image, construction and function (i.e., the Modernique Homes) and another based on the promise of "frictionless inhabitation" that looked more traditional on the outside but provided every modern amenity on the interior to streamline and ease family life (i.e., houses in the Hirsh Tract) (Smiley, 2001, p. 43).

Modernist houses were being built at various price points. The Case Study program, high Modern experimental houses sponsored by John Entenza and *Arts and Architecture* magazine, ran from 1945 until 1966, with a goal of testing efficient, economical and replicable model homes that could address the postwar housing crisis. About 30 were built, but none went into production. Architects Charles and Ray Eames, Richard Neutra, Sumner Spaulding and William Wurster all built case study houses in Los Angeles during the late 1940s, featuring open planning, floor-to-ceiling glass and indoor/outdoor connections. Modernist tract housing was also being built in Mid-Century Modern at this time, with perhaps less stylistic integrity than the Case Study houses but with more impact. Joseph Eichler built thousands of single-family homes in both Northern and Southern California, originally working with the architecture firm Anshen and Allen but eventually also working with Los Angeles architects Raphael Soriano, A. Quincy Jones and Jones & Emmons. Los Angeles architects William Krisel, Edward Fickett and Cliff May also worked on Mid-Century Modern tract housing for various developers in Los Angeles.

Hugh Gibbs

Hugh Gibbs, architect of the Hirsh Tract, had a prolific architectural practice, designing everything from custom single-family homes to office buildings to hospitals. He designed tract homes for many large subdivisions during the postwar era, including 560 homes in Silverado Park near Long Beach, 174 homes in Crenshaw Villa near Gardena and 175 homes for Rosecrans Rancho in South Los Angeles, so a tract of 57 houses in West Los Angeles was a relatively small project for him (Display Ad 68, 1948; Final Plans, 1950; New Second Unit, 1951). Large subdivisions at this time typically had five to nine different house plans that could be clad in up to 30 different elevations. Gibbs designed these homes in an incredibly wide variety of styles, including Monterey, Ranch, Cape Cod, Salt Box, Contemporary and even "Lanai."

In addition to the houses Gibbs designed for specific developer clients, he was also a part of a team that developed an "economy house plan" for Los Angeles, one that would be "economical yet adequate" (Cohan, 1948, E3). In 1948 the Home Builders Institute of Los Angeles brought together builders, lenders, FHA representatives and three consulting architects to study the problem of low-cost housing (Lower Cost, 1948).[7] Housing professionals across the country were discussing the pressing need for lower cost homes for families of average means. Typical U.S. house prices ranged from $15,000 to $60,000 in 1948, a big jump from the $7,000 average home price in 1947 (The Race, 1949, G5). The Los Angeles two-bedroom, one-bath economy house averaged 750 square feet but with the "livability of a more spacious home" (Production Increase, 1949, E1). These house plans, nine variations in all, with specifications, were first offered to Home Builders Institute Los Angeles members in January 1949. The group hoped that these houses would shave as much as 60 days off FHA processing time, sell in the $8,000 range and require monthly payments of about $50 (Lower Cost, 1948; Trend to Economy, 1949, A1).[8] Given that houses in the Hirsh Tract were permitted the same year the economy house plan was introduced, they are very likely similar, if not identical.

Gregory Ain

Gregory Ain, architect of the Mar Vista Tract, was interested in economy housing throughout his career, which he explored via research into new construction methods and materials, inventive spatial planning strategies and large-scale cooperative housing proposals. Son of a socialist, Ain spent nine months as a child at Llano del Rio, a cooperative farm established outside Los Angeles in 1914, which profoundly shaped his perspective on architecture's purpose (McCoy, 1982, p. 1). Ain "considered historicism a waste and individualism irresponsible" and viewed Modern architecture, at its highest level, to be "a means towards social ends" (McCoy, 1984, p. 82). Ain studied architecture at the University of Southern California and worked for both Richard Neutra and Rudolph Schindler, two of Los Angeles's best-known Modernists, early in his career. He established his own office in 1935 working in the International Style on small, user-friendly, "servantless" homes for middle-class private clients who would otherwise buy a house "off the rack" (McCoy, 1984, p. 114).[9] He designed his first minimal house during this time, proposing prefabricated housing that could be erected with unskilled labor for agricultural workers, who usually lived in their cars (McCoy, 1982, p. 3). He studied prefabricated low-cost dwellings during a Guggenheim fellowship in 1940 and during the war worked with John Entenza and Charles and Ray Eames on molded plywood parts for the navy.

After the war, Ain explored low-cost housing solutions at a larger scale in partnership with architects Joseph Johnson and Alfred Day and landscape architect Garrett Eckbo. The Park Planned Homes, developed and built by contractor Shy Kaplin in Altadena from 1945 to 1947, shared driveways and paired front yards and used slightly pitched roofs with inverted clerestory windows in the center for natural light (McCoy, 1984). Only 28 of the 60 planned houses were built since labor and materials became scarce and expensive after wartime price controls were lifted. The Community Homes, designed in 1948, was a cooperative housing project that proposed 280 houses on 100 acres in Reseda. Robert Kahan organized the development and enrolled subscribers to purchase the land. Mortgage insurance was needed to build the houses, but once the FHA learned that there were racial minorities among the project's subscribers, it pulled out, terminating the development. The project ran afoul of the Federal Housing Administration's Regulation X, which prohibited the mixing of races in FHA insured neighborhoods. Luckily, the price of the land the group had purchased had appreciated so the members at least made a return on their initial investment (McCoy, 1984, p. 121).

To what degree are the Hirsch Tract and the Mar Vista Tract similar or different from a design perspective? Does the Hirsch Tract's status as a conventional subdivision mean it lacks design value? Does the Mar Vista Tract's status as a historic preservation overlay zone mean it is better designed?

Massing *Pitched Roofs vs. Flat Roofs*

Both the Hirsh Tract and the Mar Vista Tract were originally developed with single-story homes, one with pitched and the other with flat roofs.

Homes in the Hirsch Tract are rectangular (approximately 30 ft by 40 ft) in plan, employ gable and hipped roofs and place parking in detached garages at the rear of the site, with a roof shape matching that of the house. Part of the volume of each house is pushed forward on the front facade so that houses are more than mere boxes.

Houses in the Mar Vista Tract are rectangular in plan (approximately 44 ft by 26 ft) and have flat roofs that extend to cover attached garages (with the exception of the Beethoven/Moore block, where detached, flat-roofed garages are placed off the alley). Garages shift position front to back and alternate sides of the lot so that front yards are paired. Houses are pure rectangular volumes with square garages attached on the side or at a corner.

House Plans *Fixed vs. Flexible*

House plans in the Hirsh Tract are static while houses in the Mar Vista Tract have a convertible plan. Hirsh tract houses were compact and efficient, ranging from 904 square feet to 1,250 square feet. Its homes are very similar to those published in the FHA's *Principles of Planning Small Houses*, which was revised in 1948 to address the issue of the minimal house. This publication contains 17 different low-cost house plans, incrementally building on the "basic plan," a one-story with two bedrooms, all the way up to a two-story with three bedrooms and a garage. Houses in the Hirsh Tract are of a type that takes the basic plan, a square, and increases the width of two or more rooms, creating more area and a rectangular building shape. The homes then extend the length or depth of one of the front rooms toward the street to create more variation on the front elevation. Front entry doors lead directly into the living room, which is used to access the other areas of the house.

The Mar Vista Tract's 1,050-square-foot houses use a center hall plan to make all areas of the house directly accessible from the entry space without having to cross through one room to reach another. To achieve this, contrary to convention at the time, the kitchen had to be at the front of the house and the living room at the rear, connecting to the backyard. The Mar Vista Tract house plan also used flexible features to enhance functionality and overlap programs in time and space. A folding wooden panel allowed the space of the master bedroom to be an extension of the living room or an open study area. A single bedroom on one side of the house could be divided into two with a sliding panel. And a built-in dining table and pass-through were used to separate the kitchen from the living room, allowing a parent cooking to keep an eye on the children playing in the living room or backyard. When privacy was preferred, a partition could be pulled down and a panel pulled up to enclose the kitchen space, cutting the table in half.

Construction *Wood Frame vs. Post-and-Beam*

Houses in the Hirsh tract use conventional wood-frame bearing-wall construction, while the Mar Vista Tract uses post-and-beam. Houses in the Hirsh Tract are constructed on raised foundations with no basements. Wood-frame construction was (and is) very common, typically placing 2 by 4 inch wood studs 16 inches on center to create load-bearing walls that would then be clad in drywall or other sheathing material. Floor joists and roof rafters, also spaced 16 inches on center, would be somewhat deeper, 2 by 6 or 2 by 8 inches. This structural type was fast and familiar.

Houses in the Mar Vista Tract are of post-and-beam construction on slab foundations. Real estate developers began using post-and-beam in the postwar era. This method allowed for nonbearing walls since the structure relied on posts (4 in by 4 in or 6 in by 6 in) with beams spanning between them (4 in or 6 in by 16 in), allowing the space of the home to be more open and less carved up by structural walls, in other words, "open plan." It was debatable which structural system cost less, but post-and-beam did require a higher level of finish and precision since structural elements were left exposed (Caltrans, 2011, p. 82). Post-and-beam also allowed for floor-to-ceiling windows since the exterior wall did not have to be load-bearing.

Pedestrian Access and Entry *Covered Porch vs. Awning*

All houses in the Hirsch Tract had inset, covered entry porches connected to the public sidewalk by cement walkways. Most porches are about 4 feet to 5 feet long—allowing just enough space to enter and exit. Some are wider (9 ft to 12 ft) but still very shallow and meant more as ornamentation rather than for occupation. Porches are about 18″ high (three steps up to a stoop) and front doors are visible from the public realm.

Entries for houses in the Mar Vista Tract are at grade and respond to solar orientation. Houses facing southwest incorporate a canopy to shade the entrance, while houses facing northeast do not, since they are not subject to direct sunlight. This is usual in tract housing (Caltrans, 2011, p. 98). Some houses also have covered walkways leading from the garage. Most front doors are visible from the public realm.

Yards and Landscape *Conventional and Sparse vs. Progressive and Articulate*

Lots in the Hirsch Tract are improved with grass, foundation plantings and an occasional tree in the front yard (Figure 2.12). The project probably did not necessitate the services of a landscape architect since its landscaping is minimal and conventional. The parkway on May Street is planted with eucalyptus trees. There is no parkway on Woodgreen Street and

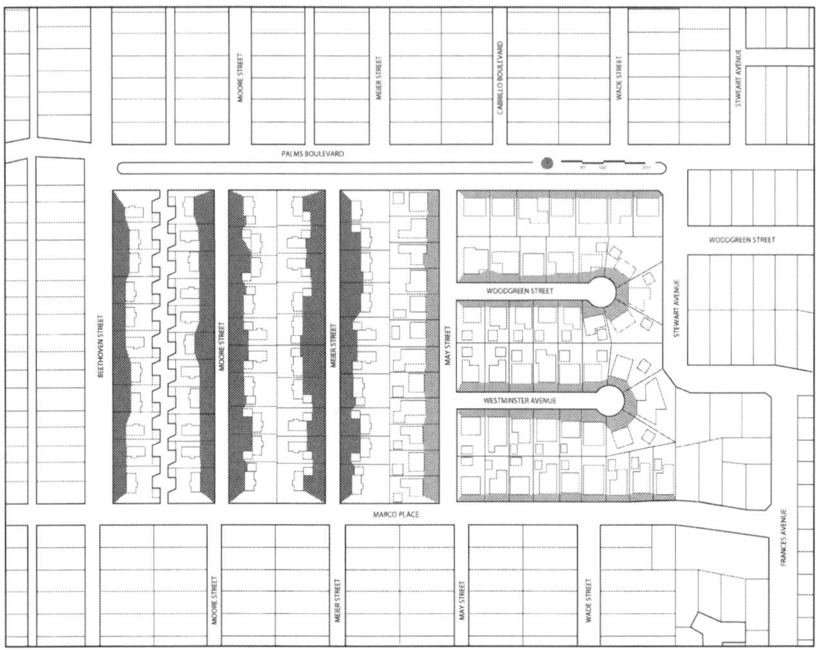

Figure 2.12 Yards and landscape diagram: The Hirsh Tract (right) contributes less space and planting to the public realm than the Modernique Homes (left) which were articulately landscaped.

Westminster Avenue. Front yards are not fenced, and homeowners were responsible for landscaping their own backyards.

Noted landscape architect Garrett Eckbo designed the landscape for the Mar Vista Tract using a wide variety of plants from diverse climates, contrasting a "curvilinear landscape against rectilinear buildings" (Denzer, 2005, p. 279). He designed front yards to create a park-like setting for the community and a sense of spatial variety. Each block was planted with a different type of street tree in the parkway between the curb and public sidewalks, melaleuca trees for Moore Street, magnolia trees for Meier Street and ficus trees for Beethoven Street (L.A. Office of Historic Resources [LAOHR], 2010, p. 22). Flowing yet geometric plantings were used to create connections between houses and create neighborly buffer zones without fencing or high shrubs, blurring property lines with drought-tolerant ground covers and flowers including lavender cotton, velvet groundsel, dwarf lantana, dusty miller and Mexican blue palm (LAOHR, 2010, p. 22). Each individual house had its own planting scheme to differentiate it from its neighbors, who might have the same house plan (Denzer, 2005, p. 278). Shade trees were planted on the rear property lines, but the backyards were mostly left to the homeowner to landscape. Initially, backyards were not fenced to create a more communal feel among neighbors.

Public Realm *Minimal vs. Park-Like*

Front yards in both tracts are private but read as part of the public realm, meaning they are an important part of the visual image of the subdivision available from the public street. Both projects are improved with public sidewalks, and the rectilinear blocks in both projects have street trees. The cul-de-sac streets in the Hirsh Tract do not include a parkway between the curb and the sidewalk. Due to the Mar Vista Tract's more thoughtful and ample landscape improvements, the public realm in the project is more park-like. The Hirsch Tracts public realm is more minimal with grass, foundation plantings and an odd tree or shrub.

Architectural Style *Minimal Traditional vs. Mid-Century Modern*

Houses in the Hirsh Tract are built in the Minimal Traditional style, stripped-down versions of the eclectic historical styles of the 1920s, including Spanish Revival, American Colonial and Craftsman. Homes have very little ornament and/or detail beyond small inset covered front porches and double hung windows. The homes are mostly stucco, with horizontal and vertical wood siding, brick wainscoting, shallow arches and window shutters to provide variety.

The Modernique Homes are built in a Mid-Century Modern style, abstract, minimal and angular but less severe than the earlier International Style. Characterized by architectural historian David Gebhard as low rather, than high, Modern, Ain's interest and emphasis was on function (Gebhard, 1980, p. 16). Large floor-to-ceiling windows connect houses to the backyard blending indoors and outdoors. Clerestory windows are used in front to daylight the interior while maintaining privacy. Side walls do not have windows, further separating one neighbor from another. Roofs are flat with overhanging eaves. Houses were also painted in different color combinations using the Plochere Color system and ironically have more detail than those in the Hirsh Tract.

Design Outcomes *Literal Minimum vs. Maximized Minimum*

The Hirsh Tract and the Mar Vista Tract both tried to create low-cost minimal dwellings but their homes are executed very differently from one another. Both are "minimal" in the sense that they are characterized by the use of simple geometries with little detail. But the houses in the Hirsh Tract aim to provide a literal minimum for postwar families while the Mar Vista Tract works to actually maximize the minimum with flexible space, overlapping programs and communal yards.

Real Estate Development

Context

Postwar Los Angeles was built tract by tract, not block by block, serving local industries and plants, especially the aviation industry which established itself in Santa Monica in the 1920s and flourished during the war (Caltrans, 2011; Hise, 1997). The pent-up demand for housing across the nation was immense and developers rushed to meet the needs of returning soldiers and those who had migrated to Los Angeles for the war and decided to stay. Pre–World War II, most developers were local, and few built more than 50 houses a year (Caltrans, 2011). After the war, Los Angeles builders, like Fred Marlow and Fritz Burns, who built large tracts in Westchester and Baldwin Hills, worked to industrialize the building industry, transforming it from a trade- and craft-based activity to one based on assembly-line production (Hise, 1997). Former agricultural land was transformed into wholesale communities by breaking down the homebuilding process into discrete, relatively unskilled tasks that could be accomplished by small teams going from house to house, allowing developers to build thousands of units a year rather than 50 to 100.

Like the Los Angeles City Planning Commission and the FHA, the Urban Land Institute (ULI), a nonprofit research and educational organization for the building industry established in 1939, encouraged homebuilding as community building, noting that the "creation of well balanced, self-contained communities should be the objective of all subdividers and operative builders" (ULI, 1947, p. 37). Its *Community Builders Handbook*, first published in 1947, echoes the physical parameters endorsed by Los Angeles planners and the FHA, from block size to street widths to landscape planning, spelling out tract development in a step-by-step process. Amplifying ULI's determination to professionalize and standardize the industry was the fear that if private real estate developers could not meet the postwar housing demand, the federal government would step in and meet it for them in projects akin to the public housing it built in the late 1930s and early 1940s. This concern intensified the industry's inherent aversion to risk and increased the skepticism of innovation. In the handbook's forward, the group warned that the "ultra-modernist and the seeker for radical, unorthodox, or socialized departures in this field will not find them here" (ULI, 1947, p. viii). The handbook also rejects the "so-called super block plan, consisting of large deep blocks penetrated by a series of cul-de-sac service drives and with sidewalks located in a common interior park area," which most government-sponsored projects employed (ULI, 1947, p. 48). The group felt that it had "not proved satisfactory in experimental project in this county" (ULI, 1947, p. 48). Lenders also felt that flat roofs were "risky" well into the late 1940s. Traditional styles, like those used in the Hirsh Tract, "represented political conservatism while flat-roofed modern architecture was perceived as being aligned with socialist Europe" (Denzer, 2005, p. 280).

Harold Hirsh

Harold Hirsh, subdivider of the Hirst Tract, was a developer and builder who worked in partnership with Arthur E. Edmunds in the Hirsh-Edmunds Building Co., which associated with many different partners on large-scale tract housing developments in Los Angeles, from modest to luxurious. At the time the company was working on the case study tract, Hirsh was working on at least three other, much larger, projects. In partnership with Todd S. Horne in the Horn-Hirsh Development Corporation, he was developing 121 homes near Pico Rivera reported to cost $1,500,000 ($1,500,000 Project, 1949). Hirsh and Edmunds were developing the last large parcel in Beverly Hills into 15 large homesites to be improved with minimum 3,000-square-foot homes, seven of which Hirsh and Edmunds built on spec (Last Portion, 1950). And the firm's development at Durfee Manor, a 193-home tract in El Monte costing $2,000,000, was nearing completion (193-Home Unit, 1950). Harold Hirsh, as an individual and the Hirsh-Edmunds Building Company, continued to produce large-scale tract housing in Southern California throughout the 1950s.

Barney M. Edelman

Barney M. Edelman was an "enlightened developer" but is perhaps better characterized as a businessman. Edelman is only known to have built two real estate projects in Los Angeles but was involved in various businesses throughout his life, some building-related and some not. During the 1920s Edelman was a shoe salesman, building materials salesman and a building contractor (L.A. Directory Co., 1921, p. 966; 1925, p. 789; 1928, p. 818). He developed and built the El Vigo Apartments at 154 North New Hampshire, a story-story steel-frame structure with 54 apartments in 1928 (Five Story Apartment, 1928). From the late 1930s into the late 1940s, Edelman was the president and manager of Sanford's Cafeteria, a health-oriented restaurant that specialized in "cooking that is kind to your stomach" (Display Ad 3, 1938). Ads for the restaurant encouraged people to "Eat for your health" and touted its healthy menu, health food store, whole wheat bakery and on-site juice bar (Display Ad

135, 1939). Edelman shared Ain's social interests and thought of the Mar Vista project as more than a speculative venture (Denzer, 2005). By the 1960s, Edelman was the president of Certified Trust Deeds Inc. in Long Beach (Long Beach, 1960, p. 206).

How do the Hirsh Tract and the Mar Vista Tract compare from a real estate development perspective? Does the Hirsh Tract's status as a by-right project mean that it was more profitable? Does the Mar Vista Tract's noted design mean that it was a poor investment?

Subdivision 1949 vs. 1948

The case study tracts were subdivided within a year and a half of one another, the Hirsh Tract in October 1949 and the Mar Vista Tract in February 1948. The area was initially developed when the railroad arrived in 1875. The Pacific Electric Railway ran on Venice Boulevard, three blocks southeast of the case study tracts, offering direct service to Venice and Ocean Park, later also connecting to downtown Los Angeles, a 30-minute trip. Land adjacent to Venice Boulevard was subdivided from the 1910s into the 1920s in response to the rail line, with houses, small multifamily and small-scale commercial buildings. At this time the neighborhood was a patchwork of small subdivisions interspersed with small farms. The need for worker housing accelerated during the 1920s when oil was discovered in Playa Del Rey and Venice and the aircraft industry began locating on former agricultural land. The area was annexed by the City of Los Angeles in 1927.

No land in the case study neighborhood was subdivided from the mid-1920s to 1940 when land directly to the northeast of the Hirsh Tract between Stewart and Centinela was subdivided into 93 lots (LACPW, 1940). The case study tracts, like much of the land in the area, were still open agricultural land at this time, with truck farms growing lima beans, lettuce and celery, two blocks from Clover Field, now the Santa Monica Airport (LADCP, 1939). Venice had become a major thoroughfare but one with uneven and unsightly development. By the time the case study tracts were subdivided and built, architectural historian Esther McCoy characterized the neighborhood as a bad one, filled with "contractor boxes" and deteriorating buildings (LACPW, 1948, 1949; McCoy, 1982, p. 13).

Construction Costs $7,500 vs. $10,000

Homes in the Hirsh Tract were significantly more cost-effective than those in the Mar Vista Tract which cost at least 33% more to build. Although the economy homes Hugh Gibbs helped design for the L.A. Homebuilders Institute were intended to be built for $5,000 (exclusive of land) and sell for $7,000 (with a garage and landscaping); a construction cost of $7,500 was listed on the Hirsh Tract building permits (LADBS, 1949b; Lower Cost Homes, 1948, E1). The tract was completed in nine months.

Although a cost of $7,000 was listed on the building permits, historian Anthony Denzer reports that the architects of the Modernique Homes were disappointed that they were not able to reduce the construction cost of the houses below $10,000 (Denzer, 2005, p. 284). Although contractor Barnett Poles used many of the streamlined techniques of the large homebuilders, including precut studs, assembly-line job scheduling and off-site construction of built-in cabinetry, they didn't provide meaningful efficiencies (One Convertible Plan, 1949). It took over 13 months to complete all the Modernique Homes.

Mortgage Insurance *FHA Insured vs. FHA Insured*

Tracts of similar homes built by Harold Hirsh were FHA insured so it is very likely that houses in the Hirsh Tract were as well. The Mar Vista Tract struggled for and finally obtained FHA approval with the concessions described earlier. Loan applications for some potential buyers of the Modernique Homes, however, were rejected due to the tract's flat roofs and unconventional architecture, which banks assumed was a fad (Denzer, 2005, p. 280).

Marketing and Absorption *Limited Marketing vs. Sustained and Evolving Marketing*

No advertisements for the Hirsh Tract could be found, while the Mar Vista Tract was heavily advertised. Although many large tracts built by Harold Hirsh and the Hirsh-Edmunds Building Company were documented by and advertised in the *Los Angeles Times*, the Hirsh Tract was not, though market comparables suggest that the homes would have sold for about $8,500 to $9,000. The project was clearly not significant for the firm, and the houses must have sold quickly with minimal promotion. The Hirsh Tract was successful enough that it didn't hinder Hirsh's ability to go after much-larger projects soon after it was built. By 1953, Hirsh and Edmunds had purchased 196 acres in south Los Angeles, planning to build 1,045 homes and multifamily units, an investment of $15,000,000 (Johnson Ranchos, 1953). This project became the very successful Inglewood Knolls and Morningside Heights neighborhoods in Inglewood (Display Ad 87, 1954).

The Modernique Homes were initially intended for subscribers only, people who ascribed to Edelman's and Ain's beliefs about the importance of "a vital, harmonious environment for the whole human community" (Ain, 1964, n.p.). Only 20 people had signed on by the start of construction, so the remaining 32 houses had to be offered for sale to the public. Printed marketing materials invited prospective buyers to the "World

Premiere" of the Modernique Homes, held in September 1948, to see the project's "unique blending of convertible living area and moderate costs" (Invitation to World Premiere, ADC, 1918). The invitation lauded the project's FHA approval, movable walls, space-saving kitchens, "windowed panoramic interiors" that "merge patio, living and garden areas" and large two-car garages (Invitation to World Premiere, ADC). No price was mentioned, but Esther McCoy cites an initial sales price of $11,000, with the cost of land, a relatively small margin over their $10,000 per unit construction cost, especially given the risk of cost overruns when building an atypical house design. Advertisements for the Modernique Homes were also run in both the classified and display ad sections of the *Los Angeles Times* (Classified Ad 8, 1949a; Display Ad 67, 1949) (Figure 2.13).

Sales stalled in late 1948 with 23 homes remaining, and Edelman used various marketing tools to spur interest (Denzer, 2005). He ran multiple display ads in the *Los Angeles Times* encouraging people to visit the tract's model home at 3508 Moore Street, which more than 2,000 did by April 1949, as reported in the *Times*, though an adjacent article on the same page reports that more than 5,000 people visited a development in the San Fernando Valley in a single day (Classified Ad 8, 1949b; Crowds Visit, 1949). Advertisements, which had always mentioned architect Gregory Ain, now also noted that he was a "Guggenheim Award Winner" (Classified Ad 8, 1949a). More elaborate display ads running through June 1949 touted the homes' central planning, connections to the outdoors and flexible space and encouraged buyers to "check these features against homes twice the cost" (Display Ad 67, 1949). Despite concerted marketing efforts, which also included vibrant new color schemes, additional front landscaping, fencing to make the rear yards more private (all of which cost money) and even raising the price from $11,000 to $12,950, the Modernique Homes did not sell quickly enough or at a high enough profit margin to remain a going concern (Denzer, 2005; Display Ad 67, 1949). Developer Edelman sold the remaining land intended for the project's second phase to Mr. Hirsh.

Market Timing and Competing Supply *Well Targeted vs. Off the Mark*

The Hirsh Tract was well-timed to market with small homes affordable to buyers in the surrounding area that sold quickly. The Mar Vista Tract may have been well-timed, in general, in the sense that single-family homes were in great demand, but the product it offered was out of sync with the surrounding market. The tract was the first significant development in the vicinity since 1940, at which time the area was considered a marginal neighborhood with small bungalows for oil and airplane manufacturing workers. Its homes looked unfamiliar, included unproven features and were more communal than the typical tract home. And the homes cost much more than anything else available in the neighborhood at the time. As Esther McCoy asked, perhaps with some exaggeration, "[w]ho want[s] an $11,000 house in a $5,000 neighborhood?" (1982, p. 13).[10]

Figure 2.13 Advertisement for the Modernique Homes published in the *Los Angeles Times* (Display Ad 74, 1948, p. E5).

Investment Performance Profitable vs. Insolvent

The Hirsh Tract was a successful development project for Harold Hirsh and his associates while the Mar Vista Tract was a financial failure. Although the Modernique Homes employed superior urban planning and design strategies, these merits could not overcome market misalignment and construction cost overruns. Developer Edelman could not remain a going concern, but historian Esther McCoy quotes Ain: "[Edelman] carried out the plan without changes, he planted every tree and shrub Eckbo called for in the landscaping" (1984, p. 130). Edelman is not known to have completed another development project.

Development Outcomes Value Out of Balance

While it may not have been a significant project for its developers, the Hirsh Tract created significantly more short-term financial value than the Mar Vista Tract. By 1950, equivalently sized homes in the area were selling for $8,500 to $9,000, creating a reasonable margin over the average $7,500 cost to build these more traditional homes, exclusive of land. Comparatively, the Modernique Homes cost at least 33% more to build and sold at or below cost. In the end, the FHA's concerns about the Modernique Homes were warranted, maybe not because of their approach to architecture and planning, but certainly because of their price point. As innovative and wonderful as the Mar Vista Tract is from a design and urban planning perspective, it had no real impact on future housing production since its innovations were not financially feasible enough to be replicated.

The outcome might have been different, however, had the Mar Vista Tract been built just two years later. The neighborhood was quickly improving and builders were developing larger, more expensive homes by 1951. A large tract of land directly northwest of the Mar Vista Tract, for example, was subdivided and improved in 1952 with 550 homes by Mark Taper of Biltmore Homes, Inc., with 43 different 3-bedroom, two-bath designs priced from $13,350 (Construction Grows at New Development, 1952, F10; LACPW, 1952).

Conclusion

When Short-Term Costs Doom Further Development But Ensure Greater Future Value

When the Hirsh and Mar Vista Tracts are evaluated from a purely design perspective, the only factor that could account for the financial failure of one and financial success of the other is the belief that consumers were not ready to embrace Modernism as mainstream (McCoy, 1984, p. 130). Expanding our point of view to evaluate the interaction of design, development and planning, we understand that, while acceptance of Modernism could have been part of the issue, the fact that the developer overreached in terms of sales price was likely the decisive factor. On the margin, few consumers were willing or able to pay nearly 50% more for the project's design features compared to surrounding homes available for sale at the same time, though these attributes were surely desirable in the abstract to some. This understanding shifts our perspective away from blaming the consumer for his or her lack of progressiveness (as well as regulators and lenders), to acknowledging that design innovation, if it is to be successful, has a stake in the real estate development and community planning strategies in which it is employed. Architects must recognize that design advancement, whether driven by cultural interests, market growth or evolving community need, must be employed judiciously, balancing future design innovation with past design precedent.

Lessons Learned *Development Matters*

Development matters. The United States has a market-based system of housing production. Good design and good planning cannot be implemented unless they are sensitive to the issues impacting financial performance and are employed in projects that are financially feasible. The Hirsh Tract versus Mar Vista Tract case study illustrates how design innovation can outpace financial and market capacity. Although the Mar Vista Tract represented an "enlightened" approach to development that valued innovative design and planning strategies, the local housing market did not translate the higher cost of these innovations into higher sales prices. The $12,950 Modernique Homes were competing with $8,500 homes in the immediate neighborhood, including those developed on the adjacent tract, and ultimately the project could not meet minimum standards for development profit. Sixty years later, however, with interest in mid-century planning and design high and the Historic Preservation Overlay Zone in place, the Modernique Homes began selling at consistently higher prices per square foot than those in the adjacent tract for the first time. The Modernique Homes was a real estate development failure in the short-term but an eventual real estate investment success in the long-term, demonstrating the limits of planning and design innovation in market-rate development yet the important role such innovations play in shaping future housing preferences.

Case Study Projects Today

In the time since the case study projects were built, Mar Vista has become a very desirable neighborhood thanks to its westside location and Los Angeles's current housing crisis. Although the Modernique Homes were doomed by short-term cost overruns, they created significant long-term investment value and today are valued higher than homes in the Hirsh Tract.

Homeowners have added onto many of the houses in the Hirsh Tract. Some have been torn down and completely rebuilt as much-larger homes in more contemporary styles. In June 2018, all the homes in the tract were valued at well over $1 million by both Redfin and Zillow. 3531 May Street, a 1,184-square-foot house in the Hirsh Tract near its original state was valued at $1,377,671 on Redfin and $1,588,080 on Zillow, or $1,164 to $1,341 per square foot.[11]

Many Modernique homes have been altered as well, but none have been torn down and rebuilt. The distinctive architectural character of the tract has been protected since the development was designated a Historic Preservation Overlay Zone (HPOZ) in 2004, Los Angeles's first postwar HPOZ (Ordinance No. 175133). In June 2018, all the homes in the Mar Vista tract were valued at well over $1.25 million by both Redfin and Zillow. A 1,016-square-foot Modernique home near its original state on 3514 Meier Street was valued at $1,614,938 on Redfin and $1,651,943 on Zillow, or $1,590 to $1,626 per square foot.[12]

Notes

1. At the end of 1950, 55.5% of land in Los Angeles was zoned for residential, 37.46% as single family (R1) and 18.04% as multifamily (R2, R3, R4 and R5) (LACPC, 1951, p. 36). A substantial part of the city remained unzoned.
2. Building permit fees are based on estimated building cost, so applicants often undervalue. The valuations were increased on all Hirsh Tract permits by the Building and Safety official, from $5,500 to $6,700 for the houses and $400 to $800 for detached garages.
3. Joseph Johnson was the son of architect Reginald Johnson who was the lead designer of Baldwin Hills Village. See Chapter 3: Lost in Translation.
4. A size of 1,016 square feet is listed on the building permits. The L.A. County Tax Assessor also lists 1,016 square feet at the original house size, not 1,050 square feet as originally designed.
5. Building costs were originally listed at $5,500 and $6,000 for the Mar Vista Tract, upped to $7,000 by Building and Safety.
6. The racial composition of a community was also an FHA underwriting criterion. At the time, the organization believed homes in mostly black neighborhoods to be too risky to insure. See *Housing Policy in the United States, An Introduction* by Alex F. Schwartz.
7. Robert Alexander, one of the principal designers of Baldwin Hills Village, was also on the team. See Chapter 3: Lost in Translation.
8. The homebuilding industry was motivated to provide economy houses, in part, because many believed if they didn't, the "government [would] step in and supply it—at the expense of increased taxes" ("Trend to 'Economy House' Construction Seen in 1949," Jan 13 1949, p. A1).
9. A servantless house is one where the kitchen is accessible from the front of the house rather than via a back entrance. The kitchen participates in the life of the household and the living spaces of the home.
10. Ironically, Hugh Gibbs, architect of the Hirsh Tract designed a flat-roofed, low-cost, convertible house in Los Altos Terrace in 1948. It cost $6,500 on a $1,200 lot and was easily expandable. The partition between the living room and a bedroom was non-load-bearing and could be removed to enlarge the living area, and the carport could be converted into two additional bedrooms (Low Cost House for Los Altos Terrace Development, 1948, p. 14).
11. www.zillow.com/homes/3531-May-St,-Los-Angeles,-CA-90066_rb/www.redfin.com/CA/Los-Angeles/3531-May-St-90066/home/6746573
12. www.zillow.com/homes/3514-meier-st-CA-90066_rb/www.redfin.com/CA/Los-Angeles/3514-Meier-St-90066/home/6746559

References

193-Home Unit Near Completion. (1950, December 24). *Los Angeles Times*, A16. Retrieved from www.proquest.com

$1,500,000 Project Planned to Provide 121 New Houses. (1949, April 24). *Los Angeles Times*, E7. Retrieved from www.proquest.com

Advance Development Company (ADC). (1948). "Invitation to World Premiere." Gregory Ain Papers, Architecture and Design Collection. Art, Design & Architecture Museum, University of California, Santa Barbara.

Ain, G. (1951, April 15). The Flexible House Faces Reality. *Los Angeles Times*, F4. Retrieved from www.proquest.com

Ain, G. (1964). Letter to the Editor. *Arts and Architecture*, *81*(12), np.

California Department of Transportation. (2011). *Tract Housing in California, 1945–1973: A Context for National Register Evaluation*. Sacramento, CA: Caltrans. Retrieved from www.dot.ca.gov/ser/downloads/cultural/tract_housing_in_ca_1945-1973.pdf

Classified Ad 8. (1949a, January 30). *Los Angeles Times*, B8. Retrieved from www.proquest.com

Classified Ad 8. (1949b, February 6). *Los Angeles Times*, B8. Retrieved from www.proquest.com

Cohan, C. C. (1948, October 10). Fact and Comment. *Los Angeles Times*, E3. Retrieved from www.proquest.com

Construction Grows at New Development. (1952, September 28). *Los Angeles Times*, F10. Retrieved from www.proquest.com

Crowds Visit Model Homes. (1949, April 17). *Los Angeles Times*, E12. Retrieved from www.proquest.com

Denzer, A. (2005). *Gregory Ain and the Social Politics of Housing Design*. Doctoral Dissertation. Retrieved from https://search-proquest-com.libproxy1.usc.edu/docview/305000860/fulltextPDF/924EEF928C6140DAPQ/1?accountid=14749

Display Ad 3. (1938, July 26). *Los Angeles Times*, 4. Retrieved from www.proquest.com

Display Ad 67. (1949, June 19). *Los Angeles Times*, E4. Retrieved from www.proquest.com

Display Ad 68. (1948, October 10). *Los Angeles Times*, E4. Retrieved from www.proquest.com

Display Ad 74. (1948, November 7). *Los Angeles Times*, E5. Retrieved from www.proquest.com

Display Ad 87. (1954, February 7). *Los Angeles Times*, E7. Retrieved from www.proquest.com

Display Ad 135. (1939, February 26). *Los Angeles Times*, J23. Retrieved from www.proquest.com

Federal Housing Administration. (1936). *Technical Bulletin No. 5, Planning Neighborhoods for Small Houses*. Washington, DC: FHA. Retrieved from https://catalog.hathitrust.org/Record/100710825

Federal Housing Administration. (1938). *Technical Bulletin No. 7, Planning Profitable Neighborhoods*. Washington, DC: FHA. Retrieved from https://catalog.hathitrust.org/Record/100887915

Federal Housing Administration. (1940). *Land Planning Bulleting No. 1, Successful Subdivisions, Principles of Planning for Economy and protection against neighborhood blight*. Washington, DC: FHA. Retrieved from https://catalog.hathitrust.org/Record/001719313

Final Plans Approved for Rosecrans Homes. (1950, January 29). *Los Angeles Times*, E3. Retrieved from www.proquest.com

Five Story Apartment Opens. (1928, January 22). *Los Angeles Times*, E2. Retrieved from www.proquest.com

Gebhard, D. (1980). *The Architecture of Gregory Ain*. Santa Barbara, CA: UCSB Art Museum.

Hise, G. (1997). *Magnetic Los Angeles, Planning the Twentieth Century Metropolis*. Baltimore, MD: Johns Hopkins University Press.

Home Building Here Speeded. (1948, February 1). *Los Angeles Times*, 23. Retrieved from www.proquest.com

Jackson, K. T. (1985). *Crabgrass Frontier: The Suburbanization of the United States*. Oxford, England: Oxford University Press.

Johnson Ranchos Sold for Over $11,300,000. (1953, April 16). *Los Angeles Times*, 4. Retrieved from www.proquest.com

L.A. City Planning Commission. (1928). *Annual Report for Year Ending June 30 1928*. Los Angeles, CA: L.A. City Archive.

L.A. City Planning Commission. (1931). *Annual Report for Year Ending June 30 1931*. Los Angeles, CA: L.A. City Archive.

L.A. City Planning Commission. (1932). *Annual Report for Year Ending June 30 1932*. Los Angeles, CA: L.A. City Archive.

L.A. City Planning Commission. (1935). *Annual Report 1934–1935*. Los Angeles, CA: L.A. City Archive.

L.A. City Planning Commission. (1938). *Annual Report 1937–1938*. Los Angeles, CA: L.A. City Archive.

L.A. City Planning Commission. (1949). *Accomplishments 1948*. Los Angeles, CA: L.A. City Archive.

L.A. City Planning Commission. (1950). *Accomplishments 1949*. Los Angeles, CA: L.A. City Archive.

L.A. City Planning Commission. (1951). *Accomplishments 1950*. Los Angeles, CA: L.A. City Archive.

L.A. City Planning Commission. (1952). *Accomplishments 1951*. Los Angeles, CA: L.A. City Archive.

L.A. County Public Works. (1940). Tract Map 12450, M.B. 235–20–21. Retrieved from http://dpw.lacounty.gov/sur/nas/landrecords/tract/MB0235/TR0235-020.pdf

L.A. County Public Works. (1948). Tract Map 14444, M.B. 316–33. Retrieved from http://dpw.lacounty.gov/sur/nas/landrecords/tract/MB0316/TR0316-033.pdf

L.A. County Public Works. (1949). Tract Map 15663, M.B. 355–1–2. Retrieved from http://dpw.lacounty.gov/sur/nas/landrecords/tract/MB0355/TR0355-001.pdf

L.A. County Public Works. (1952). Tract Map 18140, M.B. 441–19–25. Retrieved from http://dpw.lacounty.gov/sur/nas/landrecords/tract/MB0441/TR0441-019.pdf

L.A. Department of Building & Safety. (1948, February). Permit #s 7701–7774. Los Angeles, CA: LADBS, Building Records Section.

L.A. Department of Building & Safety. (1949a, January–February). Certificate of Occupancy #s 7701–7774. Los Angeles, CA: LADBS, Building Records Section.

L.A. Department of Building & Safety. (1949b, November). Permit #s 3010–3104. Los Angeles, CA: LADBS, Building Records Section.

L.A. Department of Building & Safety. (1950, July). Certificate of Occupancy #s 3010–3104. Los Angeles, CA: LADBS, Building Records Section.

L.A. Department of City Planning. (1930). *Annual Report for year ending June 30, 1930*. Los Angeles: L.A. City Archive.

L.A. Department of City Planning. (1939). *WPA Land Use Survey Maps, Los Angeles, Maps 111/153, 111/161 and 117/153*. Retrieved from http://digital-library.usc.edu/cdm/landingpage/collection/p15799coll120

L.A. Department of City Planning. (1946). *Comprehensive Zoning Plan, Zoning Ordinance No. 90,500*. Los Angeles: L.A. City Archive.

L.A. Department of City Planning. (1948). *Comprehensive Zoning Plan, Zoning Ordinance No. 90,500 (Amended to and including Ordinance No. 93,346)*. Los Angeles: L.A. City Archive.

L.A. Directory Co. (1921). *Los Angeles City Directory*. Los Angeles, CA: L.A. Directory Co.

L.A. Directory Co. (1925). *Los Angeles City Directory*. Los Angeles, CA: L.A. Directory Co.

L.A. Directory Co. (1928). *Los Angeles City Directory*. Los Angeles, CA: L.A. Directory Co.

L.A. Office of Historic Resources. (2010). *Gregory Ain Mar Vista tract HPOZ Preservation Plan*. Los Angeles City Planning Department. Retrieved from http://preservation.lacity.org/files/Mar%20Vista%20PP.pdf

Last Portion of Historic Rancho Sold. (1950, December 10). *Los Angeles Times*, G10. Retrieved from www.proquest.com

Long Beach, California, City Directory. (1960). *206*. Retrieved from www.ancestry.com

Low Cost House for Los Altos Terrace Development. (1948). *Architectural Forum*, *32*(12), 14–15.

Lower-Cost Homes Gain Inpetus Here. (1948, October 24). *Los Angeles Times*, E1. Retrieved from www.proquest.com

McCoy, E. (1982, March 11). *Ain, UCLA Lecture Notes: Esther McCoy papers, Archives of American Art*. Retrieved from https://www.aaa.si.edu/collections/esther-mccoy-papers-5502/subseries-4-4/box-23-folder-42

McCoy, E. (1984). *The Second Generation*. Salt Lake City, UT: Peregrine Smith Books.

New Second Unit Has 88 Homes. (1951, September 9). *Los Angeles Times*, E8. Retrieved from www.proquest.com

One Convertible Plan, the basic design for a 100-unit subdivision, allows the customer to change a standard house to fit his own family requirements of size and use. (1949). *Architectural Forum*, *90*(4), 126–128.

Production Increase in 1949 Aimed At by Home Builders. (1948, December 26). *Los Angeles Times*, E1. Retrieved from www.proquest.com

The Race to Build Houses. (1949, February 13). *Los Angeles Times*, SM5. Retrieved from www.proquest.com

Smiley, D. (2001). Making the Modified Modern. *Perspecta*, *32*, 38–54.

Trend to 'Economy House' Construction Seen in 1949. (1949, January 13). *Los Angeles Times*, A1. Retrieved from www.proquest.com

United States Census Bureau. (2011). *Historical Census of Housing Tables*. Retrieved from www.census.gov/hhes/www/housing/census/historic/owner.html

Urban Land Institute, Community Builders' Council. (1947). *The Community Builders Handbook*. Washington, DC: Urban Land Institute. Retrieved from https://catalog.hathitrust.org/Record/000648803

Weiss, M. A. (1987). *The Rise of the Community Builders, The American Real Estate Industry and Urban Land Planning*. Washington, DC: Beard Books.

3 Lost in Translation, Garden Apartments

Chesapeake Rodeo Apartments vs. Baldwin Hills Village

Figure 3.1 Case Study 3: Garden Apartments, Chesapeake Rodeo Apartments (left) vs. Baldwin Hills Village (right).

Credit: Imagery Copyright 2013 DigitalGlobe, US Geological Survey, USDA Farm Service Agency, Map Data Copyright 2013 Google.

Introduction

When Urban Planning Regulation Fails to Translate an Innovative "Design Precedent" into a Viable "Product Type"

Garden apartments were built throughout the United States in the 1930s, 1940s and 1950s, translating British urban planner Ebenezer Howard's concept for "Garden Cities of To-morrow" into an American context

(Howard, 1902). This common housing type shapes communities around shared landscape and open space, creating a version of Howard's idealized middle ground between city and country. Architect and urban planner Clarence Stein and members of the Regional Planning Association of America advanced the type privately beginning in the 1920s with experimental projects on the East Coast. The federal government publicly supported garden apartments in the 1934 National Housing Act. And subsequent federal legislation encouraged the construction of garden apartments across the nation as public housing, housing for war workers and private rentals for returning veterans, all as local planning, zoning and building codes in most cities were being first implemented, amended and refined. How did these local and national policies shape specific outcomes, and what can these outcomes tell us about effective relationships between urban planning, design and development? A comparison between two garden apartment projects built in Los Angeles, the Chesapeake Rodeo Apartments (1951) and Baldwin Hills Village (1942), now called The Village Green, offers insight (Figure 3.1).

Garden apartments were built in Los Angeles between 1937 and 1955 and are characterized by modest low-rise buildings grouped in a landscaped setting (Chase, Horak, & Keylon, 2012). Projects prioritize site planning and landscape design over expressive architecture and are typically arranged in courtyards on large scale, irregularly shaped sites. Buildings are repetitive, creating economies of scale, but differentiated by orientation, color and planting to create identity. Garden apartments in Los Angeles were built privately, like the case study projects and Park La Brea in Miracle Mile, and publicly, including Aliso Village, Pueblo del Rio and Estrada Courts, all in East Los Angeles. Examples of private garden apartments are concentrated in the case study area, Los Angeles's Baldwin Hills neighborhood, largely due to the availability of open land during the type's period of significance (Figure 3.2). Other garden apartments in Baldwin Hills include Baldwin Gardens (now Cameo Woods), Crenshaw Village, Fairfax Park Apartments and the Gloria Homes (Chase et al., 2012) (Figure 3.3).

The Chesapeake Rodeo Apartments is located at 4616 Rodeo Road (now Obama Boulevard) on a triangular site, halfway between downtown Los Angeles and the beach. The project was built in 1951 by Chesapeake-Rodeo Apartments, Inc., led by developer Herbert Kronish. It was designed by architect Max Maltzman and built by W. E. Robertson Company. Baldwin Hills Village is located 1,500 feet to the west at 5300 Rodeo Road, on a large rectangular site. The project was a joint venture between the heirs to the Lucky Baldwin Estate for whom the neighborhood is named, and a group of more than 30 investors, including project architects Reginald D. Johnson, Lewis E. Wilson, Edwin E. Merrill and Robert E. Alexander, as well as Clarence S. Stein, who acted as a consulting architect (Kane, Keylon, & Loe, 2013, p. 35). The project was built by the Baruch Corporation and completed in 1942.

Figure 3.2 Garden apartments in the Baldwin Hills neighborhood.

Credit: Imagery Copyright 2013 DigitalGlobe, US Geological Survey, USDA Farm Service Agency, Map Data Copyright 2013 Google.

Figure 3.3 Baldwin Hills Village and Garden Apartments in the Baldwin Hills neighborhood, mapped, including The Chesapeake Rodeo Apartments (1).

The case study projects share identifying garden apartment characteristics:

- Large-scale sites of three acres or more
- Organization of the site into a "superblock," a unified tract with a distinct urban pattern markedly different from that of the surrounding context
- Long, horizontal buildings, usually two stories
- Minimal Modern architectural style with few details
- Buildings assembled to define courtyards, outdoor rooms and other large open spaces
- Open spaces simply landscaped with native ground cover, shrubs, climbing vines and trees (Chase et al., 2012)

The Chesapeake Rodeo Apartments arranges 424 one- and two-bedroom units in 23 two-story buildings across a 17.4-acre site.[1] The site is bisected by Rodeo Lane, an L-shaped public street, creating two, smaller "mini-superblocks." Individual garages, one per unit, are placed in the center of these blocks while the edges are lined with residential buildings, organized around front courtyards facing the street and rear courtyards facing the parking areas.[2] Buildings are designed in a simple Modern style, employing low-pitch roofs, stucco, batten-board siding and metal-frame windows (Figure 3.4). Units are accessed

Figure 3.4 By-right case study project: The Chesapeake Rodeo Apartments, located at 4616 Rodeo Road in the Baldwin Hills neighborhood of Los Angeles.

with common stairways that are covered but open to the elements.[3] A narrow central green space separating two perimeter housing blocks is located on axis to an administration building. Units are compact but functional with separate dining rooms, ample windows and minimal hallways.

Baldwin Hills Village organizes 627 one-, two- and three-bedroom units in 92 one- and two-story buildings across a 67.7-acre site.[4] The site is bounded, but not penetrated, by public streets, allowing for the creation of an approximately 13-acre, nearly half-mile-long central green spine, called the Village Green (Stein, 1957, p. 190). Seventeen parking courts link to the surrounding streets but limit the depth to which the car can access the development. These courts (also called "garage courts" or "service courts") alternate with pedestrian-only garden courts ("finger courts" or "green courts"), at minimum 100 feet wide, connecting to the central Village Green (Figures 3.5 and 3.6). Buildings are designed in an understated "modern vernacular" style and contain 3 to 10 apartments ranging from three-and-a-half to six rooms (Bauer, 1944, p. 53). Units are spacious with park views, private ground-floor entries and walled patios. The project also included an administration building and clubhouse. The original plans incorporated a neighborhood retail center on La Brea, which was not built until 1959, developed by different groups of investors without any physical connection to the residential project.[5] Although the city planning department was beginning to focus on planning for deteriorated close-in neighborhoods by this time, neither case study project involved slum clearance, and both were built on greenfield sites.

The Chesapeake Rodeo is a vernacular example of the garden apartment type, a conventional building representative of a common form constructed in large numbers, usually by lesser known architects, developers and contractors. Such buildings, often called "product types" by real estate developers, typically pare down and streamline basic design, approval, funding and construction processes, making these structures both quicker and easier to build. More than 50 similar vernacular garden apartment projects were built throughout Los Angeles, many now demolished, most, like the Chesapeake Rodeo Apartments, built by-right (Chase et al., 2012). By contrast, Baldwin Hills Village is a significant garden apartment design precedent, i.e., a singular example of a specific, usually innovative, strategy built by well-known professionals, that subsequently serves as a model. Baldwin Hills Village, then called "Thousand Gardens," was recognized as precedent-setting before it was even built:

> International authorities on large-scale housing pronounce "Thousand Gardens" to be the most outstanding housing project in the

Figure 3.5 By-design case study project: Baldwin Hills Village, located at 5300 Rodeo Road in the Baldwin Hills neighborhood of Los Angeles.

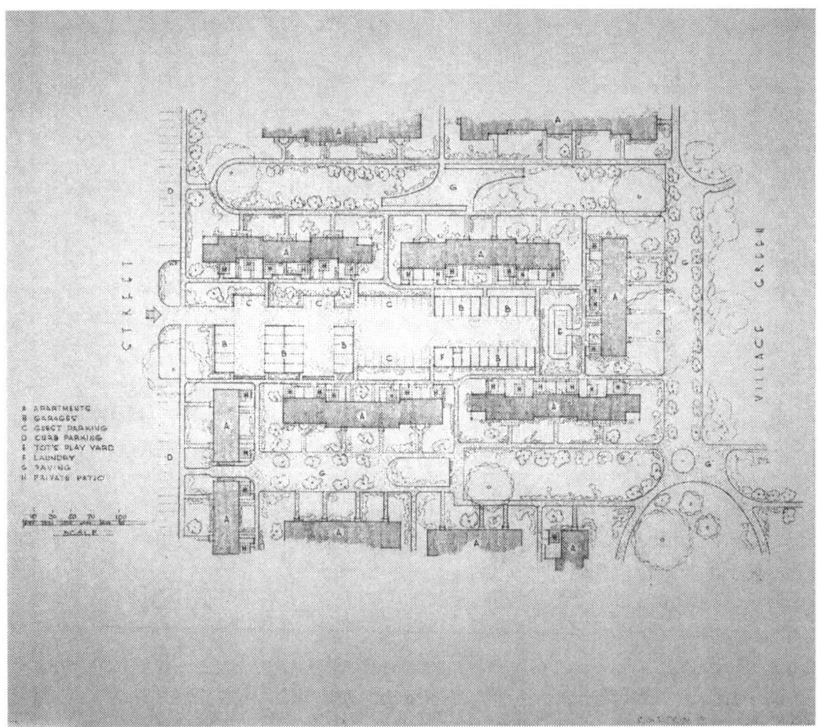

Figure 3.6 Detailed site plan of the design of two garden courts and one interlocking garage court at Baldwin Hills Village.

Credit: Clarence S. Stein papers, #3600. Division of Rare and Manuscript Collections, Cornell University Library.

> nation due to its excellence of plan. It is pointed to as the first instance in which any such development has been designed along lines that will succeed in accomplishing what city planners consider the ideal, a "super-bloc."[6]
>
> (Cohan, 1939, A1)

The project was well documented in the national architectural press and was evaluated by noted urbanists Lewis Mumford and Catherine Bauer soon after completion. Mumford believed Baldwin Hills Village to be

> [o]ne of the handful of projects that stand out as a fundamental advance in both planning and architecture. . . . Here every part of the design speaks the same robust vernacular: simple, direct, intelligible.
>
> (Mumford, 1944, p. 45)

Baldwin Hills Village's absence of through streets, large landscaped open spaces and circulation separating cars and pedestrians were all precedent-setting, helping to define garden apartments as a type, but these features made it much more difficult to gain the required governmental approvals. The project spent more than three years in the planning and design phase because the Los Angeles City Engineer and City Planning Commission repeatedly denied its proposed plan (Stein, 1957, p. 192). Their main concern was emergency access for fire and life-safety personnel given the 1,100-foot depth of the superblock, as well as the inclusion of commercial and residential uses on the same site (Stein, 1957). The project's conditions of approval mandated an intervening road, Sycamore Avenue, disconnecting the planned residential and commercial portions of the project and required that the garage courts be deeper than originally planned for emergency vehicles. The lack of through streets was only approved because the hills for which Baldwin Hills was named effectively acted as a cul-de-sac where these streets would have ended anyway (Bauer, 1944).[7]

Design

Context

The belief that good design is for everyone, rich, poor and middle-income alike, was prevalent at the time Baldwin Hills Village was built. The Depression and World War II spurred a transition from costly period styles to a more streamlined architectural language and motivated socially oriented housing experimentation along the garden apartment model. The first such experiment in Los Angeles was Wyvernwood, designed by David J. Witmer and Loyall F. Watson and built in

Boyle Heights in 1939, providing 1,187 units on 70 acres for middle- and working-class families (Wallach, 2015, p. 111). Work for architects was scarce at this time, so as the garden apartment evolved, most projects were designed as joint ventures, ensuring that opportunities were spread among many.[8] Although these efforts produced mostly vernacular buildings, many well-known architects participated, including Victor Gruen, Richard J. Neutra and Paul R. Williams. Garden apartments were mostly built in California Modern, but some were also Minimal Traditional, stripped-down versions of more traditional styles like Colonial or Spanish Revival.

By the time the Chesapeake Rodeo Apartments were built in 1951, however, the country was experiencing a postwar boom in single-family housing and the experimental ethos in multifamily housing had waned. Garden apartments built after 1946 were predominantly private, with singular architects and a more formulaic approach to design (Wallach, 2015, p. 122). The last garden apartments in Los Angeles were built in 1955, just as the dingbat apartment, a small stucco box building organized around parking and vehicular access with little to no garden space, was emerging.

Architect Max Maltzman, designer of the Chesapeake Rodeo Apartments, is known for dozens of Hollywood Regency–era apartments designed in Period Revival styles, including the Charmont Apartments in Santa Monica (1928) in a blended Art Deco and Mission/Spanish Colonial Revival style and The Ravenswood in Hollywood (1930) in Art Deco. Maltzman designed at least two other garden apartments in addition to Chesapeake Rodeo, the Alvern Apartments in Westchester in 1949 (now demolished) and the Hollypark Knolls Apartments in Inglewood in 1951. He also designed many buildings for the Jewish community in Boyle Heights.

Reginald D. Johnson, Fellow of the American Institute of Architects (FAIA); Clarence S. Stein, FAIA; and Robert E. Alexander, FAIA, were the principal architects of Baldwin Hills Village. Johnson had a successful Pasadena practice designing period-style estates for wealthy Southern California clients, but he also designed important institutional buildings, including the Good Samaritan Hospital in Los Angeles (1926) and the Hale Solar Laboratory and Solar Observatory in Pasadena (1924). Stein advanced the Garden City Movement in the U.S. through his publications and projects, which included Sunnyside Gardens in New York (1924–1928), Radburn in New Jersey (1928–1932), and Greenbelt in Maryland (1935). And Alexander, in partnership with various architects, designed a wide range of projects from housing, including Bunker Hill Towers; to institutional, including buildings at the University of Southern California, the University of California, Los Angeles, and the California Institute of Technology; to urban design, including plans for Juarez, Mexico.[9]

Inspired by his friend Stein, Johnson began looking for an appropriate large-scale housing site on the Baldwin Estate in 1934. He had been considering retirement when the Depression made better housing a national concern and shifted his focus. To this new venture, Johnson attracted the firm of Wilson, Merrill and Alexander, a company created expressly for these types of collaborative opportunities. Alexander made the first sketch for what became Baldwin Hills Village in August 1935, then envisioned as a single-family neighborhood on more than 200 acres organized around cul-de-sacs (Laskey, 1989). With Alexander acting as chief designer, the team began design studies in earnest when Stein was officially brought in as a consulting architect in 1938. The project had been reduced in scale by half by this time and envisioned as multifamily rental housing. As described by Alexander, the goal was

> to make the automobile accessible—which it had to be in Southern California—but to make it a servant instead of a master, and to somehow create a serene environment in which the automobile would not intrude.
>
> (Laskey, 1989, n.p.)

With Stein on board, the project more specifically built off his earlier garden apartment projects, refining the essential elements of his "Radburn Plan:"

- Use of a superblock
- Complete separation of cars and pedestrians for safety and better enjoyment
- Houses facing gardens and parks
- Park as the heart of the community (Stein, 1957, p. 189)

Time devoted to planning and design was three times that typically spent, during which the team generated at least 50 site plans and redrew the units at least 10 times (Berry, 1966; Laskey, 1989). Stein himself believed that his Radburn ideas were "crystalized into a more functional unity" in the design of Baldwin Hills Village (Stein, 1957, p. 189).

To what degree are the Chesapeake Rodeo Apartments and Baldwin Hills Village similar or different from a design perspective? Does the Chesapeake Rodeo Apartment's vernacular status mean it lacks architectural value? Does the fact that Baldwin Hills Village is a nationally recognized design precedent mean its design is exemplary in all respects?

Site Strategy Through Street vs. Superblock

The case study projects take opposite approaches to site design, one connected to, but buffered from, the surrounding neighborhood and the other creating an inwardly focused neighborhood of its own. The Chesapeake Rodeo Apartment's flat triangular site is approximately 500 feet deep by 1,750 feet long and is organized around Rodeo Lane, an L-shaped local street. This street cuts the site into a rectilinear block surrounded by public streets and a triangle with street frontage on two sides and a long tail against an adjacent property. Two edges of the triangle include parallel access roads, buffering the project from busy surrounding streets.

Baldwin Hills Village's flat rectangular site is approximately 1,100 feet deep by 2,500 feet long and is organized as a single superblock with no through streets.[10] The property is bordered by public streets on all sides but has a private access road, like that at the Chesapeake Rodeo, buffering the community from Rodeo Road on the northern edge of the property.

Building Organization and Massing *Homogeneous vs. Diverse*

Both case study projects distribute two-story buildings around the perimeter of their sites using a "Greek fret" pattern to create alternating courtyards, some facing "out" and others facing "in." Courts at the Chesapeake Rodeo are undifferentiated from in to out and court to court, each creating the same type of pass-through space regardless of orientation or location. Buildings are two stories with hipped roofs and cover 25% of the site area (Apartment Development Due, 1950, E2).

Courts at Baldwin Hills Village are highly differentiated. Two basic types are used, garage courts (facing out) linked to the surrounding streets and garden courts (facing in) linked to the central Village Green. Courts are also differentiated by shape, location and articulation, creating rectangular, splayed and triangular courts in different zones of the project, using the same essential elements but in varied combinations. Buildings are one or two stories with low-hipped and gabled roofs. Some two-story buildings have one-story extensions to vary their massing. Residential buildings cover 14% of the site area (Cohan, 1941, A1).

Unit Types and Amenities *Standard vs. Superior*

The case study projects use similar unit types, but those at Baldwin Hills Village are more spacious and better appointed. The Chesapeake Rodeo has 254 one-bedroom and 171 two-bedroom units, all flats, that average 731 square feet per dwelling unit (L.A. Department of City Planning, 2018). Units featured oak floors, separate stall showers, garbage disposals and TV outlets (Classified Ad 22, 1951).

Baldwin Hills Village has 275 one-bedroom, 312 two-bedroom and 40 three-bedroom units, with various layouts within each unit type (Bauer, 1944, p. 51). Most units are flats, but 216 are two-story townhouses. Interiors average 1,080 square feet per dwelling unit (Bauer, 1944, p. 52). Units in Baldwin Hills Village also had oak floors and separate stall showers as well as stainless steel drainboards and, at minimum, five closets. One-third of the units have wood-burning fireplaces. Living spaces in the units (bedrooms and living rooms) overlook garden courts or the central green while service spaces (bathrooms, kitchens and sometimes dining rooms) overlook parking courts.

Pedestrian Access and Entry Neglected vs. Protected

The Chesapeake Rodeo Apartments lacks a protected realm for the pedestrian while pedestrians are prioritized at Baldwin Hills Village (Figure 3.7). At the Chesapeake Rodeo, pedestrians access units either from street-facing courtyards linked to city sidewalks or from similar courtyards oriented toward large internal parking areas. Units are entered from a common stairway that connects the public realm to the private garage area through an open breezeway.

Pedestrian pathways are the primary mode of circulation at Baldwin Hills Village. Front doors of most units are directly accessible from the

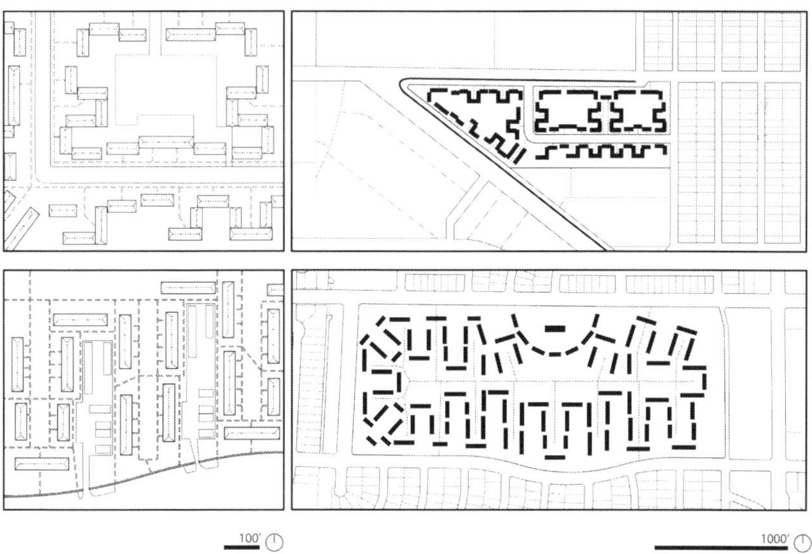

Figure 3.7 Pedestrian circulation diagrams: The Chesapeake Rodeo Apartments (top) vs. Baldwin Hills Village (bottom).

Village Green or the 17 green courtyards, all of which are accessible from the surrounding public sidewalks via four large entry portals through street-facing buildings. Entries for second-story flats are placed off the garage courts by design, but are protected by ample landscaping to allow for individual ground-floor entries for all units.

Vehicular Access and Parking *Center vs. Periphery*

Cars are at the center of the Chesapeake Rodeo Apartments and restricted to the periphery at Baldwin Hills Village (Figure 3.8). Central parking areas at the Chesapeake Rodeo are located in the middle of each block and off an alley on the southern edge of the property. Space for one car per unit was provided in garages aggregated into long rows. Parking was not initially included in the rent and required an extra charge (Classified Ad 22, 1951). Fewer than 20 guest parking spaces were provided and parking areas were not significantly landscaped.

Cars are kept at bay in Baldwin Hills Village by limiting all car access to the periphery of the superblock. Garage courts allow cars to penetrate the exterior boundary of the site but not travel through it, reducing automobile sounds and smells with generous landscaping and fencing. Carports were originally provided, one per unit, included in the rent, as well as head-in guest parking in excess of one car per unit in both the garage courts and in large indentations off the surrounding streets on the

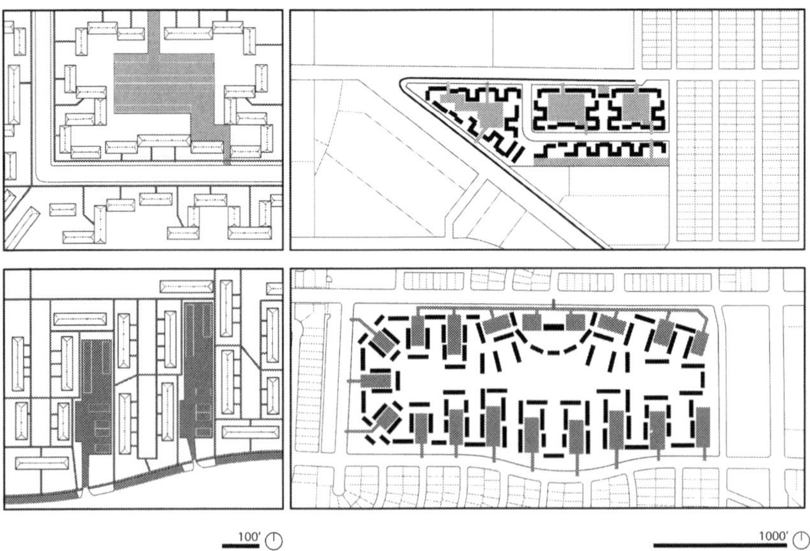

Figure 3.8 Vehicular circulation diagrams: The Chesapeake Rodeo Apartments (top) vs. Baldwin Hills Village (bottom).

northern, western and southern edges. Carports were enclosed as garages during the first few years of operation (Bauer, 1944).[11]

Common Open Space Periphery vs. Center

The Chesapeake Rodeo Apartments locates common open space at the periphery while Baldwin Hills Village places it at the center (Figure 3.9). Perimeter inward- and outward-facing courtyards make up most of the common open space provided at the Chesapeake Rodeo. These spaces are currently unprogrammed although the 18 play spaces originally included in the project, now demolished, would have been located here (Apartment Development Due, 1950). A common linear green space, 55 feet by 350 feet, or 19,250 square feet (0.44 acres), also bisects the rectilinear block transversely.

Common open space is at the heart of Baldwin Hills Village, with three large open spaces linked by allées of trees, forming the backbone of the project, approximately 250 feet wide by 2,300 feet long. These spaces, approximately 13 acres in total, are thoughtfully landscaped and intended for both active and passive recreation. Many units have direct access to this space, while other units can access it via green courts, also together totaling approximately 13 acres. The project included many active recreation spaces, located in the semicircular space framing the administration building, which have since been replaced with additional parking.

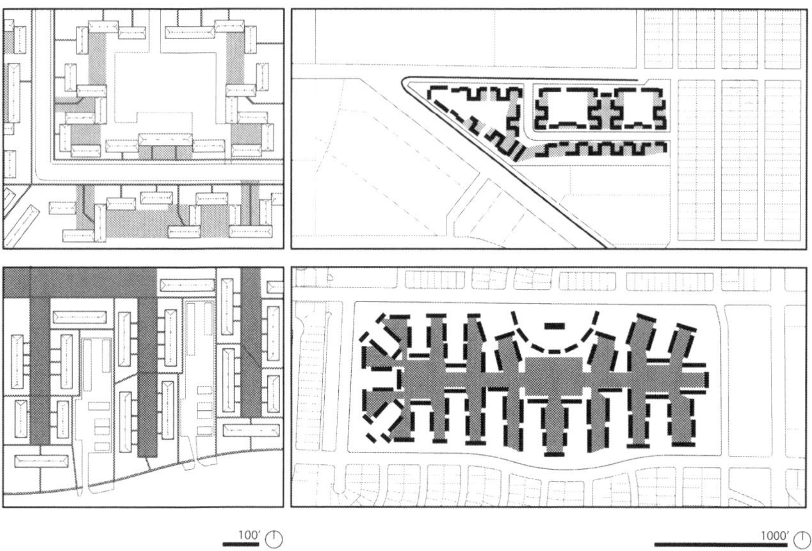

Figure 3.9 Common open space diagrams: The Chesapeake Rodeo Apartments (top) vs. Baldwin Hills Village (bottom).

Private Open Space *Absent vs. Ample*

Private open space is effectively nonexistent at the Chesapeake Rodeo Apartments but is maximized at Baldwin Hills Village. Although balconies were mentioned as a selling point when plans for the Chesapeake Rodeo Apartments were announced, few were included in the project as built, and the nine that exist today are only 3 feet deep (Apartment Development Due, 1950). They are not easily accessible and serve more as entry overhangs.

Private open space was a driving issue that shaped the design of Baldwin Hills Village from its inception. All units have ground-floor patios that function as outdoor living rooms, ranging from 250 square feet to 400 square feet (Bauer, 1944, p. 53). The patios extend off the dining room and kitchen spaces in ground-floor flats and townhouse units and provide a ground-level entry space for second-story flats. Patio spaces are either walled with 6-foot wooden fences (ground-floor flats and townhouse units) or enclosed with serpentine brick walls (second-story flats).[12] All patios are intensively landscaped around their external edges but were maintained by the tenant on the interior. The 126 upstairs flats have 6-foot-wide balconies suitable for lounging or outdoor dining.

Landscape *Incidental vs. Intrinsic*

The Chesapeake Rodeo Apartments approached landscape as an afterthought while Baldwin Hills Village used it as an opportunity to address identity and lifestyle. After building roads and parking areas, about 25% of the site area is available for landscaping at the Chesapeake Rodeo Apartments. No project records indicate that a landscape architect was employed, so, more likely, a nursery was used to create a planting plan. The grass, trees and shrubs that were used were minimal yet high-maintenance.

Baldwin Hills Village devoted more than 40% of its site to landscape (not counting landscaping in parking areas), which is used to enhance the image, social environment and functionality of the project. The design, by landscape architect Fred Barlow Jr., Fellow of the American Society of Landscape Architects (FASLA), uses a palette of native trees, shrubs and ground covers to differentiate courtyards, define pathways, frame vistas, create privacy and create spaces for active and passive recreation, 77 plant species all told (Kane et al., 2013). The landscape is informal yet orderly, and relatively low maintenance. Plantings were designed to amplify the horizontality of the site and integrate the buildings into the landscape. A 20- to 30-foot strip of ground cover (usually ivy) was used in front of ground-floor units to ensure privacy.

Architectural Style *Vernacular Modern vs. Vernacular Modern*

The architectural style of the two case study projects is similar, making them seem more alike at first glance than they are on closer inspection. Now called "Vernacular Modern" or "Minimal Modern" by architectural historians (Chase, Horak, Davis, Slater, & Bubnash, 2010, p. 26), both use straightforward materials such as stucco, batten-board siding, wood lattice/fins and overhanging roofs in a pared down vocabulary. In her evaluation of Baldwin Hills Village, Bauer noted that

> [c]onsidering the buildings individually, one must admit that while they are contemporary in feeling, relatively simple and honest, they are nevertheless not exactly exciting as "modern" architecture.
> (Bauer, 1944, p. 51)

Design Performance *Everyday Example vs. National Exemplar*

The case study projects perform as expected from a design perspective given their product type versus design precedent status. The Chesapeake Rodeo Apartments has been recognized as a vernacular garden apartment in a historic context statement prepared by Architectural Resources Group in 2012, establishing it as a member of the garden apartment type and evaluating its possible future designation. Baldwin Hills Village has been lauded throughout its existence. The project was included in the Museum of Modern Art's (MOMA) "Built in the USA" exhibit in 1944 and was named by MOMA as one of America's most significant works of architecture in 1946. It went on to win a Distinguished Honor Award from the Southern California Chapter of the AIA, also in 1946, and the National AIA 25-year award for superior community design in 1972. The project became a Los Angeles Historic Cultural Monument (#174) in 1977. Its notable status culminated in 2001 when it was designated a National Historic Landmark by the National Park Service.

Outcomes *Underachieving vs. Setting New Standards*

A shared architectural style and seemingly similar site design mask deep differences between the case study projects.[13] Ultimately, the innovations of Baldwin Hills Village are turned inside out at the Chesapeake Rodeo Apartments, providing the image of a tranquil community without the functionality of one. At the Chesapeake Rodeo, design strategies that maximize the quality of life at Baldwin Hills Village, including extensive and varied landscaping, a protected pedestrian realm, generous private and common open space and generously sized units, are either not utilized at all or not used to their fullest extent. In other words, it is not Max Maltzman's best effort and was an underachiever from a design perspective from the start. The project does have "good bones" and it's underlying unit types and site organization are relatively easy to improve. The biggest differences between the two projects are the same as those Bauer noted in her evaluation of Baldwin Hills Village and the garden apartments built as public housing projects in Los Angeles, namely, site design, improvements and landscape, all of which have enriched Baldwin Hills Village as it aged, boosting its value (Bauer, 1944, pp. 57–59). Appraising the project 25 years after it was built, architecture critic Richard Berry notes how "[l]andscaping and site planning accrue value with age; style sooner or later obsolesces toward a liability" (1966, p. 218).

Real Estate Development

Context

The Chesapeake Rodeo Apartments and Baldwin Hills Village were both privately developed as the nation was experiencing an unprecedented housing shortage and measures to increase the quality, affordability and supply of housing were under intense debate. The Depression, World War II and the flood of returning veterans postwar increased migration to cities, changed the character of demand and limited construction, all of which impacted the cost of housing. In Los Angeles, the population grew by 31%, or 466,073 people, from 1940 to 1950, and 2,412 acres were added to the city in 33 annexations (Ethington, 2007, p. 689; L.A. City Planning Commission [LACPC], 1952, p. 7). All while the development of new housing was inhibited by high land costs, scarce materials and controlled rents, which encouraged the conversion of existing housing into other uses. Los Angeles even had to house people in converted streetcar "trolley cottages" (Streetcars Converted, 1946).

A diversity of solutions to the national housing crisis were sought and the stimulation of privately built rental housing was an important piece of the New Deal housing program. The Federal Housing Administration (FHA) promoted rental housing as a sound investment, arguing that housing for low- and moderate-income families addressed a wider market and was therefore more secure (FHA, 1937, p. 13). Beginning in 1934, Section 207 of the National Housing Act responded to the need for better quality, more affordable rental housing after the Depression by providing mortgage insurance for private housing with restricted rents and rates of return. Section 608, added to the National Housing Act in May 1942, responded to the need to house defense workers during World War II, also providing mortgage insurance for private rental housing on terms similar to Section 207. Section 608 was substantially amended in 1946 in reaction to the housing shortages experienced by returning soldiers and their families, giving priority occupancy to veterans and increasing allowable construction costs per room/unit. Ultimately, under Section 608 alone, the federal government insured 465,683 units in 7,045 projects before the program ended in 1950, a commitment of nearly 3.5 billion dollars (US Senate, 1955, pp. 4, 70, 127). Mortgage insurance was issued for a total of 21,575 dwelling units in California (US Senate, 1955, p. 70).

Herbert Kronish, president of Chesapeake Rodeo Apartments, Inc., was a prominent real estate developer working in Los Angeles in the 1950s and 1960s, building primarily tracts of single-family homes and commercial office projects.[14] Right after he developed the Chesapeake Rodeo, Kronish built a tract of 850 single-family homes called the Newport Vista tract, all FHA compliant (New Tract, 1953). And he built a new three-story office building in Miracle Mile at Wilshire and Burnside Avenue (New Building, 1953).

Ray Kinsey, manager of the Baldwin Estate, was effectively the client for Baldwin Hills Village and was an enlightened one to some degree. He was very conservative but could see the need for housing for all middle-income groups (Laskey, 1989). As Anita Baldwin's representative, Kinsey had been selling off the Baldwin land incrementally since the beginning of the Depression. Architect Alexander recounted that "[h]is economic objective was investment rather than speculation, which is the number one, perhaps the most important thing that separated Baldwin Hills Village from any other housing that went on after it" (Laskey, 1989, n.p.).

How do the Chesapeake Rodeo Apartments and Baldwin Hills Village compare from a real estate development perspective? Does Chesapeake Rodeo's status as a typical product type mean it was more profitable? Does Baldwin Hills Village's celebrated design mean it underperformed as an investment?

Land Acquisition *Baldwin Estate vs. Baldwin Estate*

Both the Chesapeake Rodeo Apartments and Baldwin Hills Village were built on ranch land once owned by Elias Jackson "Lucky" Baldwin. Property for both case study projects was annexed into the City of Los Angeles as part of the 4,672 acre Palms Annexation on May 22, 1915 (Ethington, 2007, p. 687). Land for the Chesapeake Rodeo Apartments was owned by the Baldwin family until 1948. It changed hands twice before being purchased by Chesapeake Rodeo Apartments, Inc. in October 1950. Land for Baldwin Hills Village, a former bean field then owned solely by the Baldwin Estate, was contributed to the Baldwin Hills Village project as equity. The southern edge of the project remained the boundary line for the City until the actual Baldwin Hills to the south were annexed in 1947 (L.A. County Department of Public Works, 1947).

Land and Construction Costs *$8,255 per Unit vs. $4,911 per Unit*

Land and construction costs for the case study projects were roughly equivalent considering the 5.6% average annual inflation rate experienced between 1940 and 1950. The Chesapeake Rodeo Apartments' total cost was reported to be $3,500,000, or $8,255 per unit (Apartment Development, 1950). Baldwin Hills Village's total cost was reported to be $3,079,197, or $4,911 per unit (Bauer, 1944, p. 59).[15] In 1940, $4,911 has the same purchasing power as $8,434 in 1950 dollars, just $179 more than the Chesapeake Rodeo (www.calculator.net/inflation-calculator.html).

Although overall costs were aligned, the construction quality obtained for that outlay diverged significantly. Baldwin Hills Village clearly added more value for their money, providing a lush, diverse landscape, private balconies and patios, generously sized units and a clubhouse for just a few dollars more than were spent at Chesapeake Rodeo, which had none of these amenities.

Funding *Section 608 vs. Section 207*

Both case study projects qualified for mortgage insurance from the federal government, without which they likely would have been perceived as too risky to build.[16] The Chesapeake Rodeo Apartments, Inc. raised $381,100 in equity and obtained a $2,967,000 loan from the Irving Trust Company of New York City under the provisions of Section 608 of the National Housing Act (70 FHA 'Windfall' Projects, 1954; Apartment Development, 1950). Section 608 allowed the federal government to guarantee 30-year mortgages for up to "90 percent of the [FHA] Administrator's estimate of 'reasonable replacement cost' of the completed project," including land, fees and improvements (US Senate, 1955, pp. 7–8). In return, the government regulated rents, capital structure and rates of return. In 1950, for example, the FHA set an $80 rent ceiling for Section 608 projects in Los Angles (Apartment Boom, 1950, p. 100). The Chesapeake Rodeo Apartments, Inc.'s loan represented an 88.6% loan-to-value ratio.

Rancho Cienega Properties, Inc., the ownership vehicle for Baldwin Hills Village, raised $712,000 in equity and obtained a $2,600,000 loan under the provisions of Section 207 of the National Housing Act. At the time it was funded, the project was "the second largest enterprise of the kind ever insured by the large-scale division of the F.H.A." (Building Starts Today, 1941, p. 13). The project's architects and builder contributed their services, valued at $241,000. $241,000 in cash was raised from nearly 30 investors. (Rancho Cienega Properties, Inc, Annual Report, As of March 31,1942, Clarence Stein Papers). And the Baldwin Estate contributed the land, which was valued at $230,000, computed last using a residual land value method (Baldwin Hills Village, A Moderate Cost

Housing Project, Los Angeles, California, 1942, Clarence Stein Papers). Alexander said the team did dozens of "financial setups" (i.e., proformas) with the biggest variable being the land cost (Laskey, 1989, n.p.).

Under the provisions of Section 207, projects were underwritten assuming 90% occupancy and investments were set up as limited dividend corporations, capping the annual return on investment at 6%. In addition to requiring that interest on loans did not exceed 4.5% (4% interest + 0.5% for the insurance and mortgage insurance up to 80% of estimated value), the FHA had standards governing physical development as well as rent levels, capped at $12.27 per room (Bauer, 1944). Any funds exceeding an annual 6% return were placed on reserve for future amortization and replacement of important building components at the end of their useful life. Baldwin Hills Village originally sought funding from the New York Life Insurance Company but was ultimately rejected so it was (ironically) publicly financed by the National Mortgage Association (Reconstruction Finance Corporation). The $2,600,000 loan was mortgaged over 28 years and represented a 78.5% loan-to-value ratio.

Market Timing Free Market Rents vs. Wartime Rent Control

Both case study projects opened to significant and sustained housing demand, but the Chesapeake Rodeo Apartments was better timed to market from an investment standpoint since it did not have to manage operations under wartime restrictions. By the time the Chesapeake Rodeo Apartments opened in 1951, material restrictions had ended, and a bitter fight for rent decontrol had just been won by Los Angeles landlords when the US Supreme Court threw out a union-sponsored appeal of a City Council vote to revert to market rents (Francis, 1951).

Baldwin Hills Village opened in December 1941, right after Pearl Harbor, just as the War Production Board banned all nonessential construction and froze rents to prevent gouging (Stein, 1957). Rents were retained at an average of $12.27 per room/$52 per unit for almost a decade (Stein, 1957). Los Angeles would add 301,410 people (20%) between April 1, 1940, and January 28, 1946, ensuring that demand remained high during the project's early war years (LACPC, 1947, p. 7). Population in the Baldwin Hills area increased more than 25% during the same period (LACPC, 1947, p. 6).

Marketing Model Apartment (1) vs. Model Apartments (3)

The Chesapeake Rodeo Apartments and Baldwin Hills Village were marketed similarly. Both projects ran classified and display advertisements in the *Los Angeles Times* in addition to distributing on-site promotional materials. Ads for the Chesapeake Rodeo Apartments cite their location near the

Crenshaw Center shopping area, ample storage and separate stall showers in all units, as well as 18 automatic laundry rooms and play equipment areas for children (Classified Ad 20, 1951, A20). But Baldwin Hills Village had all these things and more. Its promotional materials advertised "City Living" in "Country Club Style," promising "a true adventure in modern living" (Baldwin Hills Village Brochure, Clarence Stein Papers) (Figure 3.10). Units were noted for their privacy and individualized entrances in addition to their refrigerators and occasional wood-burning fireplaces. Activities available on the project grounds included tennis, badminton, croquet and horseshoes. The project also provided a variety of playgrounds, a wading pool, a community building with a photo darkroom and library, a nursery school, 2,500 trees and optional maid service (Display Ad 29, 1942, B2). Both projects also marketed sections for adults only (Model Apartment, 1951).

Both case study projects used model apartments furnished by local department stores to entice potential renters. At the Chesapeake Rodeo, the Broadway Department Store decorated "The Chesapeake" apartment in "moderately priced" furniture in the 18th-Century style (Display Ad 6, 1951, p. 8) (Figure 3.11). The unit's living and dining rooms were painted in "rancho rose" and bedrooms in "Catalina green" (Model Apartment, 1951, E5). Baldwin Hills Village had three units furnished by Bullock's, including one in the "Swedish Modern Style" and another in "Wishmaker Modern" (Architects' Dream, 1942, p. 20).

Rents and Absorption *Middle-Income Housing vs. Upper Middle-Income Housing*[17]

Both case study projects were built for moderate-income tenants but had asking rents at the high middle and upper end of the range (Figure 3.12). The Chesapeake Rodeo Apartments originally advertised rents at $70 to $85 per month for one- and two-bedroom apartments (Apartment Development, 1950, E2). These rates were reduced by mid-1951 to $67.50 to $82.50 (Model Apartment, 1951, E5). Based on the content and frequency of advertisements in the Los Angeles Times, the Chesapeake Rodeo leased up relatively quickly and remained full during initial operations.

Initial asking rents at Baldwin Hills Village ranged from $45 to $80 for three-and-a-half- to six-room apartments with one-, two- or three-bed rooms (Display Ad 29, 1942, B2). Although controlled because of the war, these rent levels were substantially higher than the median rent in Los Angeles in 1940, $27.83, a time when most housing in the city was renting for between $30 to $39 (LACPC, 1943, p. 11). In December 1951 dollars, Baldwin Hills Village rents ranged from $76 to $135, significantly higher than those at the Chesapeake Rodeo.[18] The project was 100% occupied during its initial operation (Bauer, 1944; Stein 1957).

Figure 3.10 Advertisement for Baldwin Hills Village that appeared in the *Los Angeles Times* on January 2, 1942 (Display Ad 29, 1942, B2).

Credit: Courtesy of the Village Green Owners Association, Los Angeles, CA, USA.

Figure 3.11 Advertisement for the model apartment at the Chesapeake Rodeo Apartments that appeared in the *Los Angeles Times* on June 28, 1951 (Display Ad 6, 1951, p. 8).

Operating Costs *Lower vs. Higher*

The operating costs at Baldwin Hills Village were significantly higher than those at the Chesapeake Rodeo Apartments, partly because wartime hampered initial operations and ensured that they were costlier than expected, but also because the project had more amenities to maintain. For example, Baldwin Hills Village did not have a war-related need for individual telephones so its owners had to pay to have a telephone

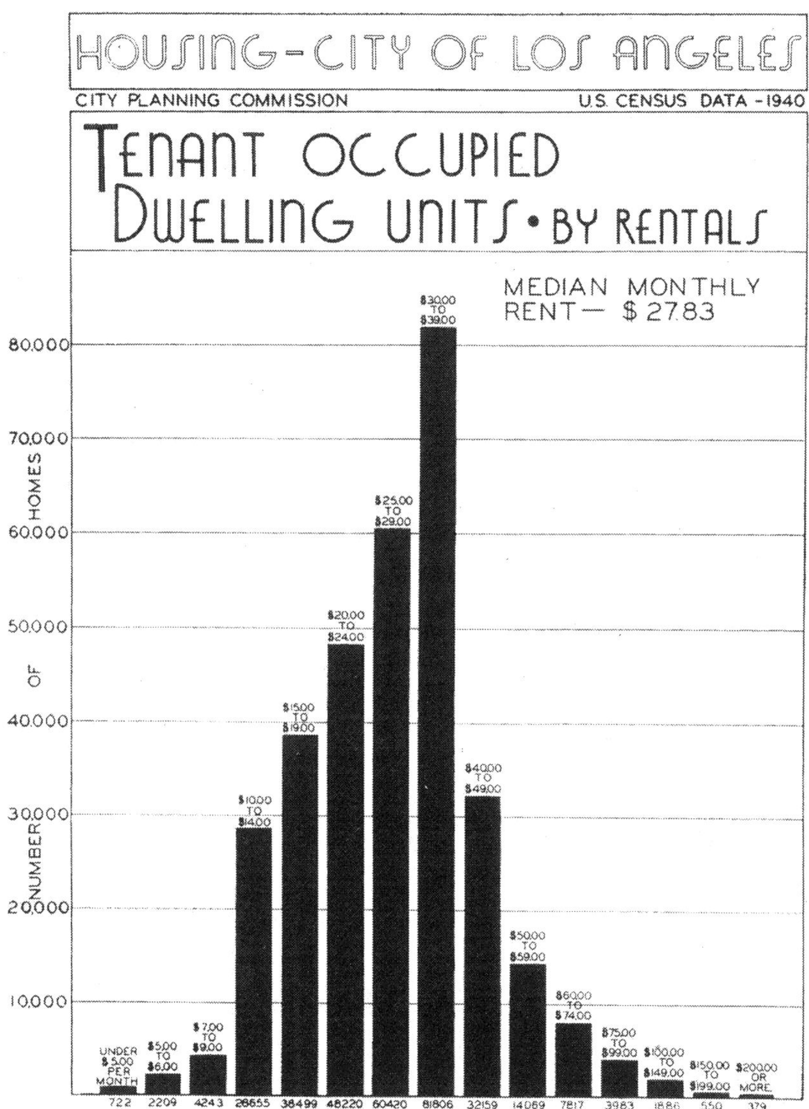

Figure 3.12 Price range of tenant occupied dwelling units 1940: Most of the rental housing in Los Angeles rented for much less than Baldwin Hills Village at the time it was being planned and built (LACPC, 1943, n.p.). Median monthly rent in Los Angeles in 1940 was $27.83.

Credit: Los Angeles City Archives and Records Center.

exchange at the office manned 24 hours a day. A planned bus line to the project was also canceled by the War Production Board, meaning that the owners had to pay for a shuttle service to a shopping center at Crenshaw and Rodeo Road and to Adams and La Brea for the streetcar service (Architects' Dream, 1942). The "services of 20 full-time gardeners" were also "required to maintain the area's country-like appearance" (Picturesque Little City, 1941, E1).

Investment Performance *Poor vs. Sustained*

The Chesapeake Rodeo Apartments and Baldwin Hills Village have experienced divergent investment outcomes. Little is known about the investment history of the Chesapeake Rodeo Apartments, but its sponsors were accused of FHA fraud in 1954, along with many others in Los Angeles and throughout the nation (70 'Windfall' Projects, 1954).[19] Herbert Kronish, Max Maltzman and several other associates were accused of inflating project costs to raise the mortgage amount guaranteed. Once a loan for this amount was obtained, the extra proceeds were distributed to investors as capital gain, not income. "Surplus" mortgage funds of $94,000 were distributed to Chesapeake Rodeo investors, an immediate 25% profit on what was to have been a limited 6% investment, all taxed at the lower capital gains rate (Anatomy of a Certified, 1955, p. 140; 70 'Windfall' Projects Named, 1954). Since this time the project has remained a rental and has changed ownership at least 10 times, most recently in 2007. Since the project was built before October 1978, it is currently rent controlled. A two-bedroom apartment today rents for about $1,800.

It was common for Section 608 projects to "mortgage out" in this manner and it was not initially clear that the practice was fraudulent. The opportunity to do so certainly accounted for the Section 608 program's popularity, but "at what point, does a 'hefty profit' become fraud?" (Welfeld, 1992, p. 13). Some argued that this was really the only way to incentivize investment in rental housing since it was a low-yield venture with slow recovery of capital that could not compete with other investment opportunities (Colean, 1955, pp. 110–111). If sponsors of Section 608 projects mortgaged out, they could effectively build rental housing with 0% equity investment and a 100% loan (Colean, 1955, pp. 110–111). But others felt that the 608 "apartment boom [was] floated on public risk and private profit," which resulted in poor quality housing (Apartment Boom, 1950, p. 97):

> Although they are certainly not intended to do so, FHA minimums actually serve as a general agreement to restrain competition. Because the buildings are protected from the normal hazards of future rentability by government insurance, nobody needs to build any bigger rooms than anybody else.
>
> (Apartment Boom, 1950, p. 101)

Both of these perspectives were proved right. Indeed, the expiration of Section 608 program spelled the end of the large-scale garden apartment typology in the US. And many that were built in the early 1950s, the height of "mortgaging out," are the projects struggling today with poor construction, unmarketable unit types and long-term underinvestment.

Baldwin Hills Village has remained a good investment throughout its history. Although its rents were initially stabilized, the project's 100% occupancy rate and long waiting list helped it stay in the black throughout the war and immediate postwar years. For the first eight years, the owners were able to pay for all operating expenses, maintenance costs and debt service payments, though interest and payback of equity were delayed until the project was sold to New England Mutual Life in 1949 for $4,500,000, a profit of approximately $1,188,000, a 21% annual return on investment, after the repayment of the loan and return of equity. (Baldwin Hills Village, 1949, p. 1).[20] New England made some changes, enclosing patios for the upper flats (which undoubtedly improved long-term value) and turning the community building into two very luxurious units (which arguably deteriorated it). Baldwin M. Baldwin, heir to one of the original project developers, repurchased the property in 1962 for an undisclosed price (Cameron, 1962). The project was bought by Terramics in 1972 and condo-ized in stages from 1973 through 1978, initially marketing units from $19,500 to $34,500 (Turpin, 1974, F1). The condominium developers updated kitchens and bathrooms and changed the project's name from Baldwin Hills Village to the Village Green.[21] Today units sell for $500,000 to $600,000.

Outcomes Speculation vs. Investment

While the Chesapeake Rodeo Apartments and Baldwin Hills Village were built using shared investment tools and development strategies, from a real estate development perspective the projects are opposites. The Chesapeake Rodeo was built for short-term (and perhaps ill-gotten) gain while Baldwin Hills Village was built as a long-term investment. It is difficult to assess whether the Chesapeake Rodeo would have been a sound investment if it had played by the rules. Clearly, however, playing by the rules and implementing innovative design did not detract from Baldwin Hills Village's solid investment performance. Its ample parking, large units, good storage, access to common and private green space, and extensive landscape have all enhanced value over time.

Urban Planning

Context

By the time Baldwin Hills Village was in the planning stages, Los Angeles was well into its recovery from the Depression and building permits and valuations were on the upswing. Housing production was crucial as the city geared up for World War II and then accommodated a postwar flood of returning servicemen and their families. A master plan for the city was incrementally developed throughout the 1940s, including separate plans for housing, parkways, parks and recreation, traffic arteries and airports, among others (LACPC, 1946, p. 9). Zoning and subdivision standards were key components of this plan, and both changed significantly to better address housing needs during the time the case study projects were built.

Subdivision standards changed the most radically. The City Planning Commission initially recommended that land be subdivided in gridiron pattern of through streets (LACPC, 1928, p. 12). But by the time Baldwin Hills Village was under construction, the grid pattern was increasingly thought to be monotonous, uneconomical and unsafe. Chief land planning consultant for the FHA Charles D. Clark noted just how resolutely planners advocated for this change in perspective:

> Not so long ago it was a primary objective of every public official concerned in subdivision matters to see to it that all streets were continuous through streets. Such an attitude is now considered to be utterly ridiculous by the very people who formerly gave it strong support.
>
> (Clark, 1941, p. 164)

Planners were now more interested in the creation of peaceful residential streets within the boundaries of busy through streets. By the time the Chesapeake Rodeo was being built, department recommendations had fully shifted to a system of internalized neighborhoods of cul-de-sacs, curvilinear streets and service roads, all turning their backs to bordering collector streets.

To what degree are the Chesapeake Rodeo Apartments and Baldwin Hills Village similar or different from an urban planning perspective? Does the fact that Chesapeake Rodeo Apartments was developed as of right while the design innovations of Baldwin Hills Village required discretionary approval mean that one met planning goals better than the other?

Housing Needs *Family Rental Housing vs. Family Rental Housing*

Both the Chesapeake Rodeo Apartments and Baldwin Hills Village met the growing need for rental housing affordable to middle-income families. Most upper- and middle-income families intended to become homeowners, but rental housing for those not in a social or financial position to buy a home was in high demand. “By 1944 one quarter of

Los Angeles County residents had arrived since 1940," many as a result of World War II, some of whom decided to stay but others were short term (Brackman, 2007, p. 389). By 1949, new construction had begun to address the local housing shortage, but "estimates at the end of the year revealed a need for about 55,000 new dwelling units to restore normal conditions, exclusive of substandard units needing replacement" (LACPC, 1950, p. 4). By 1950, Baldwin Hills, unmeasured in 1940, had a population of 7,019 that was expected to grow to 31,894 by 1980 (LACPC, 1953, p. 6). While both projects met critical housing needs, Baldwin Hills Village's more spacious units in a broader range of types were suitable for a wider range of families than those at the Chesapeake Rodeo.

Development Standards *Medium-Intensity Development vs. Low-Intensity Development*

Both case study projects created lower intensity development than they were regulated for at the time they were built. Land for both projects was originally classified as "B" zone under the city's 1921 zoning code, multiple family dwellings, and was transitioned to "R4" under the city's new 1930 zoning code. By the time the Chesapeake Rodeo Apartments were built in 1951, its site had been redesignated R3 under the 1946 comprehensive zoning ordinance. The project met all the standards of the zone, as amended in 1948: no more than two-and-a-half stories or 35 feet in height, 25-foot front and 20-foot rear setbacks and 800 square feet to 1,200 square foot of lot area per dwelling unit depending on unit size. Although the project is dense at 424 units (~24 DU/Acre), it did not come anywhere near the allowable density for the zone, which ranged from 631 to 947 units (36 to 54 DU/Acre).

Baldwin Hills Village was well under the standards for the R4 zone, which allowed up to six-story apartment buildings, but ran afoul of other City Planning and City Engineer standards relating to streets and subdivisions (LACPC, 1931, p. 18; Stein, 1957, pp. 190–192). Although its superblock strategy maximized elements planners believed to be ideal, for example, access to private and common open space, safety for pedestrians and ample space for the car, at the time it was built

> [t]he system of continuous through-streets [still] had official recognition and legal backing. Municipal engineers had nailed down the typical pattern of streets in official maps. They recognized no other arrangement. Change meant work—and making up one's mind—and possibly courting disapproval of superiors. In fact they looked upon new-fangled arrangements such as cul-de-sacs as dangerously revolutionary—or just the crazy idea of impractical architects.
>
> (Stein, 1957, p. 190)

Although city planners were transitioning to a preference for cul-de-sacs over through streets at the time Baldwin Hills Village was built, the fact that the project's superblock plan was neither one nor the other caused consternation.

Density 24 Dwelling Units/Acre vs. 9 Dwelling Units/Acre

The Chesapeake Rodeo Apartments is over twice as dense as Baldwin Hills Village, 24 dwelling units per acre as compared to 9 dwelling units per acre. Densities over 20 dwelling units per acre push the limits of the garden apartment typology, increasing the area required for cars, reducing the area that can be devoted to open space and making it nearly impossible to give every unit an individual ground-floor entry. Developers consider a density of 10 units an acre and under to be suitable for single-family housing development. When used for more compact multifamily development like that seen at Baldwin Hills Village, the space that is used to isolate the single-family home on its lot (front, side and rear yards) can be aggregated into significantly sized communal open space.

Parking One Stall per Unit vs. Two-Plus Stalls per Unit

Although Baldwin Hills Village was built nearly 10 years earlier, it has more than double the parking ratio of the Chesapeake Rodeo Apartments and better anticipated future parking needs (Figure 3.13). Parking one space per unit in an on-site garage was required in multifamily zones by 1935, and car ownership in Los Angeles increased dramatically between 1940 and 1950, over 55% (*Accomplishments 1951*, p. 14; LACPC, 1935, p. 15).

The Chesapeake Rodeo Apartments met the parking requirement of one space per unit by placing long rows of garage parking (up to 26 stalls long) in the middle of housing blocks serving 80 to 120 families, accessible but hidden from the street. Use of a space was not included in the rent and required an extra fee (Classified Ad 22, 1951, A22). The parking areas are minimally landscaped and contain approximately 440 spaces (Classified Ad 22, 1951, A22).[22] The project was soon underparked.

The team developing Baldwin Hills Village knew automobile accessibility was the key to success, given the increasing popularity of automobiles and the project's relatively remote location with limited bus service and few surrounding amenities. The project exceeded the City's minimum parking requirement, including carport parking for each unit in small garage courts serving 30 to 40 families accessible from the surrounding streets and providing an additional 770 guest spaces, uncovered, in the parking courts and in spaces lining the perimeter of the project on the street.[23] One carport parking space was included in the

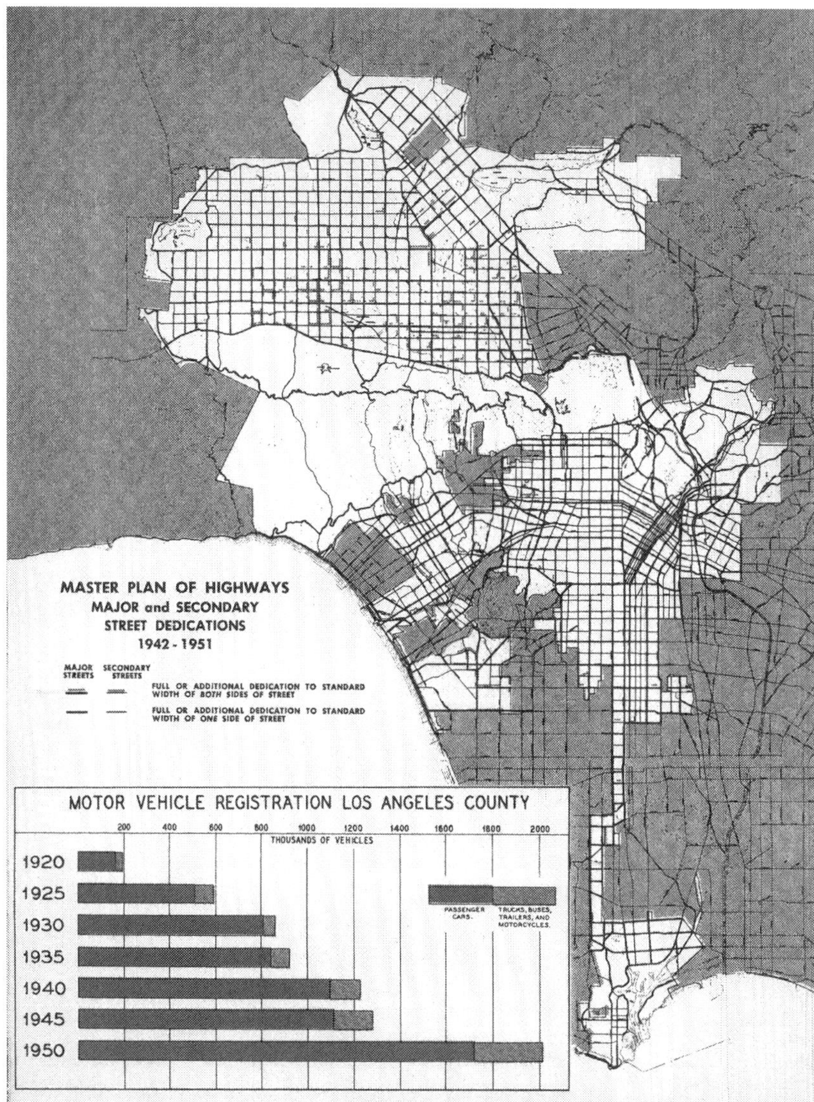

Figure 3.13 Automobile registrations rose dramatically between the time Baldwin Hills Village and the Chesapeake Rodeo Apartments were built (LACPC, 1952, p. 13).

Credit: Los Angeles City Archives and Records Center.

rent, and guest spaces were available on a first-come, first-served basis. Garage areas were extensively landscaped to reduce the smell and noise of the automobile and make the parking areas more visually attractive (Stein, 1957).

Public Realm *Admitted vs. Excluded*

The Chesapeake Rodeo Apartments incorporates the public realm while Baldwin Hills Village turns away from it. Rodeo Lane invites the larger community in and links the Chesapeake Rodeo Apartments to the surrounding neighborhood. Entries to all but a few buildings are visible and accessible from the street, which is improved with public sidewalks.

Baldwin Hills Village is an internally organized "introverted neighborhood" (Berry, 1966, p. 219). The project is not fenced, but the central Village Green and most unit entries are not visible from surrounding public streets. The project does contribute a generous setback of landscaped open space, provides a public sidewalk around the perimeter of the site and a few units have front walks and entries facing out, but the project is effectively disconnected from its surrounding context.

Internal to the project, however, the issue of public versus private is handled with more nuance, addressing community, court and individual scales, each creating a commensurate degree of openness or intimacy. The three central large greens are accessible to everyone living in or visiting the project. Many residential buildings line these open spaces, and all 17 of the garden courts feed into this green. The garden courts, coupled with their adjacent garage courts, effectively break a very large project down into neighborhoods, each serving an average of 36 households. The third, most private, scale of space is the private patios for each unit.[24]

Community Life *Limited vs. Robust*

Community-wide events and opportunities for recreation were few and far between at the Chesapeake Rodeo Apartments but were a central part of life at Baldwin Hills Village. Announcements for the Chesapeake Rodeo mention fifteen play areas and three proper playgrounds with equipment (Apartment Development, 1950). Advertisements for the project also noted that the Rancho Cienega Recreation Center and Playground were located just across Rodeo Road. It is not known whether there was any specific social programming, but none is mentioned in articles or advertisements about the property.

Recreation and social programming were robust at Baldwin Hills Village. Architect Alexander, also a resident, reported that the clubhouse was active seven days a week during the project's early years (at least partially because it was hard to get anywhere else during wartime), hosting plays, card games, a Wednesday night square dance, egg-throwing contests, a Friday night forum featuring guest speakers and debates and the annual Baldwin Hills Village Olympics (Alexander et al., 1989, n.p.). The clubhouse had a lending library, reading lounge with fireplace, Ping-Pong tables, darkroom and a large area used for dances, church services and other meetings. Outdoor space could be used just as actively, with areas for both children and adults. The project boasted six badminton courts, three horseshoe pits, two tennis courts, two croquet courts and a putting green (Letter to the Board of Directors—Thousand Gardens, Inc. from Johnson, Wilson, Merrill and Alexander, February 25, 1941). A large playground was located near the Clubhouse building and four smaller fenced play areas in sections reserved for families with children. A wading pool just south of the Clubhouse was transformed into a planter early in the project's existence (Keylon, 2011).[25]

Planning Performance Met the Code vs. Missed Opportunity to Push the Code

The design of both case study projects addressed planning regulation at the time they were built, but Baldwin Hills Village reflects shortsightedness on the part of Los Angeles planners. Since the innovative strategies used at Baldwin Hills Village, its superblock site plan, high percentage of open space and circulation separating cars and pedestrians, were not incorporated into the code, it was difficult to incorporate them into vernacular projects like the Chesapeake Rodeo Apartments that were necessarily more focused on the speed of production. All the pushing back against City regulations by the Baldwin Hills Village team only benefited their own project and could not be translated to any of the 50 other garden apartment projects built in Los Angeles in the late 1940s and early 1950s.

Outcomes

Although Baldwin Hills Village was very difficult to approve in an era biased toward single-family residential, it actually met the City's stated planning goals for single-family subdivisions better than the single-family neighborhoods that were developed around it in the late 1940s and 1950s:

> Paradoxically, despite its successes—which include superb solutions for accommodating 20th century automobile demands and Southern California's climate-generated way of living—the Village has not been reproduced nor emulated elsewhere, except in superficial aspects. Nor did it effectively influence the level of development of the urban environment around it.
>
> (Berry, 1966, p. 216)

Baldwin Hills Village meets all the performance criteria Los Angeles planners used to shape single-family neighborhoods but by other means; that is, it creates a safe, interior-focused neighborhood that has ample open space, room for the car and a family character, with a common green as opposed to a front yard, a parking court instead of a single garage, identified by communal court and building rather than individual house and block. Ironically, had Baldwin Hills Village been a single-family housing development as originally envisioned, it might have had more impact on overall Los Angeles housing outcomes.

Conclusion

When Urban Planning Regulation Fails to Translate an Innovative "Design Precedent" into a Viable "Product Type"

Lessons Learned *Urban Planning Matters*

Urban planning matters. At first glance, the Chesapeake Rodeo Apartments looks to be the same as the Village Green, with low-slung California Modern buildings defining courtyards across a large site. On closer inspection, however, the Chesapeake Rodeo reverts to conventional planning strategies, with intervening through streets instead of a superblock, parking at the heart of the project rather than park space and a complete lack of private open space, which together ensure that the project was less resilient as the markets evolved and housing expectations changed.

In this case, planning regulation failed to translate an innovative "design precedent" into a viable "product type." Although the Chesapeake Rodeo Apartments is located less than 1,500 feet from Baldwin Hills Village, it takes no lessons from the precedent-setting project next door, at least partly because the elements that made Baldwin Hills Village so successful were not incorporated into the planning and zoning code so that they could be implemented by-right. These strategies were lost in translation. Good housing often comes down to good planning since planning's domains—density, unit type, parking, open space and development pattern—arguably determine a basic quality of life. Inattention to design and planning can doom investment performance.

Outcomes

The Chesapeake Rodeo Apartments is a short-term investment that upholds disciplinary stereotypes: real estate developers only care about quick profit, planning regulation is unable to deflect bad actors and Modern architecture is for the richest or poorest. The project made negative trade-offs among disciplines. Its by-right strategy minimized market risk by creating certainty and reducing time to completion, but ultimately the project did not use planning to add lasting development value. The required public street running through the project negatively impacts safety, noise, the quality of open space and image. Design features that could have helped the project compete as the rental market evolved were not a part of the original design and were difficult to retrofit: a diversity of unit types, good storage, private open space, guest parking and more development-wide amenities. The project's singular focus on development return compromised its ability to perform long term from every perspective.

Baldwin Hills Village is a "triple-win" project that breaks disciplinary stereotypes: being well designed did not detract from its status as a profitable investment providing much needed middle-income rental housing. The project made many positive trade-offs among disciplines. Its superblock spatial organization ensures access to open space that was highly marketable at the time the project was built and continues to be highly desirable today. Time spent gaining discretionary approval, negative in the immediate term from a time value of money standpoint, was used wisely, perfecting a cost-effective and marketable design over literally hundreds of schemes produced over a 5-year period. Money that would have been spent on unremarkable street infrastructure was spent on high-quality landscape and open space instead.

Notes

1. The original site was 22 acres, which included Rodeo Lane, initially a private street. The street is now publicly owned and maintained.
2. Garages have since been demolished.
3. Entryways have since been gated.
4. Different site areas are listed in early publications, ranging from 60 to 100 acres. 67.7 acres is used here, calculated from Assessors Map 5025–7, Sheet 1. This includes the private access road parallel to Rodeo Road.
5. The commercial portion of the project was deemed "nonessential construction" due to wartime restrictions and could not immediately be built. Consequently, the Baldwin Hills Village team obtained a zone variance to temporarily operate certain commercial businesses in an existing residential building (ZA 7144, 1942). Three residential units near the circle were used to house a market and coffeeshop, a beauty/barber shop and a nursery. The commercial block only began to be developed in 1949, when theater was built (Baldwin Theater Opens Wednesday, 1949).
6. Owners of the *Los Angeles Times*, Ralph J. Chandler, Norman Chandler, and the Times Mirror Company itself were original shareholders (Kane et. al., 2013).
7. Ironically, cul-de-sacs would soon become preferred. See Case Study 2: Value Out of Balance.
8. All the architects of Baldwin Hills Village, for example, were partnered in various permutations on at least seven garden apartment projects, all of which had, at minimum, three designers (Chase et al., 2012).
9. Alexander was on the Los Angeles City Planning Commission from 1945 through 1949. He was president in 1948.
10. The shape of the overall site would have been symmetrical if the commercial parcel had been included, making the central administration building axis, semicircle of residential buildings and bump out on Coliseum Street make more compositional sense.
11. Children were playing in them and people started siphoning gas during the war (Bauer, 1944).

12. The serpentine brick walls were a later, but still early, addition, installed by New England Mutual Life Insurance, designed by Robert Alexander.
13. Notably, all except Clarence Stein lived in the project once completed to gain firsthand experience of their design work and how it might be improved going forward. Architect Robert Alexander helped the project make considered changes at points where improvements were needed, including patio walls and rebuilding after a flood in the 1960s.
14. Developer Herbert Kronish was no stranger to good modern architecture. Architect Richard J. Neutra designed a house for Kronish and his wife at 9439 Sunset Boulevard in Beverly Hills, built in 1954. See Kronish Residence, City Landmark and Evaluation Report, January 2015.
15. Although a range of costs for Baldwin Hills Village are listed in various publications, those published in Catherine Bauer's Pencil Points appraisal of the project soon after it was built are used here (Bauer, 1944).
16. One hundred percent equity would have been the only option, which is how Metropolitan Life Insurance funded its rental projects, like Park La Brea (Bauer, 1944).
17. Baldwin Hills Village essentially restricted rentals by racial minorities. There was always a long waiting list so the manager could be very "choosey" about tenants (Bauer, 1944). There was reportedly a waiting list well into the '60s (Berry, 1964).
18. www.bls.gov/data/inflation_calculator.htm
19. The Chesapeake-Rodeo Apartments, Inc., in the end, was not one of the projects thoroughly investigated by the Senate Committee on Banking and Currency, but Baldwin Gardens, just south of the Chesapeake Rodeo, was. It was found to have distributed windfall profits of $227,154 (FHA Investigation, 1954, p. 110).
20. $4,500,000 – $2,600,000 (Loan) – $712,000 (Equity) = $1,188,000. Assuming the money was invested for eight years, this represents a 21% annual return on investment (Stein, 1957, p. 190).
21. At time of condoization restrictive covenants prohibiting children under 18 and animals of any kind were put in place. The prohibition of children was struck down by the Supreme Court.
22. Garage doors at the Chesapeake Rodeo were removed in 2001 as an anticrime measure and were eventually torn down completely (May 24, 2001, *Los Angeles Sentinel*).
23. The FHA initially pushed back on this parking scenario. Given its experience with similar large-scale housing projects on the East Coast near public transportation, one garage unit per unit, plus so much guest parking seemed excessive. The Baldwin Hills Village design team really had to push for this.
24. It is worth noting that Baldwin Hills Village's inward orientation is simultaneously the source of its greatest achievement, significant common open space free from the car and its main critique, that it turns its back on the rest of the neighborhood.
25. At the last minute, the FHA also eliminated 212 benches that would have encouraged more community interaction. The original plans also called for one outdoor room per garden court with low shrubs, decomposed granite floors, benches and shade trees that were meant to draw people of each court together (Laskey, 1989, n.p.).

References

70 FHA 'Windfall' Projects Named: Five Apartments in L.A. Area Among Those Probed. (1954, June 12). *Los Angeles Times*, 5. Retrieved from www.proquest.com

Anatomy of a Certified Legal "Windfall." (1955, March). *House and Home*, 141–143.

Apartment Boom. (1950). *Architectural Forum*, 92(1), 97–106.

Apartment Development Due in Crenshaw Area. (1950, October 22). *Los Angeles Times*, E2. Retrieved from www.proquest.com

Architect's Dream Soon to Be Reality: Apartment House Project in Baldwin Hills Community Offers Luxury and Privacy. (1942, May 24). *Los Angeles Times*, 20. Retrieved from www.proquest.com

Baldwin Hills Village Sale Near Completion. (1949, June 29). *Los Angeles Times*, 1. Retrieved from www.proquest.com

Baldwin Theater Opens Wednesday. (1949, August 7). *Los Angeles Times*, 1. Retrieved from www.proquest.com

Bauer, C. (1944, September). Description and Appraisal . . . Baldwin Hills Village. *Pencil Points*, *25*, 46–60.

Berry, R. D. (1964). Baldwin Hills Village—Design or Accident. *California Arts and Architecture*, *81*, 18–21.

Berry, R. D. (1966). Experiences in a 25-Year-Old Planned Neighborhood Can Yield Lessons Applicable to "New community" Planning Today. *The Journal of Housing*, *23*(4), 214–219.

Brackman, H. (2007). Making Room for Millions, Housing in Los Angeles. In Hynda L. Rudd and Tom Sitton et al. (Eds.), *The Development of Los Angeles City Government, an Institutional History 1850–2000* (pp. 371–413). Los Angeles, CA: Los Angeles City Historical Society.

Building Starts Today on Huge Homes Project. (1941, March 25). *Los Angeles Times*, 13. Retrieved from www.proquest.com

Cameron, T. (1962, January 5). Baldwin Hills Village Sold to Earlier Owner. *Los Angeles Times*, 12. Retrieved from www.proquest.com

Chase, C. E., Horak, K. E., Davis, A., Slater, M., & Bubnash, L. (2010). *The Village Green Historic Structures Report*. Retrieved from www.villagegreenla.net/uploads/5/7/6/0/57603411/village_green_hsr_2010.pdf

Chase, C. E., Horak, K. E., & Keylon, S. R. (2012). *Garden Apartments of Los Angeles, Historic Context Statement*. Los Angeles, CA: Los Angeles Conservancy.

Clark, C. D. (1941). Land Subdivision. In W. George, L. Robbins, & T. Deming (Eds.), *Los Angeles, Preface to a Masterplan* (pp. 159–172). Los Angeles, CA: The Pacific Southwest Academy.

Classified Ad 20. (1951, July 8). *Los Angeles Times*, A20. Retrieved from www.proquest.com

Classified Ad 22. (1951, October 21). *Los Angeles Times*, A22. Retrieved from www.proquest.com

Cohan, C. C. (1939, September 29). Nation's Greatest Housing Project Announced for City: Gigantic Baldwin Hills Home Building Enterprise to Represent More Than $7,000,000 Investment. *Los Angeles Times*, A1. Retrieved from www.proquest.com.

Cohan, C. C. (1941, March 30). *Bird's-Eye View of Huge Housing Development*. Los Angeles Times, A9. Retrieved from www.proquest.com

Colean, M. L. (1955). Impotency of FHA Policies on Apartment Finance. *Architectural Forum*, 102(6), 110–111, 162.

Display Ad 6. (1951, June 28). *Los Angeles Times*, 8. Retrieved from www.proquest.com

Display Ad 29. (1942, January 2). *Los Angeles Times*, B2. Retrieved from www.proquest.com

Ethington, P. J. (2007). The Spatial and Demographic Growth of Los Angeles. In Hynda L. Rudd and Tom Sitton et al. (Eds.), *The Development of Los Angeles City Government, an Institutional History 1850–2000* (pp. 651–697). Los Angeles, CA: Los Angeles City Historical Society.

Federal Housing Administration. (1937). *Rental Housing As Investment*. Washington, DC: FHA. Retrieved from https://catalog.hathitrust.org/Record/100710352

Francis, W. B. (1951, January 3). High Court Drops LA Rent Wrangle. *Los Angeles Times*, 21. Retrieved from www.proquest.com

Howard, E. (1902). *Garden Cities of To-Morrow*. London, England: Swan Sonnenschein & Co., Ltd.

Kane, H., Keylon, S., & Loe, S. (2013). *The Village Green Cultural Landscape Report*. Retrieved from https://californiapreservation.org/wp-content/uploads/2014/03/VillageGreenCLR.pdf

Keylon, S. (2011). *Recreation Facilities and Children at Baldwin Hills Village from 1991 to the present day*. Retrieved from http://baldwinhillsvillageandthevillagegreen.blogspot.com/2011/03/as-those-of-you-who-live-at-village.html

L.A. City Planning Commission. (1928). *Annual Report for Year Ending June 30, 1928*. Los Angeles, CA: L.A. City Archive.

L.A. City Planning Commission. (1931). *Annual Report for Year Ending June 30, 1931*. Los Angeles, CA: L.A. City Archive.

L.A. City Planning Commission. (1935). *Annual Report for Year Ending June 30, 1935*. Los Angeles, CA: L.A. City Archive.

L.A. City Planning Commission. (1943). *Accomplishments 1942*. Los Angeles, CA: L.A. City Archive.

L.A. City Planning Commission. (1945). *Accomplishments 1944*. Los Angeles, CA: L.A. City Archive.

L.A. City Planning Commission. (1946). *Accomplishments 1945*. Los Angeles, CA: L.A. City Archive.

L.A. City Planning Commission. (1947). *Accomplishments 1946*. Los Angeles, CA: L.A. City Archive.

L.A. City Planning Commission. (1950). *Accomplishments 1949*. Los Angeles, CA: L.A. City Archive.

L.A. City Planning Commission. (1952). *Accomplishments 1951*. Los Angeles, CA: L.A. City Archive.

L.A. City Planning Commission. (1953). *Accomplishments 1952*. Los Angeles, CA: L.A. City Archive.

L.A. County Department of Public Works. (1947). Angeles Mesa Addition No. 4. Retrieved from http://dpw.lacounty.gov/sur/nas/SMPM_AnnexationCity/LA0100.pdf

L.A. Department of City Planning. (2018). Parcel profile report, APN# 5046034015. Retrieved from http://zimas.lacity.org/reports/9318a91264ab447d877288584787ee49.pdf

L.A. Zoning Administrator Case Number 7144. (1942, August 14). Los Angeles, CA: L.A. City Archive.

Laskey, M. L. (Interviewer). (1989). *Interview of Robert Alexander Completed Under the Auspices of the Oral History Program, UCLA*. The Regents of the

University of California. Retrieved from http://oralhistory.library.ucla.edu/Browse.do?descCvPk=27599

Model Apartment Will Be Exhibited Today. (1951, June 17). *Los Angeles Times*, E5. Retrieved from www.proquest.com

Mumford, L. (1944, September). Baldwin Hills Village. *Pencil Points*, *25*, 44–45.

New Building is Scheduled. (1953, September 6). *Los Angeles Times*, 27. Retrieved from www.proquest.com

New Tract at Beach Puts Homes on Sale. (1953, July 5). *Los Angeles Times*, D4. Retrieved from www.proquest.com

Picturesque Little City Rising at Baldwin Hills: Project Costing $3,250,000 Will Comprise 97 Apartment Buildings in a Country-like Setting. (1941, October 5). *Los Angeles Times*, E1. Retrieved from www.proquest.com

Stein, C. S. (1957). *Towards New Towns for America*. Cambridge, MA: MIT Press.

Streetcars Converted to Meet Housing Crisis. (1946, March 18). *Los Angeles Times*, 2. Retrieved from www.proquest.com

Turpin, D. (1974, April 7). Honored Housing Project Now Becoming Condominiums. *Los Angeles Times*, F1. Retrieved from www.proquest.com

US Senate Committee on Banking and Currency. (1955, January 6). *FHA Investigation, Report of the US Senate Committee on Banking and Currency, Eighty-Fourth Congress, First Session, Pursuant to Senate Resolution 229*. Retrieved from https://catalog.hathitrust.org/Record/100669583

Wallach, R. (2015). *Los Angeles Residential Architecture, Modernism Meets Eclecticism*. Charleston, SC: The History Press.

Welfeld, I. (1992). *HUD Scandals, Howling Headlines and Silent Fiascos*. New Brunswick, NJ: Transaction Publishers.

Part 2

Collaborative Models

4 Proliferating a Product Type, House Courts

Clark Court vs. Horatio West Court

Figure 4.1 Case Study 4: House courts, Clark Court (left) vs. Horatio West Court (right).

Introduction

When Housing Regulation Encodes Flexibility and Encourages Typological Innovation

House courts are a common multifamily housing type built in Los Angeles from the early 1900s into the 1930s that cluster small, detached units around a central landscaped courtyard. Courts can be found from

Highland Park to Hollywood to Venice, all essentially miniaturizing the benefits of the single-family home, the city's predominant housing type, and distributing these benefits to a wider variety of residents. Early house courts, however, provided housing only for the relatively wealthy in tourist destinations like Pasadena and Santa Monica or the markedly poor, in industrial areas like those in East Los Angeles near the Los Angeles River (Gish, 2009–2010). Ensuing state and local regulation shaped the open space, unit size and construction requirements for house courts, ensuring that they were habitable, but did not create so many requirements that the buildings' design could not respond to a range of market, social and class conditions. Far from dampening production, these urban planning policies prompted more responsible development and supported a broad array of design interpretations affordable to everyday Angelenos.

House Courts

House courts characteristically assemble a series of small freestanding houses on a single lot organized symmetrically to define a common courtyard (Figures 4.2 and 4.3). Courtyards are open to the street, providing a communal landscaped outdoor space capitalizing on the mild Southern

Figure 4.2 House courts in the Ocean Park neighborhood of Santa Monica.

Figure 4.3 Horatio West Court and house courts in the Ocean Park neighborhood of Santa Monica, mapped, including Clark Court (1).

California climate and pedestrian access to an individual entry for each house. Houses are typically one story and were executed in many styles, including Craftsman, Mission and Spanish Colonial. Homes were small, usually two to five rooms, and employed built-in furniture to maximize the use of space, including dining room buffets, kitchen breakfast nooks, window seats and, often, "disappearing" beds. Houses were customarily identical, or at least very similar to one another, and usually built of stucco over a wood frame. Sometimes units were joined together into bars on the side or in larger structures at the rear. Cars were also frequently integrated into courts, using a driveway down the center of the courtyard or down the side to garages at the back property line. By the late teens, house courts were being rented mainly by middle-class locals, tourists and retirees.

The most important characteristic of house courts, however, is the way they allowed multifamily housing to blend into single-family residential neighborhoods:

> These buildings of California have drawn the opposite poles of human habitations—a home and an apartment—into one aesthetic and practical unit, embodying the best characteristics of each.
>
> (Roorbach, 1913, p. 520)

House courts had the privacy, individuality and access to outdoor space typical of a single-family home, combined with the convenience and inherent community of an apartment. Individualized units and a clear delineation of public, semipublic and private space via entry gates, porches, landscaping and garden walls made living in a house court synonymous to living in a single-family house. Courts' "space-oriented" configuration, however, also creates room for community interaction and protection, as well as participation in the public realm (Polyzoides, 1992, p. 9). Facing units and common entry walkways ensured that house court residents knew their immediate neighbors while the common open space facing the street created opportunities to engage the neighborhood at large. Consequently, this type of low-rise, high-density housing did not have the same negative connotation as other, more collective and tenement-like apartment structures and provided desirable rental housing for those who could not yet afford a single-family home. In Los Angeles, the "City of Homes," a house court was "A Little City of Homes in Itself" (Bungalow Courts, 1921, p. 69).

Although house courts eventually won favor for their middle ground, as planning historian Todd Gish has noted, their origins are both bottom-up and top-down. (Gish, 2009–2010) Vernacular house courts were being built in Los Angeles by the early 1900s as housing for immigrants and the working poor who were laboring to build Los Angeles's rail lines, roadways and streetcar systems. While some were modest but well kept, many were essentially "horizontal tenements"—overcrowded, unsanitary and unsafe. Courts during this era were usually built by small contractors and landlords, but some were also erected by the residents themselves from found materials (paying $1.50 to $2.00 a month for ground rent) or by large employers, like the Pacific Electric Railroad, for their workers (L.A. Housing Commission [LAHC], 1908, p. 10) (Figure 4.3). Individual dwellings were sometimes built in rows around a common open space, but more often than not, as many units as possible were "packed" on to a lot with no consideration for access, privacy, daylighting or drainage (Gish, 2009–2010). Some were very large and very dense, including a court between New High and Buena Vista Streets and Sunset and Ord Streets which housed more than 170 people in 57 dwellings at a density of more than 55 units per acre (which today would require a three- to five-story building) (LAHC, 1908, p. 12). With daily wages for an immigrant worker as low as $1.50, the rents for such housing ranged from $1 to $3 a month for a single room and $10 to $16 a month for a three- to four-room dwelling (LAHC, 1908, pp. 8, 10).[1] These rents "averaged higher for worse conditions than in the slums of New York" (LAHC, 1908, p. 12). Many families had to take in lodgers just to make ends meet (Quintana, 2015, p. 61).

At the other end of the spectrum, architect-designed house courts for the upper middle-class began to appear at the end of the first decade of the 20th century. The first is generally agreed to be St. Francis Court built in Pasadena in 1909, designed by Sylvanus Marston (Bungalow Courts in Pasadena, 1994, F14). This is a "bungalow court," a house court variation that downsized the California Bungalow that was then burgeoning in Pasadena, Los Angeles and Santa Monica for upper middle-class and wealthy residents.[2] St. Francis Court arranged 11 Craftsman-style bungalows on a single site with lush landscaping, a central fountain and a driveway down the middle with a cul-de-sac at the end.[3] Each house was different, both in exterior appearance and in internal layout, and had one to three bedrooms, numerous porches and a private garden (Saylor, 1911, p. 23). These units were more luxurious than the typical Pasadena single-family home at the time, costing $3,000 per unit to build compared to $1,750 for the average Pasadena house (Bungalow Courts in Pasadena, 1994, F11). The bungalows rented, completely appointed, for $1,000 to $1,500 a year or from $900 to $1,200 for the November to May winter season ($83 to $200 per month; Saylor, 1911, p. 25). At nine dwelling units per acre, St. Francis Court was a sixth as dense as the court at New High and Buena Vista Streets and up to 200 times more expensive.

Almost simultaneously, in 1910, architect Irving J. Gill designed Bella Vista Terrace (also called Lewis Court) for F. B. Lewis, a spacious house court in Sierra Madre, just east of Pasadena. This project proposed 12 one-bedroom, one-bath houses around a large central open space with a vegetated pergola in the center, all designed in Gill's pared-down Mission Revival style with cubic forms, smooth surfaces and abstract archways. Large open loggias at unit entries housed movable beds so they could also be used as outdoor sleeping porches. Seventy percent of the site was to be open space, both private, in the form of individual walled gardens, and common, including landscaped terraces and a croquet court. The project would have been 10 dwelling units per acre if built as originally designed, but only seven houses were constructed, all of concrete and hollow tile.[4] Although these homes built on Gill's experiments in minimal dwelling and efficient living, like St. Francis Court, they were initially rented by affluent tourists, "by the week, month or year," "only five minutes to terminus of Sierra Madre car line" (Classified Ad 121, 1911, V7; McCoy, 1960).

From these disparate beginnings, the house court became a dominant, and desirable, housing type throughout Southern California in the 1910s,

1920s and into the 1930s, filtering both up and down, settling into a middle ground that worked for most (Polyzoides, 1992). The City of Los Angeles registered more than 1,200 of them by 1915 (Bogardus, 1916, p. 391).

> They're great to live in, these courts. Apartments can't hold a candle to 'em. They're cropping up like mushrooms. As bachelor quarters and homes for single or professional women, or for elderly people whose children have established homes for themselves, to say nothing of honeymooners, these courts can't be beat!
>
> (Hawkins, 1924, p. 92)

The majority of these structures were not designed by architects but were, rather, planned by building contractors using extant buildings, pattern books and trade publications for reference (Bungalow Courts in Pasadena, 1994; Rubin, 1977, p. 526; Weston, 1922). But how did these buildings make the transition from housing for the poor and the relatively wealthy to desirable housing for middle-class residents, tourists and retirees, renting from $14 to $25 a month as opposed to $1 or $200 (Bogardus, 1916, p. 396)? By what process did house courts both redeem and democratize themselves, and what can that tell us about the relationship between housing regulation and housing production? A closer look at two specific house courts, one a common model and the other an unconventional architect-designed example, offers a lens into these questions (Figure 4.1).

A TYPICAL CHOLO COURT

Figure 4.4 An example of deteriorated court conditions documented by the Housing Commission of the City of Los Angeles in 1908 (Los Angeles Housing Commission, 1908, p. 5).

Credit: Los Angeles City Archives and Records Center.

Clark Court

Clark Court, located at 2411 Third Street in the Ocean Park neighborhood of Santa Monica, is a vernacular example of a house court built in the Mediterranean Revival style (Historic Resources Group, LLC, 2004) (Figure 4.5). It was built by John N. Clark in 1922 and arranges 10 one-story freestanding houses, five to a side, with a duplex in the rear for a total of 12 units, efficiently maximizing the central landscaped courtyard and walkway and providing a homelike backdrop and setting. The building is such a straightforward example of the type that it was likely built using stock plans.[5] The size and layout of its units are not unlike those documented in *Weston's Single and Double Bungalows*, which advertised "A Bungalow Court of Six Units," "Plans and specifications furnished for $50.00" (Weston, 1922, pp. 22–23). Pacific Ready-Cut Homes also offered court units in a variety of styles and configurations, including double units, two-story buildings and even garages (Thornton & Wolicki, 2004). Mr. Clark, who ran a shooting gallery on the Ocean Front Promenade, lived on the premises during the court's first years of existence (Los Angeles Directory Co., 1923, p. 130; For Rent—Houses, Clark Court, 1922b).[6] The project was built by-right and did not require any special approvals. .

Figure 4.5 By-right case study project: Clark Court, located at 2411 Third Street in the Ocean Park neighborhood of Santa Monica.

Horatio West Court

Horatio West Court was designed by architect Irving J. Gill in 1919 and built by Horatio D. West at 140 Hollister Avenue, also in Ocean Park.[7] It arranges four units symmetrically around a narrow landscaped central courtyard with shared vehicular and pedestrian access (Figures 4.6 and 4.7). Unusually for house courts, Horatio West Court's units are two story and are designed to maximize private, rather than common, outdoor space. Mr. West and his wife, Alice, lived at 143 Wadsworth Avenue, one block south, in a single-family home on a parcel backing up to the West Court's lot (Los Angeles Directory Co., 1921, p. 500). West was a successful legal publisher in St. Paul, Minnesota, who began wintering in Pasadena for his health around 1895 (Jarvis, 2010; Real Estate and Building, 1895). Mr. West commissioned at least two houses in Altadena before the Ocean Park court. After his retirement in 1909, West seems to have been a real estate investor, frequently buying and selling property throughout the region, and a businessman with interests in oil, eucalyptus farming and cotton ginning (Another Cotton Gin at Shafter, 1930; Classified Ad 25, 1907; Kansas Takes Fight to the President, 1905). He eventually moved permanently to the beach house on Wadsworth. (Los Angeles Directory Co., 1925, p. 901) Like 2411 Third Street, West Court did not require any discretionary approvals to be built, but had it been

Figure 4.6 By-design case study project: Horatio West Court, located at 140 Hollister Avenue in the Ocean Park neighborhood of Santa Monica.

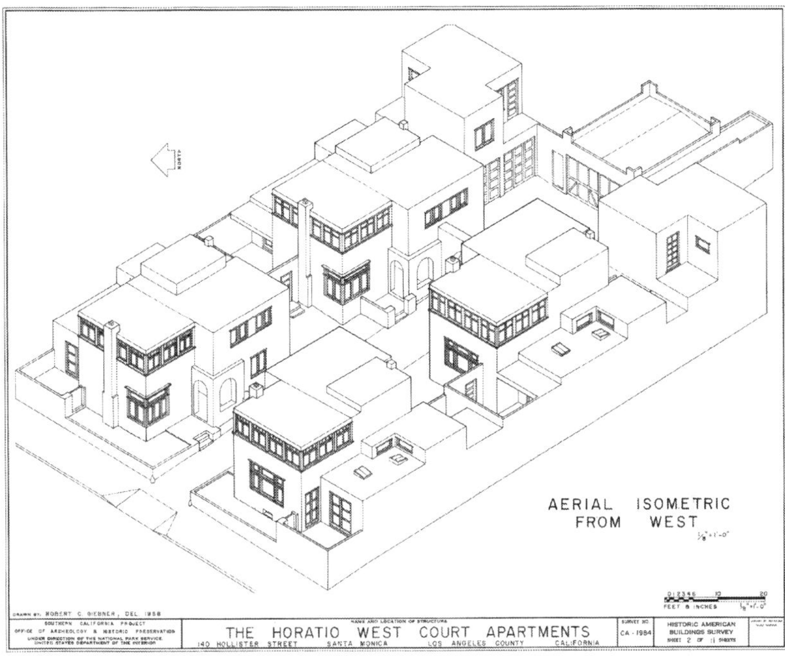

Figure 4.7 Axonometric drawing of Horatio West Court, documented in 1968.
Credit: Historic American Buildings Survey.

built just 3 years later, it would have required a variance from the Santa Monica zoning code, first established in 1922.

Mr. West made some significant changes to his court early in its existence with Gill's involvement unclear. Two additional apartments were constructed on top of the existing garages in late 1922, listed as "servants quarters" on the building permit (SMDBS, 1922). These two-room units define outdoor spaces to create irregular massing similar to that of the townhouses. In early 1923 the porches on the second story of the townhouse units were enclosed to create additional second-story rooms, turning five-room houses into six-room houses (approximately 1,350 sq ft) and facilitating their use in a more traditional configuration with the public space below and private above (Pastier, 1974; SMDBS, 1923a, 1923b). The two-story units were split into upper and lower apartments, and the name of the property was changed to El Consuelo Apartments in 1927 (HABS, 1968). And, finally, at some point between 1923 and 1950, two additional parking spaces were provided at the rear in a garage projecting into the lot behind (HABS, 1968; Sanborn Map, Santa Monica, Sheet 24, 1950). Building permits for these last two changes, if they existed, have been lost.

Design

Context

At the time Clark Court and Horatio West Court were built, noted architects from Pasadena, Los Angeles and Santa Monica were building in primarily traditional styles. Architects John Byers, Roland Coate, Reginald Johnson, Gordon Kauffmann, A. C. Martin and Wallace Neff were all building large houses for wealthy clients and important institutional buildings in period revival styles, including not only the Spanish-influenced styles of Mission, Spanish Colonial, Monterey and Mediterranean but also American Colonial, French Norman and Tudor. This period was also the era of the California Bungalow, similarly used for wealthy clients, initially those who wintered in Pasadena but eventually in Los Angeles and Santa Monica as well. Architects Charles and Henry Greene, Sylvanus Marston, Myron Hunt and Meyer and Holler all built large bungalows in the Craftsman, Japanese Craftsman, Shingle and even Swiss Chalet styles during this time.

All these styles, in more restrained terms, were also used for "common" or vernacular buildings, including small single-family homes, house courts and apartment buildings built by developers and contractors without the involvement of architects. There were many "bungalow books" and compendiums of stock plans, and there was a robust discussion of house courts, in particular, in building trade publications. *Building Age* published "A Community Court of Exceptional Attractiveness," while *American Builder* published "Bungalow Courts, New Idea in Space-Saving Construction" (Bungalow Courts, 1921; Byers, 1920a). *Hopkins Ladies Home Journal* even wrote about "A Picturesque Court of 30 Bungalows: A Community Idea for Women" (Hopkins, 1913). Along with Clark Court, at least 14 other house courts were built in the Ocean Park neighborhood during the 1920s and 1930s, most in Spanish Colonial Revival and Craftsman styles, clustered on Second and Third Streets between Pier and Pacific Avenues (Historic Resources Group, LLC, 2004, p. 44). Courts were popular with almost everyone, except, of course, prominent architects, who displayed a familiar bias against vernacular building. Indeed, Charles Greene, a master of the Bungalow Style, thought St. Francis Court was "a good example of what not to do," believing courts had "no other reason for being than that of making money for the investor" (Winter, 1980, p. 65).

Irving J. Gill, architect of Horatio West Court, built in traditional or "derivative" styles like Neoclassical, Gothic, Half-Timber and Shingle at the beginning of his career, but "he was not at home in revival styles" and quickly evolved his own distinctive architectural language based on the abstraction of indigenous California forms (McCoy, 1960, p. 63). He practiced primarily in San Diego but moved to Los Angeles in 1913 and completed many buildings in Los Angeles toward the end of his career, all in his synthetic style that blended regional Spanish traditions with pioneering Modernism. Gill believed in simplicity and eschewed ornamentation, focusing rather on the straight line, the cube and the arch as the most dignified "architectural language" (Gill, 1916). His elemental forms were then softened, not with precious architectural details, but with climbing vines, flowers and eucalyptus trees. Contrary to Greene, he thought that it would be "much better for California if there were less complicated, meaningless originality and more frank following of established good types" (Gill, 1916, p. 148).

Horatio West Court is a significant example of Gill's approach to small-scale, low-cost housing development and ideas about minimal dwelling. Gill had a "passion for simplifying," and according to historian Esther McCoy, he "was the first West Coast architect to give attention to company towns, barracks for laborers, housing for the unemployed, and that vast segment of the population who has to be content with hand-me-downs" (McCoy, 1960, pp. 59, 83). Gill designed several house courts during his career. In addition to Horatio West Court in Ocean Park and Bella Vista Terrace in Sierra Madre, he built worker housing for the Riverside Cement Company in 1911, built to an altered plan but still including Gill's courtyard design, a court of four houses in Echo Park in 1913 and housing for railroad workers in Torrance, also in 1913, much altered during construction.[8,9]

How similar or different are Clark Court and Horatio West Court from a design perspective? Does Clark Court's status as a vernacular example mean it lacks architectural value? Does the fact that a well-known architect designed Horatio West Court mean its design is exemplary in all respects?

Site and Building Organization *Central Court vs. Central Court*

Both Clark Court and Horatio West Court gather individual housing units symmetrically around a narrow central courtyard. Clark Court's freestanding units face one another across an approximately 20-foot-wide courtyard, while Horatio West Court's are separate but connected by walled patios, service porches and garden spaces, facing one another across a central space that varies from approximately 9 feet to 45 feet wide. Both projects are built on upsloping sites, creating a slight terracing effect, further defining each individual structure and increasing privacy.

Massing *Straightforward vs. Composite*

Buildings at Clark Court are simple one-story, rectilinear volumes. Buildings at Horatio West Court are two stories, characterized by interlocking volumes and irregular cubic forms. These qualities are amplified by the lack of a second story over the kitchen and entry spaces and the enclosed walls defining private outdoor spaces, both of which provide variety in exterior form as well as interior space. Roofs on both projects are flat.

Unit Types and Amenities *One-Story House vs. Two-Story Townhouse*

Ten units at Clark Court are freestanding houses while two rear units are attached to create a duplex (Figure 4.8). All are one-bedroom, one-bath and approximately 20 feet by 35 feet, or 700 square feet. The living room spans the width of the unit in front, with a dining room and kitchen to the right on one side and the bathroom and bedroom to the left on the other. All had numerous built-ins.

Units at Horatio West Court are two-bedroom, two-bath townhouses of approximately 1,250 square feet.[10] Their interior space was originally inverted, locating the living areas on the second story with a generous open balcony to capture views of the ocean and the service and sleeping areas below. Amenities at Horatio West Court included skylights in the

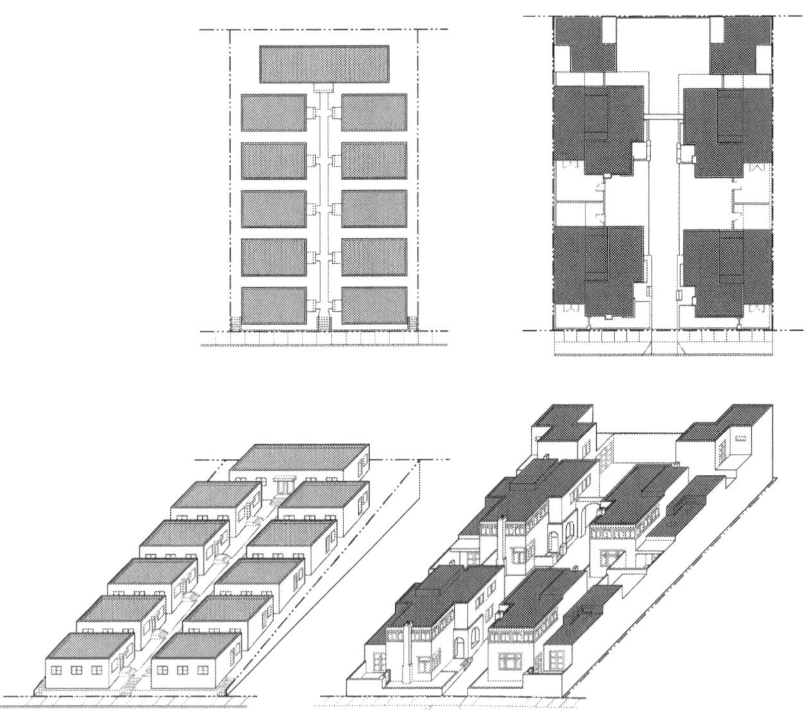

Figure 4.8 Unit aggregation diagrams: Clark Court (left) vs. Horatio West Court (right).

dining room and pantry, two private landscaped garden spaces, a walled service court and one enclosed garage space at the rear of the site.

Pedestrian Access and Entry *Central Pathway vs. Central Pathway*

Both Clark Court and Horatio West Court provide a concrete pedestrian walkway from the street down the center of their sites. Front entries for each unit are provided off these pathways with concrete stoops for Clark Court and covered porches at Horatio West Court. All West Court units and most of the Clark Court units face each other across this walkway.

Vehicular Access and Parking *None vs. One Space per Unit*

Clark Court provides no parking on site. Horatio West Court was originally parked at one space per unit, providing individual garages at the rear of the property accessed by a narrow 9-foot central driveway (which is also a walkway). The parking area is separated from the housing units with a simple archway.

Open Space *Ambiguous and Common vs. Well-Defined and Private*

The courtyard at Clark Court is common and semi-public, open to both residents and visitors (Figures 4.9 and 4.10). It is simply landscaped with grass and foundation plantings. There is no private open space individual to the units. The open space between and behind the houses is individually accessible, but it is not fenced off for private use.

Horatio West Court limits common open space to two small landscaped areas on either side of the driveway between the front and rear townhouses, the driveway itself and the rear parking area.[11] All units have private open space in the form of walled garden courtyards off front rooms and service courts off the kitchens. These outdoor spaces are meant to extend the living area of the house and give character to the downstairs space but limit the space available for more communal interaction. Second-story balcony spaces had views of the ocean, half a block away, and the mountains in the distance. Landscape at Horatio West Court is more varied and colorful than that at Clark Court but is also straightforward with geranium hedges, windbreaks of eucalyptus trees and climbing bougainvillea.

Structure *Wood Frame vs. Concrete*

Clark Court's buildings are wood frames clad in stucco, the typical construction type for the period. Horatio West Court was built using

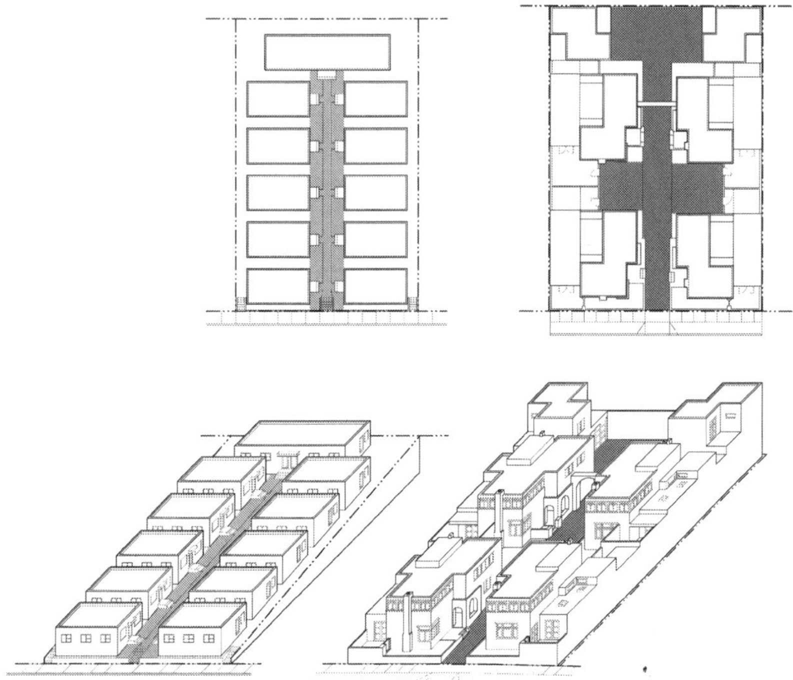

Figure 4.9 Common open space diagrams: Clark Court (left) vs. Horatio West Court (right).

"fireproof" concrete construction. Reinforced concrete foundations and bearing walls were built with sliding formwork and then covered in white stucco. Both first and second floors are constructed of concrete slabs, with the concrete underside exposed. The central staircase is also concrete. Non-load-bearing partitions are plaster on a wood frame (Historic American Building Survey [HABS], 1968).

Architectural Style *Mediterranean Revival vs. Early Modern*

Both case study projects are built in simplified architectural styles. Clark Court is designed in a Mediterranean Revival style but only minimally so. This style is suggested by Spanish tile on front roof awnings, smooth stucco surfaces on elemental volumes and the coping detail on the parapet wall. Front windows also have awnings made of Spanish tiles, and the main walkway has a series of "streetlights" down the center, both of which add character.[12]

Horatio West Court is executed in Gill's abstracted and stylized language of Spanish Colonial and Mission Revival forms. The project's flat roofs, plain white walls, cubic forms and unadorned archways, all tempered with landscaping, are typical of his approach and unusual at the time the project was built.

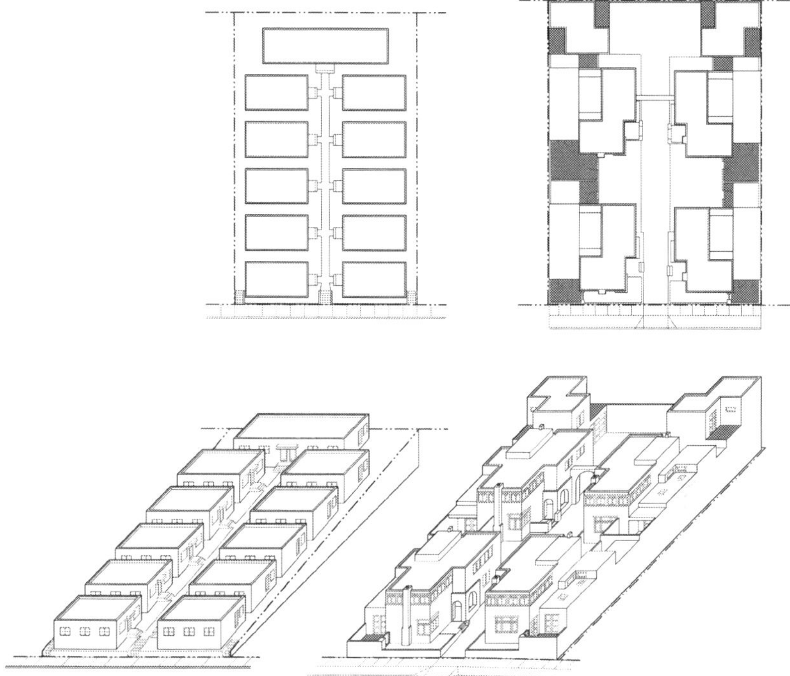

Figure 4.10 Private open space diagrams: Clark Court (left) vs. Horatio West Court (right).

Outcomes

From a design perspective, Clark Court and Horatio West Court have similar DNA but are executed much differently. Both employ the same underlying site and building organization strategy, but Horatio West Court is clearly more intensively and intentionally designed than Clark Court. The massing of its units is complex, the definition and landscaping of its open space are articulate and varied, and it tests the application of an unusual construction system. West Court is unmistakably pushing the boundaries in terms of style, space and structure in a way that Clark Court does not. However, the analysis also shows that the case study projects bookend an acceptable range of design outcomes for "good" house courts at the time they were built. Clark Court may be simple and straightforward in terms of construction, unit type and style, but it provides well-organized living space, privacy and individual identity to its residents. And improvements, such as further articulating the landscape and defining private open space, are within easy reach. The fact that Horatio West Court was built a few years before Clark Court, also illustrates a process of establishing acceptable bounds rather than a progression from simple to more complex or vice versa.

Real Estate Development

Context

Clark Court and Horatio West Court were built as Ocean Park was transitioning from a tourist destination with mostly short-term housing to a year-round neighborhood with permanent homes and activities beyond bathhouses, pleasure piers and roller coasters. Ocean Park was first established in the early 1870s as a beach resort, just south of Santa Monica, later known as Santa Monica's "South Side" (Warren, 1944, p. 35). The area was initially subdivided and connected by rail to Los Angeles in 1875, though by 1880 the permanent population of the beach area was only 417 (US Census, 1880). A rate war between the Santa Fe and Southern Pacific railways touched off a population boom beginning in 1886. Ocean Park was incorporated in 1904 and was annexed into the City of Santa Monica in 1907 (Storrs, 1974, p. 21).

The beach was big business in the late 1800s and the first few decades of the 20th century, and demand for short-term housing was high. Ocean Park hosted an ever-expanding collection of "amusements" for both local and out-of-town tourists during this time, including not only bathhouses, pleasure piers and roller coasters but also hanging gardens, casinos, golf courses, aerial circuses, ballrooms, carousels, floating boat launches, fishing spots, Ferris wheels, skating rinks, race courses and tearooms, much of it built by Abbott Kinney, who founded the Ocean Park Development Company in 1891 and later went on to develop "Venice of America," now the Venice neighborhood in Los Angeles. The coastline from Ocean Park to Venice Beach became known as the "Coney Island of the West," and Ocean Park even had its own municipal band (Historic Resources Group & Architectural Resources Group, 2018, p. 34; Ocean Park's Piers, 1921). Much of the early housing in the area took the form of intentionally impermanent beach shacks constructed on ground leases, but as the area matured, more "sightly" housing was built, often required by deed restrictions (Along the Ocean Front, 1902). By the time both case study projects were constructed, the Ocean Park neighborhood was largely built out with a range of housing types, schools, banks and churches, as well as small-scale commercial developments on Pier Avenue and Third Street. Both case study projects are close to the beach and would have been suitable for part-time rental or full-time beach living.

How similar or different were Clark Court and Horatio West Court from a real estate development perspective? Does Clark Court's vernacular status mean it was more profitable? Does Horatio West Court's innovative design mean it underperformed as an investment?

***Subdivision** Town District vs. "Sand District"*
(Ingersoll, 1908, p. 259)

Land for both case study projects was part of the 861 acres originally purchased by Nancy A. Lucas in 1874 from the Machado family of Rancho La Ballona. Clark Court's property was subdivided in 1885 by J. H. Lucas, one of Mrs. Lucas's sons, carving up the land northeast and southwest of Ocean Park's original township into 20-acre parcels (LADPW, 1885b). E. J. Vawter further subdivided the area less than a month later into lots that were 100 feet wide by 300 feet long (LADPW, 1885a). Block 6 was further split using a lot-cut process, creating Clark Court's two 50-foot by 155-foot parcels, only four blocks from the ocean and three blocks from Pier Avenue and its year-round commercial amenities (Warren, 1944, p. 37) (Figure 4.11).

By 1901, Ocean Park, "a quiet colony of summer homes, occupied by people of moderate means, for the most part, suddenly became the most popular and fashionable beach resort in Southern California" (Ingersoll, 1908, p. 255) (Figure 4.12). Three and a half blocks southwest of Clark Court's parcels, Horatio West Court's property was subdivided in April 1902 by Thomas S. Wadsworth, a contractor, and Charles W.

Figure 4.11 Commercial development on Third Street in Ocean Park in 1905, around the time the parcels for the case study projects were subdivided.

Credit: M. Reeder.

Figure 4.12 A crowded beach in Ocean Park on July 4, 1919, close to the time Horatio West Court was built.

Credit: Nicolina Karisson Collection.

Hollister, pastor of the Church of the Good Shepard in Santa Monica, creating small 25-foot by 100-foot lots for beach cottages on land once owned by Abbot Kinney (Historic Resources Group, LLC, 2004, p. 81; LADPW, 1902) With the Pacific Ocean and popular Bristol Pier a half block to the west and the Pacific Electric Rail Line half a block to the east, the subdivision was ideally situated for the booming tourist trade. Oceanfront lots originally sold for $40 per front foot, while those in the rest of the tract ranged from $20 to $34 per front foot (Classified Ad 17, 1902, A9). Lot 27 and 6.25 front feet of Lot 26, directly behind Horatio West Court's lots 7, 8 and 9, sold for $625 or $20 per front foot in November 1902, suggesting that West Court's property would have sold for $1,500 at the time (Real Estate Transfers, 1902, A5).

Market Timing and Demand *One Year Before the Peak vs. Three Years Before the Peak*

Both case study projects were built at the beginning of the 1920s housing boom and were the first permanent structures to be built on their lots (Sanborn Maps, Santa Monica, 1918, Sheet 24, 29). Santa Monica's population more than doubled from 1900 to 1910, growing from 3,057 to 7,847, and nearly doubled again between 1910 and 1920, growing from 7,847 to 15,252 (US Census, 1910, 1920). Higher costs for labor and materials were a concern after the end of World War I in 1918, but the influx of returning soldiers, new residents and tourists after the war soon put upward pressure on rents. By the end of 1919, homes for everyone were in short supply, but especially for tourists. In October 1920, 2,000 tourists a day were expected to arrive in Los Angeles during the winter season, double that of 1919, many of whom were of modest means who "will be tempted to stay" (Two Thousand Tourists, 1920, p. 1). Indeed, Wyllys S. Abbot, Chairman of the Industrial Exhibits and New Industries Committee of the Santa Monica–Ocean Park Chamber of Commerce noted the need for both tourist housing and housing for the "modern workman," ideally in small California bungalows like Clark Court's. (Abbot, 1920, p. 1). Horatio West Court had 2 extra years of the upswing, and both case study projects were on the market at the height of the real estate cycle, which peaked in 1923 and then slowly declined toward the Depression.

Construction Cost *Economical vs. Expensive*

No specific construction cost for Clark Court is available, but costs were declining at the time it was built and were, in fact, lower in 1922 than at any other time during the 1920s (Investors Appraisal Service, 1937). One prominent homebuilder reported that building costs in February 1922 were a full 25% lower than those at the same time a year earlier (Building Costs are Lower Now, 1922). Christie Court, a 24-unit house court built near Clark Court at 125 Pacific Street, now demolished but of the same conventional construction type, was built for approximately $2,050 a unit in 1924 (PCR Services Corporation, 2004, p. 2). Clark Court's earlier construction date suggests that its cost could have been lower, but its inclusion of larger and more individual units suggests that its per unit cost could have been higher, so $2,050 per unit for a total construction cost of $24,600 is a reasonable estimate.

Horatio West Court was an exclusive building of an expensive construction type which reportedly cost $32,000 to build (HABS, 1968). Adding servants' quarters over the garages in 1922 cost $2,500, and enclosing porches as additional bedrooms in 1923 cost $1,100, for a total price of $35,600 or $8,900 per unit (SMDBS, 1922, 1923a, 1923b). If Clark Court's units had been similarly expensive, it would have cost $106,800!

Funding *Mortgage Loan vs. All Equity*

Mortgage lending was on an upswing in the early twenties and it is likely that Clark Court was funded with a mortgage loan.[13] In early 1922, it was estimated that 10,000 homes needed to be built in Los Angeles to keep up with demand and that 60% of housing built that year would be financed by mortgage loans (Ten Thousand Homes, 1922, V6). In Ocean Park, for example, financing was available from firms like the Federal Bond and Mortgage Company, which advertised "Our own funds available for construction of homes, courts, apartments, stores, etc. Quick action, no waiting" and "Build! Convert Expense into Income" (Financial, 1923a, p. 3; Financial, 1923b, p. 3). Loans at this time were typically no greater than 50% loan-to-value and amortized over no longer than 5 years, requiring either refinancing or large balloon payments upon termination.

Given the volume and scale of Horatio West's investments around the time his court was built, it is likely that Horatio West Court was built with all equity, that is, without any debt. Lenders would probably have been put off by the building's unusually high cost, unconventional construction method and unfamiliar inverted unit types.

Marketing and Absorption *Houses for Rent vs. Resorts*

Both case study project addressed the high demand for housing but targeted different markets. Clark Court focused on middle-class tourists and locals. It was first advertised in the *Santa Monica Evening Outlook* in March 1922 in the "For Rent—Houses" section:

> CLARK COURT. FOR RENT—Unfurnished, new Spanish bungalows, beautiful, four rooms, modern; all built in effects. Splendid view, four blocks to ocean. Inquire on premises; 2411 3rd St., near Hollister, Ocean Park, Calif.
>
> (For Rent—Houses, 1922a, p. 6)

The project was advertised consistently through June 21, 1922, suggesting it leased up in about three months. Mr. Clark did make some changes early on, renting units furnished and saying they were closer to the beach (two blocks as opposed to four), possibly in response to the need for tourist housing (For Rent—Houses, 1923).

Horatio West Court targeted upper class, out-of-town tourists. No advertisements for Horatio West Court could be found before 1923, suggesting that the project was easily leased up with minimal advertising early in its existence, perhaps just listing with the local chamber of commerce or the Los Angeles Tourist Bureau. An advertisement for the property did appear in the "Resorts" section of the *Los Angeles Times* on April 28, 1923:

> Near Beach—Four concrete, six-room houses; sun parlor, garages and outside servants' rooms; exclusive and extraordinary. Special

> attractive terms for yearly lease. Two houses can be secured for May 1st. Very exclusive.
>
> (Display Ad 26, 1923, p. 16)

This ad ran for 2 days near the peak of the real estate cycle and could be a signal that the market was beginning to transition. Both projects were advertised periodically for the rest of the 1920s. No rental rates were ever listed for either project.

Investment Performance *Tested and Known vs. Untested and Unknown*

Since rental advertisements for neither case study project mentions price, comparables are needed to estimate investment performance. Houses in both courts were listed for rent in the *Santa Monica Evening Outlook* in October 1923, the beginning of the winter tourist season at the height of the housing boom. One hundred twelve unique ads for houses for rent that include price were found during the month. Rents for four-room houses (furnished and unfurnished), like those in Clark Court, ranged from $26.50 to $55 per month. At the median, $40, Clark Court would have generated $5,760 in gross income per year, making back the estimated project construction cost in 4.3 years. However, in an advertisement for the sale of the property, Mr. Clark claimed the gross monthly rent exceeded $600, more than $50 per month per unit (For Sale—Income Property, 1923a, p. 6). At this rate the property would gross $7,200 a year, making back its estimated construction cost in 3.4 years. Clark Court is well within the range of investment terms acceptable at the time it was built as documented in *Building Age* magazine: 2 to 14 homes each valued between $600 to $5,000 and renting between $15 to $65 (Marple, 1920, p. 41). Indeed, a house court close to the ocean generating an annual gross income of $5,500 was for sale for $45,000 (For Sale—Income Property, 1923b).

Horatio West Court timed the general housing market well, but not the luxury tourist market. Rents for five- and six-room houses (furnished and unfurnished) ranged from $35 to $150 per month during October 1923. At the median, $57.50, Horatio West Court would generate $2,760 a year, less than half that estimated for Clark Court. But its units were almost twice the size of Clark Court's and would have generated higher rents even at the same rent level. Applying the same rate per square foot as Clark Court's estimated median rent, Horatio West Court would have rented for $71.50 a month, generating $3,432 in gross income a year. But, given Horatio West Court's superior location, generous private outdoor space and provision of parking, it is reasonable to assume it would have rents at the upper end of the range. To make an equivalent annual gross income of $7,200, West Court would have to achieve rents of $150 per unit per month, making back the original construction cost in 5 years, just within the range of five- and six-room houses for rent in Santa Monica at the time.

While it's possible that Horatio West Court achieved rents of $150 per unit, the fact that it was altered so early in its existence suggests that the project was not performing as well as expected. Enclosing additional rooms and adding servants' quarters indicates that West initially tried to make the building more attractive to upper class tourists. But, by the early 1920s, North Santa Monica had become the resort of choice for the wealthy and famous. "South side" entertainments still thrived, but they were more geared for ordinary, middle-class visitors (Scott, 2004, p. 66). Splitting four units into eight around 1927 implies that West shifted his focus to middle-class tourists and may even have rented out the two-room servants' quarters as independent units.[14] Some trial and error was plainly needed to ensure that the building was marketable.

Outcomes *Early Profitability vs. Initially Struggling*

From a real estate development perspective, Clark Court and Horatio West Court are similar investments with very different risk profiles. Clark Court was a straightforward project that followed a proven formula to reduce risk from multiple perspectives. Its familiarity as a building type would have made everyone involved, from bankers to contractors to tenants, very comfortable regarding the viability of the project. Clark Court was likely profitable in the short term.

Horatio West Court was an "exclusive and extraordinary" project requiring more up-front investment to build its unproven but attractive innovations. It takes calculated risks, banking on its superior location and good market timing, both of which suggested an upper class tourist, "resort" orientation. But these assets did not outweigh the risks actually taken by Mr. West in building the project. The project's cutting-edge architecture, unusual unit types and walled gardens would have been unfamiliar to most players in the development process and unlike anything else available around it. The project also targeted a more specific, and arguably smaller, market—upper class tourists with servants and cars. However, Mr. West was able to make early changes to the building that made it more marketable to a larger audience which likely improved financial performance early in its existence.

Urban Planning

Context

Clark Court and Horatio West Court were built during a time of national, state and local interest in housing reform and the advent of zoning as a guiding tool for development. During the Progressive era, the 1890s to 1920s, middle-class reformers throughout the U.S. believed that people could and should work to improve their environment, socially, economically and physically, through scientific management, the wisdom of experts and a faith in moral environmentalism. They assumed that "physical disorder and dilapidation" seen in areas of urban poverty "determined, or helped to determine, the physical and moral condition of their inhabitants" (Hoffman, 1998, p. 2). In the City of Los Angeles, these beliefs motivated the appointment of its first housing commission in 1906 to delve into the City's housing problems, which included overcrowding, unsanitary conditions and inflated rents. The State of California began regulating tenement housing in 1909, ultimately publishing the State Housing Manual in 1917, including rules for tenements, hotels and small dwellings. All at a time when Progressive-era reformers, including Jacob Riis in New York City, Jane Addams in Chicago and Emory Bogardus in Los Angeles were all documenting poor housing conditions and formulating policy to make housing more sanitary, economical and accessible.

How similar or different were Clark Court and Horatio West Court from a planning perspective?

Needed Housing Types

Housing for citizens, tourists and immigrants alike was all in short supply throughout the Los Angeles area during the time the case study projects were built, and both projects did their part to address these needs. Many housing advocates believed that "there [was] a vital connection between good housing and good citizenship," and a broad spectrum of housing advocates believed well-built house courts to be the ideal housing solution for a wide range of people (Commission of Immigration and Housing of California [CIHC], 1923, p. 64). After studying 1,202 house courts in Los Angeles, sociologist Emory Bogardus determined that the type had social and community advantages that apartments and flats did not:

> The house-court has many splendid possibilities in the way of housing the people. The ventilation and sunshine possibilities are excellent. In a well-constructed court the danger from fire is small. . . . The inner court upon which the dwellings face offers unlimited opportunities for wholesome social contact and group development. If land values could be kept low so that rents could be kept reasonable, the house-court would offer in many ways ideal housing facilities.
>
> (Bogardus, 1916, p. 399)

Santa Monica Chamber of Commerce member Wyllys Abbot declared the building of house courts for working men and their families as both civic-minded and fulfilling:

> Building homes to rent or sell to workmen, the modern workman, is in some respects more satisfactory to the contractor and to the investor than the building of houses for the tourist trade.
>
> (Abott, 1920, p. 1)

The Los Angeles Housing Commission, as part of its work establishing new house court regulations, promoted house court development as a sound investment:

> The great need at present is the intelligent interest and co-operation of property owners, who will look upon their improved conditions not as charity, but as a business investment. The mere fact that the courts have been improved, that new courts have sprung into existence, and that others are contemplated, should be enough to convince any reasonable landlord that the matter is a safe and legitimate investment.
>
> (LAHC, 1908, p. 16)

And Charles Alma Byers, who frequently wrote about bungalow courts building trade publications, even encouraged families to group together as cooperatives to maximize both the communal and financial benefits the house court provided (Byers, 1914).

Information about how to actually go about building a good house court was readily available from many sources (Figure 4.13). In its first report, the Los Angeles Housing Commission detailed the Navarro Street Court as not only model of good housing but also an example of potential profitability, built entirely under the City's new house court ordinance for $3,000, with 18 two-room houses renting for $5.00 a month projected to earn a 6% return (LAHC, 1908, pp. 14, 16). In subsequent reports, the commission encouraged citizens to create limited dividend stock companies to take over the maintenance of existing courts or rent or buy land and construct "proper" courts, known as "Philanthropy + 6%" (Capital for House Court, 1908, I11). Building trade publications also extensively documented various house court designs and business models. Plans for an inexpensive Craftsman Style bungalow court were detailed in *Building Age* in 1920, along with design tips and rules of thumb for the house court builder, suggesting "battleship" grey with white trim as an ideal color scheme (Byers, 1920b, pp. 32–33). An example detailed in *Building Age and National Building* in 1924 ran the numbers on a 10-unit bungalow court plus a larger owners unit in Los Angeles for sale for $55,000 earning a net income of $6,600 a year:

THE FIRST AND ONLY CONCRETE HOUSE-COURT IN LOS ANGELES

Eight 3-room habitations; 8-in. wall concrete construction. Cost $1650. per habitation. The floor plan of these houses is shown on opposite page

Figure 4.13 The Housing Commission of the City of Los Angeles considered courts built out of concrete to be ideal (Los Angeles Housing Commission, 1913, p. 30).

Credit: Los Angeles City Archives and Records Center.

> In ten years [the investor] would have taken in $66,000. In other words, his purchase price of $55,000 would be back in his pocket, and a surplus of $11,000 in the bank.
>
> (Hawkins, 1924, p. 92)

There were even exhibitions contrasting slum court conditions with courts built to new standards and a "Model Village Movement," which sought to "show how this [house court] idea can be carried out in the right way" (Ellerbe, 1911, I16; Gish, 2009–2010, p. 377).

Development Standards

Los Angeles *Middle-Class Court vs. High-Class Court*

Housing regulations were evolving quickly when Clark Court and Horatio West Court were built, working to shape both better and more affordable house court outcomes. Both case study projects easily exceeded these new standards and would have met housing advocates' approval, but many other courts in the region clearly needed to be upgraded. After a year studying the city's poorest housing conditions, primarily house courts built near industrial districts, the Los Angeles Housing Commission, which included a medical doctor, settlement worker, capitalist and plumber, among others, proposed an ordinance to improve the many "slum courts" found in the city, passed by City Council on February 5, 1907. The House Court Ordinance set forth basic standards for the development and operation of house courts, defined as three or more individual dwellings on a single parcel of land with the vacant portions used in common. All house courts had to obtain and maintain a permit from the Department of Public Works, which detailed layout and materials. Minimal physical standards required that houses shed water, have floors, include windows in both sleeping and living areas, and have at least 7-foot ceilings. 30% of the ground area had to be open space, unoccupied by buildings, with accessible hydrants and sinks in the ratio of one per three dwellings, among many other provisions (Los Angeles, 1907). The goal was to improve and propagate house courts, not simply do away with them.[15] "The new law was broad enough to include projects large and small, formal and informal, high- and low-end—but the specifics clearly targeted slum courts" (Gish, 2009–2010, p. 373). Its standards weren't onerous and actually stimulated house court production. In 1915, for example, the housing commission reviewed 1,878 permit applications for house courts, 95% of which were approved (CIHC, 1916, p. 275). Although the ordinance technically did not apply in Santa Monica, its provisions would have been well known. House courts just outside its boundaries were inspected under the new regulations, and there was a robust discussion of house court construction in the local press.

California Dwelling House *vs.* Dwelling House

California was also working to regulate housing at this time in response to poor housing conditions in all parts of the state and the prospect of rising immigration. The Commission on Immigration and Housing of California was established in 1912 to "facilitate and coordinate private and local government activities in the field of immigration (and now housing) rather than impose state policy" (Issel, 1988, p. 129). From 1913 to 1917, the group made detailed surveys and inspections of housing conditions in cities throughout California, much like those begun in Los Angeles in 1906. In response to their findings, the commission organized a series of housing conferences around the state, called Housing Institutes, to gain insight and input on the improvement of the existing state tenement and hotel laws and a third proposed dwelling house act to specifically address small habitations. California cities sent a professionally diverse group of citizens to these events, from architects, to fire chiefs to social workers (CIHC, 1923, p. 75). A meeting was held in Los Angeles in February 1915, and while the City's housing commission supported the regulation of private dwellings, Los Angeles Building Superintendent J. J. Bakus and the Los Angeles City Council initially did not (Find Danger, 1915, I13). There were concerns that the regulations might retard growth and require too many approvals at the state level. The City drafted 26 amendments to the proposed State Dwelling House Act that placed the determination and regulation of certain standards with the local community (Housing Bills, 1915, p. 16). All three laws were passed in 1917.

The Commission of Immigration and Housing of California issued the State Housing Manual in 1917, which incorporated the State Tenement House Act, the State Hotel and Lodging House Act and the State Dwelling House Act into one convenient, easy-to-use, annotated volume. These laws were to be enforced locally and "fix[ed] the minimum of requirements for ventilation, sanitation, privacy and safety" but encouraged communities to amplify these laws with additional housing, planning and zoning regulations (CIHC, 1919, p. 5). Because "all apartment houses are tenement houses, except houses not more than two stories high containing not more than four apartments," house courts were "dwellings" by design (CIHC, 1917, p. 3). As such, house courts had to have raised foundations but no basement, just in case anyone was thinking of living down there (CIHC, 1919, pp. 28, 30). Every room had to be at least 8 feet in height, with an operable window opening to a street or to an unoccupied portion of the lot at least 4 feet wide, and each dwelling had to have its own water closet (CIHC, 1919, pp. 32, 34, 39). Residents could not cook in the bathroom or sleep in the kitchen (CIHC, 1919, p. 57). And horses, cows, pigs, sheep, goats, rabbits, mules, chickens, pigeons, geese and ducks were prohibited from living in the home and had to be housed at least 20 feet away (CIHC, 1919, p. 61).

Zoning *B Zone vs. A Zone*

Although the City of Los Angeles and many other local jurisdictions had been zoned by the time Clark Court and Horatio West Court were built, Santa Monica did not pass its zoning ordinance until 1922 and wasn't comprehensively zoned until December of that year, after both case study projects were built (Ordinance #148). Santa Monica's ordinance was very similar to those in Los Angeles and other Southern California cities, and indeed, the City of Los Angeles tried to annex Santa Monica in 1917 and 1924 (Richerson, 1950). Santa Monica had been discussing zoning in the press since at least 1917, evaluating, among other things, the advice of outside city planners, the need for detailed maps and data, the establishment of a city planning commission and the need for controlling beachfront development. Both case study projects were mapped in August 1922 under ordinance No. 222, Clark Court as "B" Zone, "limited to living quarters of all kinds, including bungalow courts, apartment houses and hotels," and Horatio West Court as "A" zone, limited to “single family dwelling[s] together with the usual accessories located on the same lot or parcel of land, including space for not more than four automobiles” (Rankin, 1921, p. 1; 1922, p. 1). Both blocks were already improved with a mix of single- and multifamily housing when they were zoned. Horatio West Court would have needed a variance had it been built after 1922 since it originally placed four dwellings on a single lot in a single-family residence district. Zoning at this time was primarily about use, with few, if any, associated physical standards.

Density *33 Dwelling Units per Acre vs. 21 to 55 Dwelling Units per Acre*

Both case study projects are low-rise, medium-density projects that were acceptably dense at the time they were built. Clark Court provided 12 units on a 100-foot by 155-foot, 15,500-square-foot site equaling 33 dwelling units per acre. Horatio West Court provides four units on a 75-foot by 1,050-foot, 7,875-square-foot site, or 21 dwelling units per acre. Once Horatio West Court was split into eight apartments plus the two servants’ apartments, the dwelling units per acre rises to 55.

Parking/Transportation *No Parking vs. One Parking Space per Unit*

At the time the case study projects were built, Ocean Park was connected to Los Angeles by both steam train and electric trolley, with trips from downtown Los Angeles averaging 35 to 40 minutes. Only Horatio West Court anticipated the need for parking. By 1920 Angelenos owned one car per 3.6 residents compared to one per 13 in the rest of the US (Scott, 2004, p. 62).

Outcomes

From an urban planning perspective, Clark Court and Horatio West Court are more similar than they are different. Both case study projects exceeded planning standards in force at the time they were built and were built at a time when housing reform and housing development ideals were being publicly discussed, encoded into policy and iterated. This environment shaped house courts for the better since an extreme range of house court types could be built, all under the same rules. These rules were explicitly developed to incorporate a range of voices and preserve existing housing types. In the course of making all its surveys, the Commission on Immigration and Housing

> had the opportunity to see how many different professions and occupations are touched by housing, and to become convinced that if the

> new housing laws were to be acceptable to the state as a whole and were to avoid future friction they would have to reflect the views of many people in addition to building experts.
>
> (CIHC, 1923, p. 75)

House courts were not legislated out of existence but were, rather, encouraged to improve and proliferate via new housing regulations, model examples and the establishment of well-defined multifamily districts.

Conclusion

When Housing Regulation Encodes Flexibility and Encourages Typological Innovation

In this case, housing regulation encoded flexibility and encouraged typological innovation. Bungalow courts were successful in Southern California because the type could be executed to address a range of needs and desired outcomes at a broad range of price points, from limited dividend investments for lower income families to middle- and upper-income courts like Clark Court and Horatio West Court.

Lessons Learned

Good policy planning should support a range of good design and development outcomes. State and local regulation shaped the open space, unit size and ventilation requirements for house courts, ensuring that they were habitable, but did not create so many requirements that the buildings couldn't respond to a range of market, social and class conditions. That the type could be built to house poor immigrants, middle-class tourists and upper middle-class professional families is a testament to its desirability, but also inherent flexibility. The type can stretch and change in many dimensions (unit size, style, articulation of open space, etc.) and still be considered a house court.

Case Study Buildings Today

The Ocean Park neighborhood and its entertainment attractions were in decline from the 1950s through the 1970s. The City of Santa Monica established rent control in 1979, meaning that now house courts like Clark Court are often poorly maintained and in threat of demolition. Those in other Southern California cities, especially those in Pasadena, are under greater protection by historic preservation efforts. Clark Court was converted to a condominium in 1992.

Horatio West Court became a rooming house and then a "drug den" as Gill's reputation faded in the 1940s and 1950s, only to be rediscovered in the 1960s. In 1968, Horatio West Court was documented by the Historic American Building Survey's Los Angeles Project, recording the building's configuration, construction and state of repair in measured drawings, photographs and text. In the early 1970s a partnership of six people, half architects, bought the property for $125,000 and restored it for their own use (Horatio West Court, 1976). The project was converted to condominiums in 1979. Horatio West Court was placed on the National Register of Historic Places in 1977 and was designated as a local landmark by the City of Santa Monica in 1979. It remains a private residence.

Ironically, Horatio West Court did not need discretionary approval to be built, but it did need a parking variance to convert to a condominium. The minimum parking required per unit in Santa Monica at the time was one-and-a-half spaces per unit. The only way the project could be legally parked was to use the rear yard of the beach cottage next door as a parking lot (Parcel Map 11741, 1977).

Both projects are extremely desirable now, given their proximity to the beach and Santa Monica's constrained housing supply. On March 28, 2018, Zillow valued units in Clark Court from $750,000 to $850,000 and units at Horatio West Court from $1.5 to $2.5 million, both more than $1,000 per square foot.

Notes

1. The California Commission of Immigration and Housing believed that "One day's wage of a workingman should equal one week's rent of house" (An A B C of Housing, 1916, California State Printing Office, 6).
2. Eventually *bungalow court* became a generic term used to describe courts of any style, not just bungalow or Craftsman. Courts were also commonly named for their owners, for example, Lewis Court, Clark Court, West Court (Historic Resources Group, LLC, 2004, pp. 44–45).
3. St. Francis Court, curiously, included a driveway but no on site parking.
4. The Bella Vista Terrace site was eventually filled in with additional units, not of Gill's design, in 1925 and between 1947 and 1954.
5. The building's original permit is lost so it is not known whether it had an architect.
6. The project was renamed "Sunshine Court" by 1992 (Santa Monica Parcel Map Application, PM 11741, Resolution 5203 (CCS), 1979).
7. Although the 1919 date is listed in most publications, Mr. West did not obtain the Hollister Street property until February 24, 1920, per Corporation Grant Deed, Los Angeles County, Book 7239, pages 324–25. The original building permit is lost.
8. Architects often speak about Horatio West Court as "affordable" housing since it is linked to Gill's social housing experiments. With a prime beach location and at a cost of $32,000, Horatio West Court was intended as housing for the upper middle-class at minimum, that is, those who could afford to own cars and employ servants in the early 1920s.
9. Gill's style acted as a bridge to the work of early Los Angeles modernists R. M. Schindler, Richard Neutra and Gregory Ain (Gebhard, 1967, p. 131).
10. Once the second story balcony was enclosed as a bedroom, the units averaged 1,350 square feet.
11. The driveway has since been gated.

12. It is unclear whether the awnings or the walkway "street lights" were original to the property.
13. Income properties were also commonly seller financed and traded at this time.
14. Gill does not seem to have understood how the real estate market works to set rents and prices. Discussing Lewis Court in Sierra Madre historian Esther McCoy writes, "Gill had demonstrated that he could build a good house at a price which would allow a landlord to rent if for a nominal sum. But the court was such a success that rents were fixed beyond the means of the workmen for whom it was designed. Gill was angered by this turn of events because it thwarted his hope of benefitting the low-income groups always ignored by architecture" (McCoy, 1960, p. 85)
15. The Los Angeles Housing Commission also promoted discriminatory practices by working to regulate behavior as well as form and construction quality. Under the guise of education, housing inspectors were thought of as "municipal housekeepers" who tracked court demographics, "enforced cleanliness" and encouraged assimilation and "right living" (LAHC, 1908, pp. 6, 12).

References

Abbot, W. (1920, August 26). Bungalows is Big Need of Bay District. *Santa Monica Evening Outlook*, 1. Retrieved from http://digital.smpl.org

Along the Ocean Front. (1902, September 16). *Ocean Park Daily News*, 4. Retrieved from http://digital.smpl.org

Another Cotton Gin at Shafter. (1930, September 1). *Los Angeles Times*, 8. Retrieved from www.proquest.com

Bogardus, E. S. (1916, November). The House-Court Problem. *American Journal of Sociology*, *22*(3), 391–399.

Building Costs Are Lower Now. (1922, February 5). *Los Angeles Times*, V10. Retrieved from www.proquest.com

Bungalow Courts. (1921). *American Builder*, *32*(3), 68–70.

Bungalow Courts in Pasadena. (1994). National Register of Historic Places Inventory Nomination Form, US Department of Interior, National Park Service. Retrieved from https://npgallery.nps.gov/NRHP/GetAsset/NRHP/64000063_text

Byers, C. A. (1914). The Bungalow Court Idea Shown in Practical Application. *The Craftsman*, *27*(3), 317–319.

Byers, C. A. (1920a). A Community Court of Exceptional Attractiveness. *Building Age*, *42*(7), 29–30.

Byers, C. A. (1920b). An Inexpensive Bungalow Court. *Building Age*, *42*(10), 32–33.

Capital for House Court: Housing Commission Gets an Offer to Build. (1908, September 6). *Los Angeles Times*, I11. Retrieved from www.proquest.com

City of Los Angeles. (1907). House Court Ordinance, Ordinance No. 14,113 (New Series). Los Angeles, CA: L.A. City Archive.

Classified Ad 17. (1902, October 12). *Los Angeles Times*, A9. Retrieved from www.proquest.com

Classified Ad 25. (1907, October 2). *Los Angeles Times*, I11. Retrieved from www.proquest.com

Classified Ad 121. (1911, May 28). *Los Angeles Times*, V7. Retrieved from www.proquest.com

Commission on Immigration and Housing of California. (1916). *Second Annual Report*. Sacramento, CA: California State Printing Office.

Commission on Immigration and Housing of California. (1917). *State Housing Manual Containing the State Tenement House Act, State Hotel and Lodging House Act and State Dwelling House Act*. Sacramento, CA: California State Printing Office.

Commission on Immigration and Housing of California. (1919). *State Housing Manual Containing the State Tenement House Act, State Hotel and Lodging House Act and State Dwelling House Act*. Sacramento, CA: California State Printing Office.

Commission on Immigration and Housing of California. (1923). *Ninth Annual Report*. Sacramento, CA: California State Printing Office.

Display Ad 26. (1923, April 28). *Los Angeles Times*, 16. Retrieved from www.proquest.com

Ellerbe, R. L. (1911, April 22). "Model Village" Philanthropic Los Angeles Women Have Great Project in Hand. *Los Angeles Times*, I16. Retrieved from www.proquest.com

Financial, Money to Loan, Real Estate. (1923a, May 9). *Santa Monica Evening Outlook*, 3. Retrieved from http://digital.smpl.org

Financial, Money to Loan, Real Estate. (1923b, May 18). *Santa Monica Evening Outlook*, 3. Retrieved from http://digital.smpl.org

Find Danger in Housing Bills. (1915, February 13). *Los Angeles Times*, I13. Retrieved from www.proquest.com

For Rent—Houses, Clark Court. (1922a, March 27). *Santa Monica Evening Outlook*, 6. Retrieved from http://digital.smpl.org

For Rent—Houses, Clark Court. (1922b, May 2). *Santa Monica Evening Outlook*, 6. Retrieved from http://digital.smpl.org

For Rent—Houses, Clark Court. (1923, October 30). *Santa Monica Evening Outlook*, 8. Retrieved from http://digital.smpl.org

For Sale—Income Property. (1923a, April 2). *Santa Monica Evening Outlook*, 6. Retrieved from http://digital.smpl.org

For Sale—Income Property. (1923b, May 23). *Santa Monica Evening Outlook*, 6. Retrieved from http://digital.smpl.org

Gebhard, D. (1967). The Spanish Colonial Revival in Southern California (1895–1930). *Journal of the Society of Architectural Historians*, *26*(2), 131–147.

Gill, I. J. (1916). The Home of the Future: The New Architecture of the West: Small Homes for a Great Country. *The Craftsman*, *30*(2), 140–151, 220.

Gish, T. (2010). Bungalow Court Housing in Los Angeles, 1900–1930: Top-down Innovation? Or Bottom-Up Reform. *Southern California Quarterly*, *91*(4), 365–387.

Hawkins, R., & Hawkins, R. (1924). Profit in Bungalow Courts. *Building Age and National Builder*, *46*(11), 92–94.

Historic American Building Survey. (1968). *Horatio West Court Apartments. National Park Service, Department of the Interior, HABS No. CA-1984*. Retrieved from www.loc.gov/pictures/item/ca0298/

Historic Resources Group & Architectural Resources Group. (2018). *City of Santa Monica Historic Resources Inventory Update, Historic Context Statement*. Prepared for the City of Santa Monica. Retrieved from https://www.smgov.net/uploadedFiles/Departments/PCD/Programs/Historic-Preservation/Appendix%20A%20-%20Santa%20Monica%20Citywide%20Historic%20Context%20Statement_Final_3.20.2018.pdf

Historic Resources Group, LLC. (2004). *Historic Resources Survey Update, Ocean Park*. Prepared for the City of Santa Monica. Retrieved from www.smgov.net/departments/pcd/agendas/Landmarks-Commission/2004/20040614/FINALDRAFT2004-6-8(Part1).pdf

Hopkins, U. N. (1913). A Picturesque Court of 30 Bungalows: A Community Idea for Women. *Ladies Home Journal*, *30*(4), 99.

Horatio West Court, Remodeling Portfolio. (1976). *Progressive Architecture*, *57*(11), 68–69.

Housing Bills Are Modified. (1915, April 1). *Los Angeles Times*, 16. Retrieved from www.proquest.com

Ingersoll, L. A. (1908). *Ingersoll's Century History Santa Monica Bay Cities*. Los Angeles, CA: Luther A. Ingersoll.

Investors Appraisal Service. (1937). *The Los Angeles Blue Book of Land Values*. Los Angeles, CA: Investors Appraisal Service.

Issel, W. (1988). Citizens Outside the Government: Business and Urban Policy in San Francisco and Los Angeles, 1890–1932. *Pacific Historical Review*, *57*, 117–145.

Jarvis, R. M. (2010). John B. West: Founder of the West Publishing Company. *The American Journal of Legal History*, *50*(1), 1–22.

Kansas Takes Fight to the President. (1905, February 16). *Los Angeles Times*, 11. Retrieved from www.proquest.com

L.A. County Department of Public Works. (1885a, February 16). Miscellaneous Record (MR) 6–221, Lucas Tract. Retrieved from http://dpw.lacounty.gov/sur/nas/landrecords/misc/MR006/MR006-221.pdf

L.A. County Department of Public Works. (1885b, March 3). Miscellaneous Record (MR) 6–217, Vawter's Subdivision. Retrieved from http://dpw.lacounty.gov/sur/nas/landrecords/misc/MR006/MR006-217.pdf

L.A. County Department of Public Works. (1902, April 30). Map Book (MB) 2–9–10, Wadsworth and Hollister Tract. Retrieved from http://dpw.lacounty.gov/sur/nas/landrecords/tract/MB0002/TR0002-009a.pdf

Los Angeles Directory Co. (1921). *Santa Monica, Ocean Park, Venice, Sawtelle and Westgate Directory, 1921–1922*. Los Angeles, CA: Los Angeles Directory Co.

Los Angeles Directory Co. (1923). *Santa Monica, Ocean Park, Venice, Sawtelle and Westgate Directory, 1923–1924*. Los Angeles, CA: Los Angeles Directory Co.

Los Angeles Directory Co. (1925). *Santa Monica, Ocean Park, Venice, Sawtelle and Westgate Directory, 1925*. Los Angeles, CA: Los Angeles Directory Co.

Los Angeles Housing Commission. (1908). *Report of the Housing Commission, February 20, 1906 to June 30, 1908*. Los Angeles, CA: L.A. City Archive.

Los Angeles Housing Commission. (1913). Report of the Housing Commission, July 1, 1910 to March 31, 1913. Los Angeles, CA: L.A. City Archive.

Marple, A. (1920, March 1). The Modern Bungalow Court. *Building Age*, *42*(3), 19.

McCoy, E. (1960). *Five California Architects*. New York, NY: Reinhold Book Corporation.

Ocean Park's Piers Delight Multitudes: Rivals Atlantic Resorts. (1921, July 3). *Los Angeles Times*, II8. Retrieved from www.proquest.com

Pastier, J. (1974, July 29). Price of Living in a Landmark. *Los Angeles Times*, E1. Retrieved from www.proquest.com

PCR Services Corporation. (2004). *Christie Court—Multi-Family Property, City Landmark Designation Evaluation*. Retrieved from www.smgov.net/departments/pcd/agendas/Landmarks-Commission/2004/20040614/125%20Pacific%20PCR%20Report%20w%20pics.pdf

Polyzoides, S., Sherwood, R., & Tice, J. (1992). *Courtyard Housing in Los Angeles, A Typological Analysis*. New York, NY: Princeton Architectural Press.

Quintana, I. S. L. (2015). Making Do, Making Home: Borders and the Worlds of Chinatown and Sonoratown in Early Twentieth-Century Los Angeles. *Journal of Urban History*, *41*(1), 47–74.

Rankin, G. (1921, December 29). Santa Monica City Council Plans to Adopt Protective Zoning Ordinance for City. *Santa Monica Evening Outlook*, 1. Retrieved from http://digital.smpl.org

Rankin, G. (1922, February 28). Santa Monica's Zoning Ordinances Intended to Direct Growth and Development of City. *Santa Monica Evening Outlook*, 1. Retrieved from http://digital.smpl.org

Real Estate and Building. (1895, December 19). *Los Angeles Herald*, 7.

Real Estate Transfers. (1902, November 8). *Los Angeles Times*, A5. Retrieved from www.proquest.com

Richerson, J. L. (1950). *A Critical Analysis of Zoning Ordinances in Los Angeles County* (Master's Thesis). Retrieved from http://digitallibrary.usc.edu/cdm/ref/collection/p15799coll39/id/91340

Roorbach, E. M. (1913). The Garden Apartments of California, Irving J. Gill, Architect. *The Architectural Record*, *34*(12), 520–530.

Rubin, B. (1977). A Chronology of Architecture in Los Angeles. *Annals of the Association of American Geographers*, 67(4), 521–537.

Sanborn Fire Insurance Maps, Santa Monica. (1918). *Sheets 24 & 29*. Retrieved from www.loc.gov

Sanborn Fire Insurance Map, Santa Monica. (1950). *Sheet 24*. Retrieved from www.loc.gov

Santa Monica Department of Building & Safety. (1922, November 13). Building Permit Number 273. City of Santa Monica.

Santa Monica Department of Building & Safety. (1923a, January 10). Building Permit Number 733. City of Santa Monica.

Santa Monica Department of Building & Safety. (1923b, March 14). Building Permit Number 1205. City of Santa Monica.

Santa Monica Parcel Map Application, PM 11741, Resolution 5203 (CCS). (1979). City of Santa Monica.

Saylor, H. H. (1911). *Bungalows, Their Design, Construction and Furnishing, with Suggestions also for Camps, Summer Homes and Cottages of Similar Character*. Philadelphia, PA: The John C. Winston Company.

Scott, P. A. (2004). *Santa Monica, A History on the Edge*. Charleston, SC: Arcadia Publishing.

Storrs, L. (1974). *Santa Monica, Portrait of a City*. Santa Monica, CA: City of Santa Monica.

Ten Thousand Homes Needed. (1922, January 15). *Los Angeles Times*, V6. Retrieved from www.proquest.com

Thornton, R., & Wolicki, D. P. (2004). *California's Kit Homes: A Reprint of the 1925 Pacific Ready-Cut Homes Catalog*. Alton, IL: Gentle Beam Publications.

Two Thousand Tourists a Day into Los Angeles Would Also Indicate Great Influx into S. M. (1920, October 20). *Santa Monica Evening Outlook*, 1. Retrieved from http://digital.smpl.org

US Census Bureau. (1880). *Santa Monica Population*. Retrieved from https://en.wikipedia.org/wiki/History_of_Santa_Monica,_California

US Census Bureau. (1910). *Santa Monica Population*. Retrieved from https://en.wikipedia.org/wiki/History_of_Santa_Monica,_California

US Census Bureau. (1920). *Santa Monica Population*. Retrieved from https://en.wikipedia.org/wiki/History_of_Santa_Monica,_California

von Hoffman, A. (1998). *The Origins of American Housing Reform*. Boston, MA: Joint Center for Housing Studies, Harvard University, W98–2.

Warren, C. S. (Ed.). (1944). *Santa Monica Community Book. In Two Parts, Narrative and Biographical*. Santa Monica, CA: A. H. Cawston.

Weston, R. D. (1922). *Weston's Single and Double Bungalows*. Los Angeles, CA: Rex D. Weston Publisher.

Winter, R. (1980). *The California Bungalow*. Los Angeles, CA: Hennessey and Ingalls.

5 Design Well Timed, Four-Flats

1060 S. Cochran Avenue vs. Mackey Apartments

Figure 5.1 Case Study 5: Four-flats, 1060 S. Cochran Avenue (left) vs. Mackey Apartments (right).

Introduction

When Good Market Timing Encourages Both High Design and Profitable Design

Four-unit apartment houses flourished across Los Angeles in the 1910s, 1920s and 1930s, constructed in large numbers by growth-oriented builders, landlords and owner/occupants. These buildings, also called four-family flats, four-flats and eventually, fourplexes, can be found in most Los Angeles neighborhoods, but especially those in mid-city, filling in what had been agricultural land between early population centers in downtown Los Angeles and Santa Monica. They are as beloved as the dingbat apartment is maligned. When state housing laws threatened to make building four-flats more difficult in 1915, Los Angles City administrators and councilmen pushed to have the law changed, since "four-family flats, as constructed in Los Angeles, are especially desirable" and "there should be no restriction upon the continuance of such construction" (Find Danger, 1915, I13). Four-flat construction continued to respond to the city's breakneck growth during the 1920s, and by 1926 the annual increase in multiple-family dwellings (including three-flats, four-flats and apartment houses) exceeded that of single-family homes for the first time (Los Angeles City Planning Commission [LACPC], 1929, p. 18). Building was constrained during the worst years of the Depression, but four-flat construction began to rise again by 1935, only to be eclipsed by newer multifamily housing types, namely garden apartments, by the beginning of World War II (Eberle, 1935b).

The typical four-flat aggregates four single-story units (i.e., flats), two-up, two-down in a rectangular building constructed in a Spanish Revival style. Two-flats (duplexes) and three-flats (triplexes) were also built during this time, all serving permanent residents as well as long-term tourists. A mix of houses and small-scale apartments characterizes the typical four-flat neighborhood, where flats often used their overall image as a large single-family house to blend into home districts at a time when the city was still being comprehensively zoned (Gish, 2007). Four-flats were located not only close to streetcar lines but also near increasingly convenient automobile thoroughfares, like Wilshire Boulevard and La Brea Avenue (Figures 5.2 and 5.3). Four-flats are exemplified by:

- Two-story rectilinear building forms, usually with a symmetrical facade
- Single-story flats, with two downstairs and two upstairs, mirrored in plan
- One- or two-bedroom units with one bath (though they were advertised by "rooms" as in five-room flat, or four-room flat)
- Spacious, "homelike" units with dedicated dining rooms and large living rooms
- Built-in furniture
- Access to light and air on three sides
- Parking for one car per unit at the rear of the property, often enclosed in garages, accessed by a driveway down the side
- Stucco over wood frame construction
- Period revival architecture (Architectural Resources Group, Inc. [ARG, Inc], 2015, p. 38; Gish, 2007, p. 6)

Figure 5.2 A selection of four-flats in the Mid-Wilshire neighborhood of Los Angeles.

Not surprisingly, the four-flat as a housing type evolved over its period of significance, responding to the real estate market, urban planning regulation and design opportunities. This happened most notably in terms of its entry sequence. Early in its existence, the typical four-flat had four separate entry doors at ground level, usually accessed from a common exterior porch or stoop.[1] These led directly into the lower apartments and onto private staircases for the upper units so that no interior space was shared in common. This configuration ensured that four-flats would be classified by state law as "dwellings" rather than "tenements," which were more highly regulated (Commission of Immigration and Housing of California, 1919; Gish, 2007, pp. 7–8). By the mid-1920s, however, four-flats began to be spot-zoned into predominantly single-family neighborhoods on the condition that they provide a single front entry. Interior entry vestibules with a common stair accessible from a single exterior doorway then became the norm (Gish, 2007, p. 8). Superior location outweighed the expense of providing a second means of egress, adding a rear stair accessible by all four units, as required by state law. What made the four-flat so popular with such a wide range of housing actors? How did the needs of design, development and planning work to shape the type?

Figure 5.3 The Mackey Apartments and four-flats in the Mid-Wilshire neighborhood of Los Angeles, mapped, including 1060 S. Cochran Avenue (1).

This chapter evaluates a typical four-flat located at 1060 South Cochran Avenue, as compared to the Mackey Apartments, another four-family building located halfway down the block and across the street at 1137 South Cochran Avenue (Figure 5.1). 1060 South Cochran, built in 1926, is a normative example of the type. It arranges four five-room apartments, two-up, two-down, in a two-story rectilinear block, built in the Spanish Colonial Revival style. The Mackey Apartments, with its Early Modern architectural style, three-story massing and generous private outdoor space, does not look like a four-flat at first glance, but it shares many important four-flat characteristics (Sheine, 1998, p. 162). Built in 1939, it contains three five-room flats and a double-height owner's unit with an optional standalone studio. Both buildings are located in a mid-city neighborhood that was developed primarily in the 1920s and 1930s with small apartment houses that has recently been designated as a Historic Preservation Overlay Zone by the City of Los Angeles (Miracle Mile HPOZ, 2017).

Development Histories

1060 South Cochran was built by William B. Miller, who also acted as its architect and contractor (L.A. Department of Building and Safety [LADBS], 1926) (Figure 5.4). Its location, year built and the building itself indicate a development history typical of the era. During the 1920s, subdividers, builders and lenders all made it easy to build small-scale apartments, even for novice landlords and owner-users. A huge amount of land was subdivided during the 1920s, following the Standard Subdivision Guide adopted by the planning commission in 1926, which suggested the creation of 50-foot by 130-foot parcels suitable for flats (LACPC, 1928, p. 12). More than 30,000 lots were subdivided in 1926 alone (LACPC, 1931, p. 16). Plans for flat buildings were readily available in compendiums of stock plans and bungalow books, including *Weston's Single and Double Bungalows*, which offered four-family flat plans

Figure 5.4 By-right case study project: 1060 South Cochran Avenue in the Mid-Wilshire neighborhood of Los Angeles.

and specifications for $50 in 1922, including an "[i]n-a-door-bed in [the] dining room and a breakfast nook in the kitchen" (Weston, 1922, p. 24). Pacific Ready-Cut Homes, which delivered precut kit houses in pieces ready to be put together on-site, also provided two-family and four-family flats (Thornton & Wolicki, 2004, p. 53). And lenders provided ready-made plans and other architectural services, along with construction and mortgage loans. All at a scale of investment that was attainable for many, especially for owner-users since they would have the cash flow from three units to help cover their mortgage.

1060 South Cochran was built "by-right" since it did not require any discretionary approvals to be built and conformed to the development standards in force when it was constructed. It is considered to be an "altered contributor" to the Miracle Mile Historic Preservation Overlay Zone since its modifications are reversible, including the replacement of its original smooth stucco with textured and several side windows. (LACPD, 2017; State of California, 2015a). The building's front facade, however, retains a high degree of architectural integrity and exhibits a relatively high degree of detail and variety.

The Mackey Apartments was built by owner/user Pearl Mackey, designed by architect Rudolph M. Schindler and constructed by general contractor Ray L. Hommes (Figure 5.5). Mrs. Mackey hired Schindler

Figure 5.5 By-design case study project: Mackey Apartments, located at 1137 South Cochran Avenue in the Mid-Wilshire neighborhood of Los Angeles.

to design an apartment building for her and her adult daughter, Winnie Mae, in late November 1938 (Standard Form of Agreement, 1938). Both women were teachers in Los Angeles City schools and wanted to live together but separately, in a situation that would allow some flexibility since both had long vacation periods (L.A. City Directory, 1938, p. 1296; Mackey, 1939a). Mackey, widowed by 1936, was originally interested in building a duplex or triplex, but after studying the neighborhood, Schindler convinced her that a four-flat would be the most profitable route (Pearl Mackey Letter, April 30, 1940). He produced a back of the envelope proforma that estimated a 15% return on a total investment of $17,000 (Schindler, 1939a) (Figure 5.6).

Schindler designed the building with a large owner's unit that was really two units in one, making the building a four- and sometimes five-flat (Figure 5.7). It contained a small studio apartment for Miss Mackey connected by a side corridor to a double-height living room and third-floor "study," actually a bedroom, for Mrs. Mackey. This created a spacious and distinctive owner's unit that defined the front facade of the building. The three additional units were all more conventional one-story flats, two of which had dining rooms convertible to a second bedroom by a sliding wall. All five units utilized built-in furniture for more efficient use of space, and transom windows and skylights to bring more light to interior spaces. All also had substantial access to private outdoor space in the form of large patios for the two ground-floor units, a front balcony for the second-floor flat and a large roof garden for Mrs. Mackey's unit and Winnie Mae's studio.

Mrs. Mackey was a detail-oriented client who communicated with Schindler often during the design phase of the project, reminding him about shoe racks, bookshelves, day beds and several times about a special cabinet for her mixer (Schindler, 1939b). The design and permitting of the project, delayed by the need for discretionary approval for the building's partial third story, took much longer than Mackey anticipated, and she grew more worried as time extended. Eventually Schindler stopped returning her phone calls so she communicated with him via detailed letters and lists. The building permit was finally approved on June 14, 1939, already well behind schedule in Mrs. Mackey's opinion (L.A. Building Permit No. 23497, 1939a; Mackey, 1939a). The building was permitted as a four-unit, not a five-unit as was the intended eventual use, demonstrating the sleight of hand architects often use in the face of building and zoning codes (Los Angeles Department of Building and Safety [LADBS], 1939a, 1939b).

Construction did not go well. Although Schindler typically oversaw the construction of his projects himself, Mrs. Mackey had hired a general contractor, causing much consternation (McCoy, 1960, p. 150). In Schindler's opinion, the contractor needed "more than the usual watching," and he asked to be released from the job if Mrs. Mackey did not

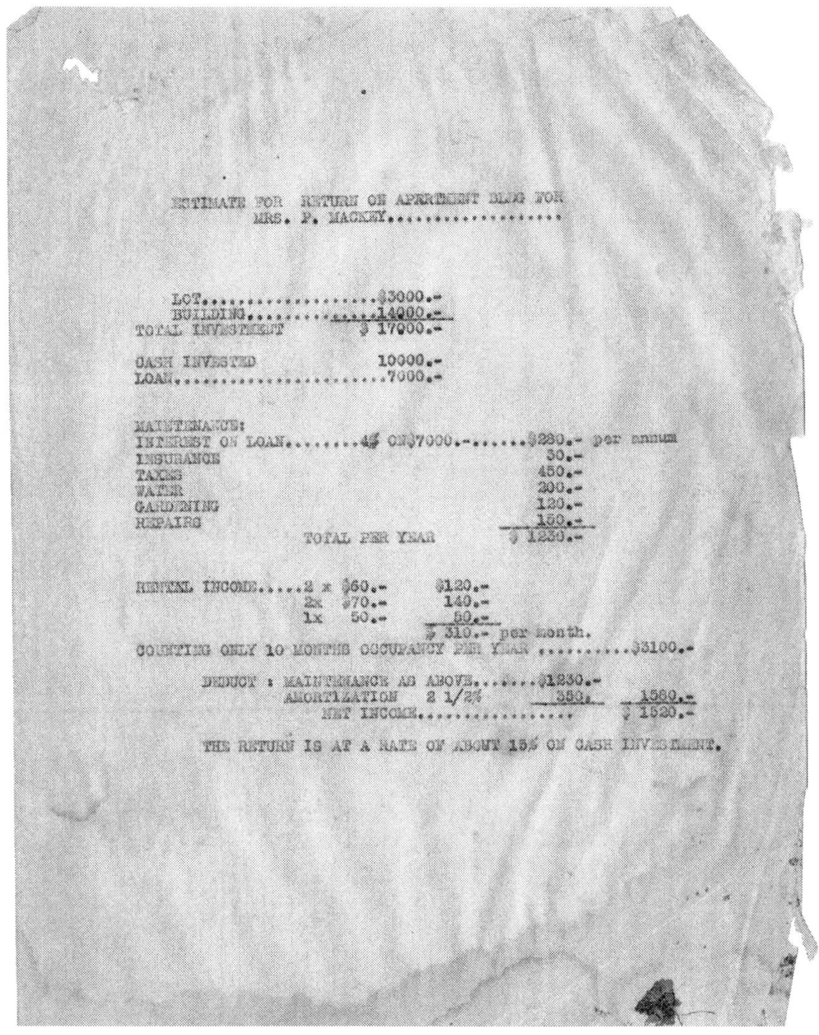

ESTIMATE FOR RETURN ON APARTMENT BLDG FOR
MRS. P. MACKEY.....................

LOT.......................$3000.-
BUILDING..................14000.-
TOTAL INVESTMENT $ 17000.-

CASH INVESTED 10000.-
LOAN.......................7000.-

MAINTENANCE:
INTEREST ON LOAN........4% ON $7000.-......$280.- per annum
INSURANCE 30.-
TAXES 450.-
WATER 200.-
GARDENING 120.-
REPAIRS 150.-
TOTAL PER YEAR $ 1230.-

RENTAL INCOME.....2 x $60.- $120.-
2x $70.- 140.-
1x 50.- 50.-
$ 310.- per month.
COUNTING ONLY 10 MONTHS OCCUPANCY PER YEAR $3100.-

DEDUCT : MAINTENANCE AS ABOVE.......$1230.-
AMORTIZATION 2 1/2% 350. 1580.-
NET INCOME.................. $ 1520.-

THE RETURN IS AT A RATE OF ABOUT 15% ON CASH INVESTMENT.

Figure 5.6 The proforma for the Mackey Apartments prepared by architect R. M. Schindler estimated a 15% cash-on-cash return.

Credit: R. M. Schindler papers, Architecture and Design Collection. Art, Design & Architecture Museum, University of California, Santa Barbara.

pay him for supervision (Schindler, 1939c).[2] Construction commenced and then was almost immediately stopped by a lumber strike that began on June 19, 1939 and was not resolved until July 15 (Employers Seek, 1939; Harbor Strike, 1939; Schindler, 1939b). Then, the third-story portion of the building was actually built to a depth of 25 feet from the

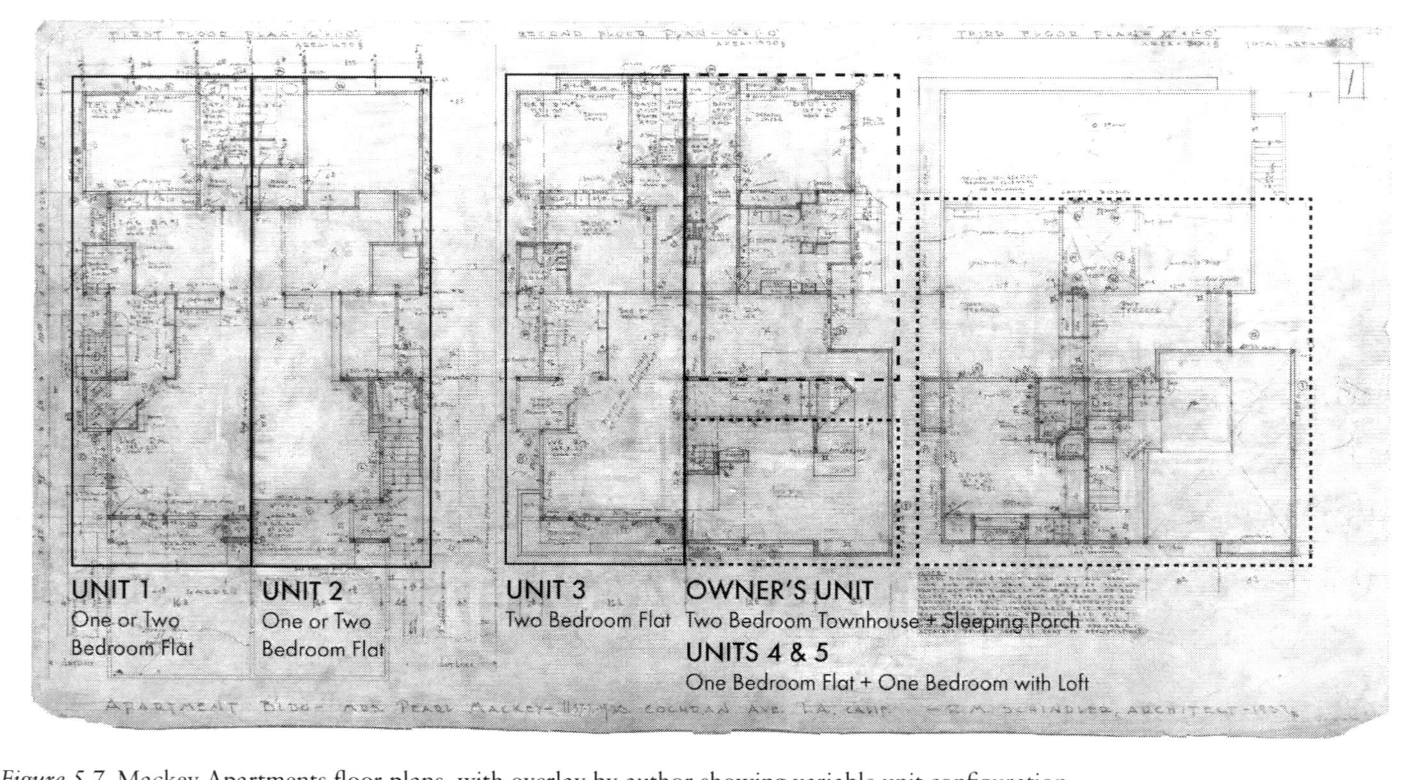

Figure 5.7 Mackey Apartments floor plans, with overlay by author showing variable unit configuration.

Credit: R. M. Schindler papers, Architecture and Design Collection. Art, Design & Architecture Museum, University of California, Santa Barbara.

front façade, instead of the approved 19 feet. The City building inspector caught the discrepancy (among others) and forced Schindler to apply to the City Planning Commission for reapproval, which was granted on February 1, 1940 (L.A. Board of Building and Safety Commissioners, 1940).[3] The Certificate of Occupancy, allowing the building to be inhabited, was filed on February 28, 1940 (LADBS, 1940).

The Mackey Apartments was built "by-design" from the perspective of this analysis because its signature design strategies required discretionary approval from the Los Angeles City Planning and Building Commissions. The double-height living room and second bedroom of the owner's unit boosted the front portion of the building to three stories, over the height limit for its housing type per state and local law. The City Planning Commission considered the issue and eventually granted permission because the third story was to be built over a relatively small portion of the building. The commission required an increased south side setback, 3.5 feet, and granted the right to build this portion of the building to a depth of 19 feet from the front façade (L.A. Board of Building and Safety Commissioners, 1940; Niederhofer, 1939). The third story also triggered the need for a second means of egress. After some negotiation, the Building and Safety Commission allowed Schindler to add a 3-foot-wide exterior stair from the third-story roof garden (L.A. Building and Safety Commissioners, 1939a, 1939b). The Mackey Apartments has been deemed a "contributor" to the Miracle Mile Historic Preservation Zone (LACPD, 2017; State of California, 2015b).

Design

Context

Throughout the 1920s, Los Angeles architects were busy responding to the city's unprecedented population growth designing single-family homes and small-, medium- and large-scale multifamily housing. These were built mainly in Eclectic Revival styles that dominated the interwar period, including Spanish Colonial, American Colonial, Mediterranean, French Norman, Craftsman and Tudor, all based on romantic ideas and liberal interpretation of "foreign" architectural styles. Well-known Los Angeles Architects Roland Coate, Reginald Johnson, Wallace Neff and Paul Williams all worked in Period Revival styles during this time, though the 1920s was also a time of early Modernist experimentation seen in the work of not only Schindler but also Irving Gill and Richard Neutra. Housing continued to be designed and constructed throughout the 1930s, but the Depression slowed the pace of building and ended the Period Revival era by the close of the decade, ceding to the use of more stripped-down, modern styles including Art Deco, Streamline Moderne, Zig Zag Moderne and the International Style.

This multiplicity of styles characterizes the case study block where eleven buildings, including 1060 South Cochran, were constructed in the 1920s, built mainly in Spanish Colonial Revival, but also Tudor Revival, American Colonial Revival and Moorish Revival. The owner/architect/builder of 1060 South Cochran was not a practicing architect, but a variety of professional architects did design similar buildings on the block. In 1925, for example, four-flats designed by architects Harry H. Lincoln, Charles A. Gault and Wilbur W. Campbell were all built (State of California, 2015a). Both Lincoln and Gault designed numerous apartment buildings in the neighborhood, Gault in the 700 block of Cochran and Dunsmuir and Lincoln the 1000 block of Redondo and Meadowbrook, all in the 1920s (State of California, 2015a).

Although few buildings were built during the worst years of the Depression, 1929 to 1933, more buildings on the block were built in the 1930s than the 1920s (12), including four four-flats, all in more stripped-down versions of revival styles. During the 1930s, the most prolific architect working in the neighborhood was R. S. Loring, who designed 1120 and 1112 South Cochran on the case study block, both in 1938, and many other four-flats close by including 1222 South Cloverdale in 1934, 1202 South Cochran in 1939 and 1048 Stanley in 1940 (State of California, 2015a). In 1939, the Mackey Apartments was the last building to be built on the block until 1947, in an Early Modern style. Six lots remained unbuilt by the close of the 1930s.

Rudolph Schindler, the Mackey Apartment's Viennese Modernist architect, established his architectural practice in Los Angeles in 1920, building many of his best-known houses during the decade, including his own "double-family" house in West Hollywood. Schinder also began a serious interest in multifamily housing during this time, designing the Pueblo Ribera Court in La Jolla and the Sachs Apartments in Silver Lake. These reflected his former employer Frank Lloyd Wright's influence, as well as Irving Gill's stripped-down Spanish Colonial/Mission style (Gebhard, 1971). Schindler's office, which was always small, was sustained by modest projects throughout the Depression (McCoy, 1960). He designed more than a dozen multifamily apartment projects in the 1930s, three of which were built by the end of the decade, the Bubeshko and Falk Apartments, both located in Silver Lake and the Mackey, all spatially complex, with maximal private outdoor space and clever built-in furniture. While Schindler may have championed the "artist architect," writing in 1934,

> Modern architecture cannot be developed by changing slogans. It is not in the hands of the engineer, the efficiency expert, the machinist or the economist. It is developing in the minds of the artists who can grasp "space" and "space forms" as a new medium for human expression.
>
> (Gebhard, 1971, p. 149)

he often operated as a more practical contractor/architect, working out construction details in the field rather than with drawings made in the office (McCoy, 1960).

To what degree are 1060 South Cochran and the Mackey Apartments similar or different from a design perspective? Does the fact that 1060 South Cochran is a vernacular building, while the Mackey Apartments was designed by a well-known architect mean that it lacks architectural value?

Site Strategy and Massing *Two Stories vs. Partial Third Story*

Both case study projects site a rectilinear volume at the center of their lots, set back from the front, side and rear, with detached garage structures on the back property line.[4] The building at 1060 South Cochran is two stories with a gabled roof in front and flat roof on the rest of the structure. The Mackey Apartment's building is three stories in front and two stories at the rear with a flat roof that steps down from three- to two-and-a-half- and then two-stories.

Unit Types and Aggregation *Rental Flats vs. Owner Townhouse + Rental Flats*

Unit types and their method of aggregation are conventional at 1060 South Cochran but more spatially innovative at the Mackey Apartments. The building at 1060 South Cochran aggregates four two-bedroom, one-bath flats, two-up, two-down, all with useful built-ins. Although the plans are mirrored, units are essentially identical and organize rooms linearly, stacking the living room, dining room, kitchen and then bedrooms and bathroom from front to back. The building does not have a more expansive owner's unit, but many four-flats did.

The Mackey Apartments aggregates two one-bedroom, one-bath flats side-by-side on the ground level; one two-bedroom, one-bath flat on the second level; and one two-story, two-bedroom, two-bath owner's unit on the second and third levels. Ground-floor units are mirrored and contain a flexible space that can either be used as an open dining room or as a second bedroom enclosed by a sliding wall. The second-floor flat is similar to those on the ground floor but with a permanent second bedroom instead of the flexible space. Rooms are organized similar to 1060 South Cochran, stacked linearly from the most public in front to the most private at the rear. The owner's unit includes a one-and-a-half-story living area that connects to a dining room, kitchen, bedroom and bathroom (mirroring these rooms in the second-story flat) and a "study" (i.e., bedroom) with a second bathroom on the third story (on top of the second-story flat). The unit also has two roof terraces on the third level, one accessible from the living area and the other directly from the third-floor study, both of which were configured as outdoor sleeping porches, covered with a pergola and including closets and sinks. A kitchen on the third floor was installed after the fact but is not on the original plans.[5] All units have built-in furniture in the form of dining nooks, bookcases, window seats and flower boxes. Upstairs units have skylights to daylight the interiors. Unusually, the second-floor dining room, kitchen, bedroom and bath of Pearl Mackey's unit can be rented as a standalone studio, effectively adding a fifth unit. A hallway bumps out over the driveway connecting the studio unit to the front two-story space.[6]

Pedestrian Access and Circulation *Common vs. Individual*

Pedestrian access and circulation are used in common for all residents at 1060 South Cochran but are more individualized at the Mackey Apartments. 1060 South Cochran provides centralized pedestrian access from a single door near the center of the front facade. Individual apartment entry doors are not visually accessible from the public sidewalk, making the building look more like a private single-family home. Each unit is accessed from a common, interior entry vestibule with an L-shaped stair to the second story. All units have back doors providing accessibility from the parking area in the rear.

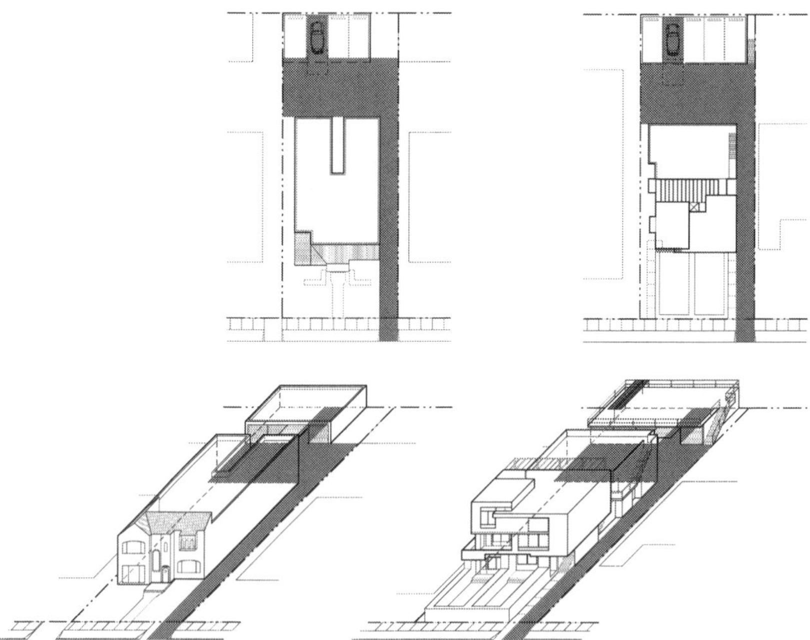

Figure 5.8 Vehicular access and parking diagrams: 1060 S. Cochran Avenue (left) vs. The Mackey Apartments (right).

Unit entries in the Mackey Apartments are organized asymmetrically and are accessed on either side of the building. One ground-floor flat is entered from a side door on the left and the other from a door on the right. An L-shaped common stairwell to the upper units, enclosed yet open to the elements, is also located on the right, providing access to the second-floor flat and owner's unit. There are two entry doors to the owner's unit, one to the right of the landing, providing entry into the dining room and kitchen area, and the other to the left, providing entry into the living area. This configuration gave Winnie Mae Mackey some privacy and allows the unit to be rented as two. All front entry doors are hidden from public view, and all units have back doors providing accessibility from the parking area.

Vehicular Access and Parking *Four Cars vs. Five Cars*

Both case study projects use a side driveway (approximately 8 ft wide) for vehicular access to garages at the rear of the property (Figure 5.8). 1060 South Cochran was parked at one car per unit, as is the Mackey Apartments if rented as a five-flat. If operating as a four-flat, the extra parking space is allocated to the owner's unit.

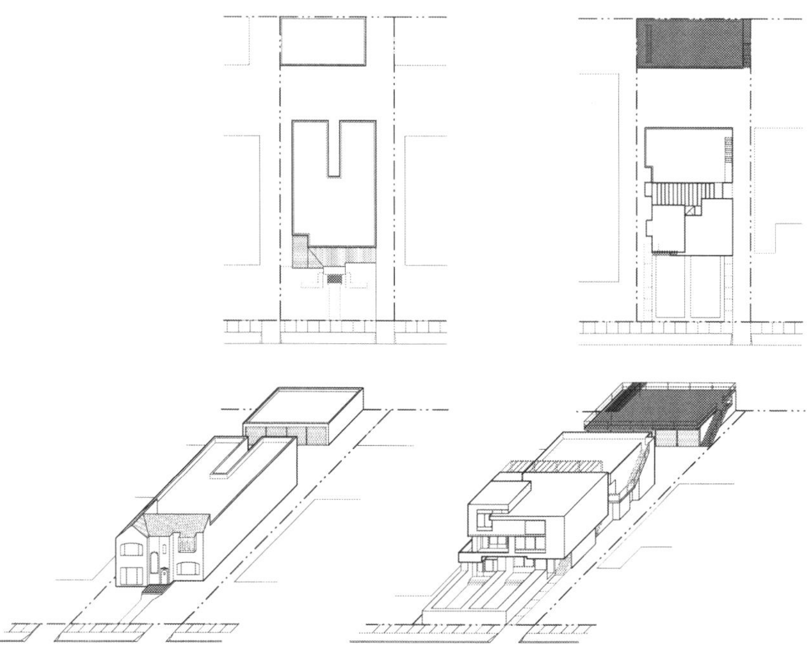

Figure 5.9 Common open space diagrams: 1060 S. Cochran Avenue (left) vs. The Mackey Apartments (right).

Common Open Space *Token vs. Utilitarian*

The common open space included in both case study projects is minimal (Figure 5.9). 1060 South Cochran provides a front stoop and patio area accessible to all units (approximately 3 ft by 18 ft, 54 sq ft), currently defined by hedges. The Mackey Apartment's garage rooftop was accessible to all units, originally used for clothes drying (45 ft by 20 ft, 900 sq ft).[7]

Private Open Space *Absent vs. Ample*

The case study projects are maximally different in terms of the provision of private open space (Figure 5.10). The building at 1060 South Cochran provides no private open space, though some four-flats did, in the form of small balconies, porches and patios.

The Mackey Apartments provides an uncommon amount of private open space for each unit. Ground-floor units have large front patios occupying almost all of the front setback, originally grass and enclosed by fences and envisioned as "outdoor living rooms," now decomposed granite enclosed by hedges (approximately 12 ft by 20 ft, 240 sq ft) (Mackey, 1939b).[8] The second-floor flat has a front balcony (approximately 4 ft by 16 ft, 64 sq ft). There is a large roof terrace with pergolas and flower boxes for owner's unit (approximately 35 ft by 35 ft, 1,225 sq ft).

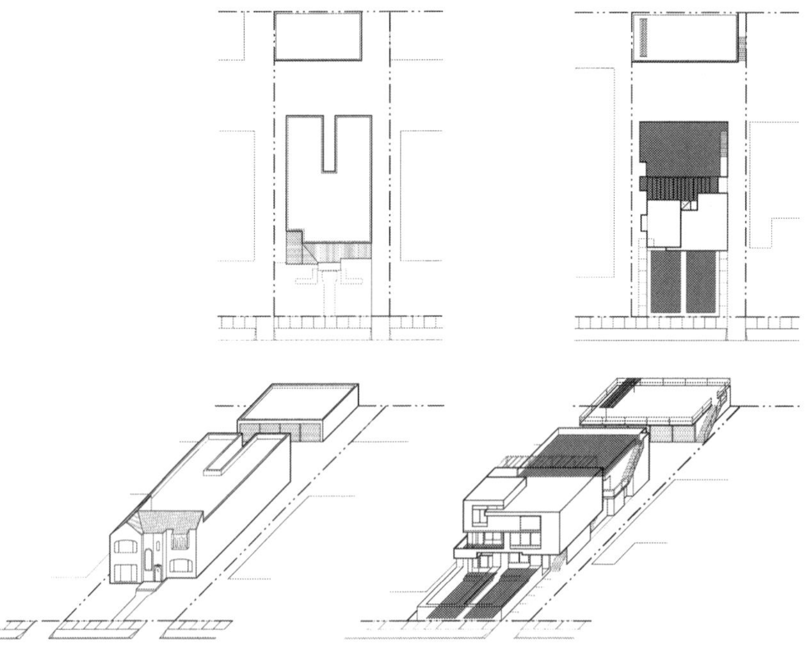

Figure 5.10 Private open space diagrams: 1060 S. Cochran Avenue (left) vs. The Mackey Apartments (right).

***Landscape** Spare vs. Sufficient*

The landscape at 1060 South Cochran's is limited to hedges, lawn and a eucalyptus tree in front and foundation plantings on the side. No street trees are extant.

Schindler specified a variety of plants for the Mackey Apartments including ivy, lantana, viburnum suspensum, hibiscus whitewing, euonymus japonica and vitis capensis to be used in foundation plantings and planting boxes and hedges, among others (Schindler, 1940b). Three pittosporum rhombifolium street trees were permitted, but it is unknown whether they were actually planted (L.A. Board of Park Commissioners, 1940). No street trees exist today. Pearl Mackey seems to have been more interested in the project's landscape than the architect, pushing Schindler to finalize planting boxes and roof garden so that she could start gardening.

***Architectural Style** Spanish Colonial Revival vs. Early Modern*

1060 South Cochran is built in the Spanish Colonial Revival style, one of the most popular architectural styles in Southern California during this era. The style is characterized by shaped roofs, roofs or roof trim of clay tile, use of arched shapes for windows and doors and leaded windows, all of which are exhibited by the project. The style is also typified by compound massing and integration of balconies, covered porches and patios and other types of outdoor space. It was used for housing of all types since it could be as cheap or expensive as one wanted by adding more or less detail on more or less complex spatial volumes.

The Mackey Apartments is designed in Schindler's Early Modern style that translated the International Style into a California context. His style was characterized by the use of clean geometric shapes, interlocking volumes, asymmetrical massing and minimal detailing. This is most evident at the Mackey Apartments on the front of the building, where asymmetrical interlocking L's shape the facade, giving it added depth, shade and movement. Unlike other Modernist architects, Schindler "maintained that color was an architectural element" (McCoy, 1960, p. 175). He specified colors for the Mackey Apartments, and even though the exterior was white, unlike most Modernist architects, the built-in furniture was brightly colored with shades of orange and blue.

***Outcomes** Vernacular Type Done Right vs. Modern Four-flat at Heart*

The Mackey Apartments is clearly more intensively and innovatively designed than 1060 South Cochran, but that does not mean that 1060 should not be considered a well-designed building. Its units are large and functional. Its Spanish Colonial revival style is expressed with an appropriate level of detail and authenticity. Its common entry sequence is enough to engender some neighborliness. It's a vernacular type done right.

Conversely, although it looks quite different from 1060 South Cochran and the other four-flats on its block on the surface, the Mackey Apartments is a four-flat at heart. The project accepts important characteristics of the four-flat development type, including its site and unit aggregation strategies, parking scenario, interior spatial organization and use of built-in furniture. But it also literally builds upon that type in many dimensions, from its double-height owner's unit to expansive private open space to its Modern Style and color palette. Here, the by-design approach is clearly an inflection or extension of the typical by-right strategy, which points the way to an improved development type. The use of a known type allowed for meaningful design innovation.

Real Estate Development

Context

The boom and bust of the real estate cycle characterized the environment in which both case study projects were built. Housing was already in short supply when the boom began in 1921, and even though Los Angeles led the nation in homebuilding in 1920 and continued to build in increasing numbers, the city was still short on housing of all types in 1923 when "hundreds of persons use[d] the hotel and dwelling directory of the Chamber [of Commerce] each week" (City Leads, 1921, V6; City Takes Good Care, 1923, H12). At the end of 1922, the *Los Angeles Times* reported that never in the history of the city had so much subdividing been done and that an "Average of One New Tract per Day Opened in Los Angeles City During the Year" (Subdivision Activity, 1922, V1). By 1923 the city was in "a period of unbridled speculation" (Findley, 1958, p. 170). Much of this subdividing occurred in the Wilshire District, the case study neighborhood, which had the most annual buying power per home in the city in 1925, at $5,399 per year per family (Family Incomes, 1925, p. C23).

By 1925, however, a year before 1060 South Cochran was built, real estate developers were overbuilding in relation to population and income growth. A University of Southern California study in January 1924 warned that the 6.8% vacancy rate for existing dwellings and those under construction would rise precipitously if the present rate of subdividing and building continued (Warn Against, 1924, p. 14). By 1927, rents were falling and subdivision activity fell from a high of 43,980 lots in 1923 to 13,318 in 1927 (LACPC, 1953, p. 33; New Construction, 1927, p. 18).

During the late 1920s, building and real estate sales activity continued but at the much slower pace, so there was not as much overbuilding as there might have been. By the end of the 1920s, nearly a third of the lots on the case study block were still vacant.

The worst part of the Depression was experienced from 1929 to 1933, but Los Angeles fared better than many other cities. A survey of construction costs from 1919 to 1931 made by Ira J. Smith, cost estimator, found that building costs in Los Angeles were lowest in the nation, on average 40% less than cities on the East Coast and in the Midwest (Cohan, 1933, p. 19). And Los Angeles buildings lost only 32% of their value over that same period as compared to 41.6% in other cities. With more robust valuations and better value per construction dollar, Los Angeles had less distance to cover to resume normal operation (Cohan, 1933, p. 19). Land costs, construction costs and rents all began to slowly increase by 1934 and 1935 but were still below peak levels in 1937 (Trend Study, 1939, E2; Uptrend of Rents, 1937, E2) (Figure 5.12). Russel G. Creviston, president of the Los Angeles Producers' Council noted, "a 1937 house costing $6,500 offers more to its owner than a house costing $7,500 in the 1926–1929 period" (Building Costs, 1937). At the beginning of 1939 when Mrs. Mackey was contemplating her flats, it was still a very good time to build.

To what degree are 1060 South Cochran and the Mackey Apartments similar or different from a real estate development perspective? Does the vernacular status of 1060 South Cochran mean it was more profitable than the Mackey Apartments? Does the Mackey Apartment's well-known architect mean it was a poor investment?

Subdivision *December 1922 vs. November 1922*

The case study properties were subdivided within days of one another and are essentially the same in terms of their initial development (L.A. County Department of Public Works, 1922a, 1922b). 1060 South Cochran is built on Lot 380 of Tract No. 5070, recorded on December 13, 1922, as part of the Mansfield Knoll Tract. The Mackey Apartments was built on Lot 74 of Tract No. 4031, recorded on November 14, 1922. Both lots are located on parallelogram-shaped blocks and are of a similar size, 50 feet by 138 feet (6,897 sq ft) and 50 feet by 130 feet (6,475 sq ft), respectively.

1922 was a time of intense subdivision activity in Los Angeles, especially in the mid-city "New Wilshire District," responding to the development of Wilshire Boulevard and its growing importance as a commercial corridor (Figure 5.11). David Barry & Company, subdivider of the Mansfield Knoll Tract and much of the surrounding area, promoted the neighborhood as a "veritable Gridiron of Important Thoroughfares," highlighting the tract's "high grade through streets," access to future public transportation (near two yellow and one red line) and distance from the oil district (far) (Display Ad 204, 1922, V3). Subdivision activity in the area was so

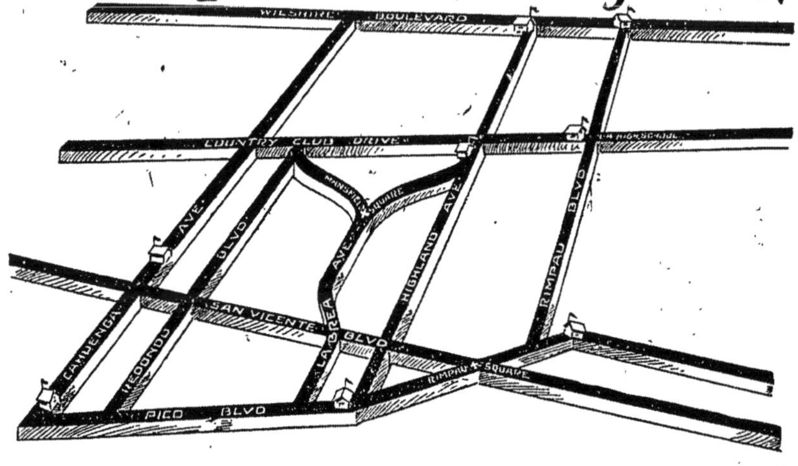

Figure 5.11 A David Barry & Company advertisement for subdivisions in the new Wilshire District (Display Ad 204, 1922, p. V3).

swift that street names on tract maps were not consistent. What eventually became Cochran Avenue was called Edgemar Avenue on Tract 4031 but was called Cahuenga Valley and Ballona Creek Road on Tract 5070.

Market Timing and Demand *End of Peak vs. Approaching Full Recovery*

Both case study projects were built at times of transition in the real estate market (Figure 5.12). 1060 South Cochran was built toward the end of the peak of the 1920s' boom, while the Mackey Apartments was built just as the next cycle was gaining speed. By the time 1060 South Cochran was built in 1926, the outlook for flats in Los Angeles was already weakening. Vacancy was the lowest it had been in 2 years, with

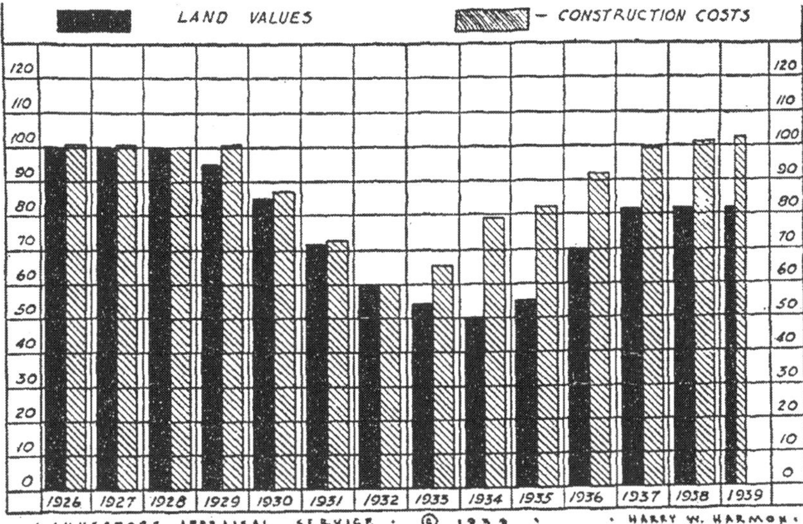

GRAPH GIVES INDEX—Trend of land values and building costs in Los Angeles metropolitan area since 1926 is charted above. The index figures at the margins give basis of comparison, with the basic figure of 100 indicated for the year 1928. The graph was prepared for The Times by the Investors Appraisal Service, publishers of the Los Angeles Blue Book of Land Values.

Figure 5.12 Relative land and building values at the time the case study projects were built. Construction costs returned to pre-depression levels more quickly than Los Angeles land values (Trend Study, 1939, p. E2).

Credit: Investors Appraisal Service.

9.2% vacant, half that of apartment houses (18.7%) and less than bungalow courts (10.1%), but the property type was experiencing increased seasonal vacancy, and it was not nearly as popular as single-family homes (3.7% vacant) (Eberle & Riggleman, 1926, p. 295). By the end of 1927, four-flat vacancy was up to 14.8%, and Los Angeles had accumulated an excess of 32,603 family units (Eberle, 1927, p. 311; LACPC, 1928, p. 47). From 1928 to 1935, vacancy for flats ranged from a low of 7.8% in 1930 to a high of 11.7% in 1933, ameliorated by the fact that construction waned significantly in the early years of the Depression (Eberle, 1935a, p. 15).

By 1939, the real estate market was approaching full recovery and coming back to the levels of activity seen at the peak of the boom. Rents for flats were still 20% below their 1928 height in 1937 but on the rise (Uptrend of Rents, 1937, E2). Leonard F. Hammel, head of the real estate department at Union Bank & Trust, said, "Today we are close to the bottom of the cycle" (Building and Land-Cost, 1938, E1). By the end of 1939, state real estate commissioner Clarence Urban foresaw a better market, stating "the market for all types of property, including homes, office buildings, vacant land and factory sites is beginning to show an immediate incline" (Outlook Sound, 1939, E2).

Land and Building Costs *Relatively Higher vs. Relatively Lower*

Despite the 13-year time difference, important development costs were the same or lower in 1939 than they were in 1926. Land in Los Angeles lost 50% of its value during the Depression, falling from a peak seen between 1925 and 1928 to its low point in 1934 (Trend Study, 1939). By 1939, land values had risen, but only to 80% of those seen at the height of the boom. The exact price paid for 1060 South Cochran's lot is unknown, but lot prices in the neighborhood ranged from $4,000 to $6,750 in 1926 based on an analysis of advertisements in the *Los Angeles Times*. Given this, we would expect land prices in the area in 1939 to range from $3,200 to $5,400. The land price listed on the Mackey Apartments proforma is $3,000. Mrs. Mackey likely bought the land earlier than 1939 (Mackey, 1939a).

Construction costs in Los Angeles rose more quickly than land values after the Depression and were back at 1926 levels by 1939, having fallen to their lowest value in 1932 (Trend Study, 1939). On its building permit, 1060 South Cochran lists a cost of $9,000 (LADBS, 1926). This likely underestimates building costs since fees are based on valuation, but Mr. Miller acted as his own architect and contractor, which would have saved him some money. However, *The Los Angeles Blue Book of Land Values* calculated per square foot costs for the construction of four-family flats of speculative construction in 1928 to be $2.80 per square foot. Given that the square footage of 1060 South Cochran is 5,572, its construction costs could have been as high as $15,600 (*Blue Book*, 1938). In 1926, $9,000 spent had the same buying power as $7,000 in 1939.[9]

Schindler reported a building cost of $12,000 on the permit but used $14,000 in the pro forma he prepared for the project. In 1939, $12,000 spent had the same buying power as $15,000 in 1926, more in line with the Los Angeles Blue Book valuations.[10] Bottom line, the Mackey Apartments was effectively cheaper to build and achieved better construction value for the money spent.

Funding *Construction Loan vs. Construction Loan*

Many Los Angeles firms offered short-term construction loans and longer term mortgages on all types of property in 1926, and this is likely how 1060 South Cochran was funded. W. Ross Campbell Company, for example, extended "Building Loans" on both "Residential and Business Property, Straight or Amortized" (Display Ad 91, 1926, E2). Consolidated

Mortgage advertised "[p]lenty of money for residence, apts., flats in sums of $2,500 and up, building loans" (Classified Ad 7, 1926, p. 23). And the California Mortgage Company offered building loans from $25,000 to $50,000 at 7% interest, promising "liberal appraisals" (Classified Ad 8, 1926, p. 21). At this time, funds for construction were generally loaned for 6 months to 3 years at rates from 5.5% to 7%. First mortgages on improved property were also available but were still relatively short term, needing to be refinanced in 3 to 15 years (Classified Ad 7, 1926, p. 23).

By 1939, when the Mackey Apartments was built, rates were down, loan-to-value ratios were up, and loan terms were much longer. With the help of Schindler's static pro forma, Pearl Mackey obtained a $7,000 building loan at 4% from California Bank, a good rate considering that construction loans advertised in the *Los Angeles Times* then ranged from 4.5% to 6% (Schindler, 1939a). The loan represented just 41% of the total required investment in land and building, which was expected to be $17,000. Mrs. Mackey likely refinanced at the end of construction with a longer term mortgage, also available at California Bank, "the bank to see for loans" where there were "no commissions to pay" (Display Ad 5, 1939, p. 8).

Marketing and Absorption Likely Delayed vs. Quick

Asking rents for unfurnished four- and five-room flats in the case study neighborhood in 1926 and 1939 were comparable. At the end of 1925, an Eberle and Riggleman study found that the Wilshire District had the most apartments in the city renting from $55 to $85 while the average rental for a two-bedroom apartment in the city of Los Angeles at this time was $40.70 (Home Rentals, 1925, E9). No specific advertisements for 1060 South Cochran could be found, but competing supply in the "West and Northwest" area advertised in the *Los Angeles Times* on May 1, 1926, ranged from $30 to $75, with a median of $50 (Classified Ad 6, 1926, A12). Flats experienced double-digit vacancy rates for the rest of the 1920s and rents were falling by 1927 (Holden, 1927, p. 18).

The first advertisement for the Mackey Apartments appeared in the *Los Angeles Times* on April 21, 1940:

> $55. NEW 4–5 rm., Schindler designed studios, patios. 1137 Cochran.
>
> (Classified Ad 10, 1940a, B8)

Later ads dropped the Schindler reference and touted the building's "ultra mod" architecture, indirect light and refrigerators (Classified Ad 5, 1940, A13). Ads for four- and five-room flats in the "Wilshire and West" neighborhoods ranged from $40 to $80 on the first day Mrs. Mackey advertised, with a median of $50 (Classified Ad 10, 1940, B8). The rents assumed by Schindler in his financial analysis, ranging from $50 to $70 and averaging $62, were well within range. A total of 5 advertisements for the Mackey Apartments appeared in the *Los Angeles Times* from April 21 to May 5, 1940 by which time the building must have been leased up (Classified Ad 4, 1940; Classified Ad 5, 1940; Classified Ad 9, 1940; Classified Ad 10, 1940a; Classified Ad 10, 1940b). It couldn't come too soon for Mrs. Mackey, who complained to Schindler that the units were difficult to rent, just a week into the process. Schindler responded,

> I warned you ahead of time that an unusual building might take longer to rent but would prove a superior investment in the long run. I am told that your attitude antagonizes prospects and advise you let somebody else handle the renting. Why show the worst apartment? Whatever happens I am vitally interested in the building and will do all I can for it.
>
> (Schindler, 1940a)

Outcomes *On the Bubble vs. Profit not Patronage*

The building at 1060 South Cochran was a speculative investment built just as the boom was transitioning to bust, while the Mackey Apartments was built in time to benefit from the lower costs experienced during the downturn but capture all the upside of recovery. This does not mean that 1060 South Cochran was unprofitable, but given the higher land and construction costs in 1926, it was likely less profitable than buildings built in the late 1930s into the 1940s.

The Mackey's well-known architect and status as a design precedent did not inhibit its investment performance and the building arguably performed better than 1060 South Cochran and the other conventional four-flats on its block built in the 1920s. It was better timed to market, was cheaper to build and, with a fifth unit, had the potential for higher revenue. And the assumptions used by Schindler in his proforma to project a 15% return were actually quite conservative: a 17% vacancy rate, achievable rent levels and a thorough estimation of maintenance costs (Schindler, 1939a). The building was clearly built for profit, not patronage.

Planning

Context

The Los Angeles City Planning Commission spent the time between the construction of 1060 South Cochran and the Mackey Apartments addressing the consequences of the city's phenomenal growth. Between 1920 and 1925, Los Angeles experienced a massive increase in both subdivision and construction activity, peaking in 1923 and then gradually declining into the Depression in 1929. The valuation of building permits in 1919 for all types of construction was $28.2 million, higher than during the war years but still $3 million less than the valuations seen in the 1912–1913 boom (Findley, 1958, p. 165). Valuations were $60.0 million in 1920, up to $200.1 million in 1923 and then back down to $152.6 million in 1925 (Findley, 1958, pp. 177–178). Similarly, only 5,217 lots were recorded in the city in 1920, increasing to 43,980 in 1923 and then down to 9,955 by 1925 (LACPC, 1952, p. 9). Although this growth was regulated, improvements were clearly needed given the number of poorly planned subdivisions, uneconomical use of land and substandard construction of temporary "unkempt little dwellings" (Fact and Comment, 1922, V1). Luckily, the City had reduced its number of Planning Commissioners from 51 to 5 in 1925, and organized the Department of City Planning ready to conduct the work of planning the city:

> The economic chaos of the Depression brought a reassessment of the real estate business with consequent greater emphasis upon the development of community planning, and subdivision and zoning regulations were strengthened to insure better standards.
>
> (Findley, 1958, p. 197–198)

Early subdivision in Los Angeles was haphazard at best. The City Planning Commission had been trying to regulate subdivisions from its inception in 1920, but until the State Map Filing Act of 1929 was passed, subdividers did not have to submit their map to the City Planning Department for review, too late in the game for the Wilshire District which was mostly subdivided in the early 1920s (LACPC, 1930, p. 48). Although the City Planning Commission adopted a "Standard Subdivision Guide" in 1926, "showing street dedications required and typical lot layout for varying degrees of land subdivision," and began to actively educate subdividers, many lots were still inaccessible, unbuildable and uncoordinated with adjacent subdivisions (LACPC, 1928, p. 12). Even worse, Angelenos were subdividing but not building (Figure 5.13). The *Los Angeles Times* reported in 1924 that almost 65% of subdivision sales were to buyers who intended to hold the property in hopes of quick appreciation rather than immediately developing it (Frank, 1924, D10). By 1925 the city had more than 600,000 vacant lots (Brackman, 2007, p. 385). It would take the post–World War II boom to finally absorb them all.

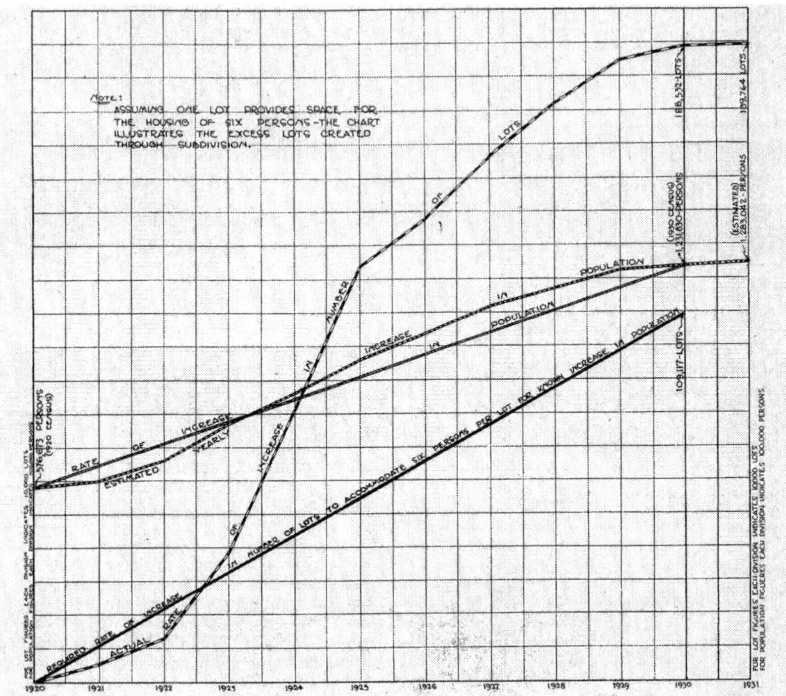

Chart showing exhorbitant increase in ratio of lots to population 1920 to 1931 and the falling off of subdivision activity in accordance with the law of supply and demand.

Figure 5.13 Ratio of lots to population: Los Angeies needed only 109,117 lots to house six people per parcel in 1930 but had a total of 188,532 lots, an excess of nearly 80,000 (LACPC, 1930, p. 51).

Credit: Los Angeles City Archives and Records Center.

If Los Angeles was oversubdivided, it was also overzoned. William L. Pollard, chairman of the city planning committee of the real estate board noted,

> The overzoned condition of Los Angeles, with 60 per cent of the city for large-type apartment houses, is the result of a speculative attitude of certain Los Angeles people whose ideas are governed by the amount they can get from a lot sold for speculation, rather than the amount that the lot will earn when used to its fullest economic capacity. The latter is the true test of value.
>
> (Zone Condition, 1928, E1)

Los Angeles passed its first complete zoning code in 1921 using an A, B, C, D, E nomenclature to identify areas for single-family housing, multifamily housing, commercial and industrial. By 1926, however, how the city was zoned versus how property was actually used was considerably out of sync. Of land that had been zoned in the city, 45.6% was used for single-family dwellings while only 9.5% of property was zoned for it (A zone) (LACPC, 1928, p. 6). Conversely, 59.3% of zoned land in the city was designated for multifamily housing (B zone) while only 10.5% of property was actually used that way (LACPC, 1928, p. 6). Clearly, zoning needed to respond to facts on the ground as well as guide future development. Los Angeles passed a new zoning code in 1930, providing greater differentiation within the residential zones, acknowledging that two-, three- and four-flats were very different than larger scale apartment houses. B zone properties were transitioned to the R4 zone, suitable for large-scale residential and institutional uses (LACPC, 1928, p. 20). Two new zones, R2, two-family, and R3, multiple dwelling, were added in between, so the code could better capture the scale of residential development (LACPC, 1928, p. 20). By 1936, only 0.3% of the land zoned R4 was used as such, with 46.4% used for single-family homes, 25.7% used as R2 and R3 and 21.9% vacant (LACPC, 1938, p. 17).

To what degree are 1050 South Cochran and the Mackey Apartments similar or different from an urban planning perspective?

Zoning and Development Standards

Zoning *B Zone vs. R4 Zone*

When they were subdivided in 1922, both case study parcels were zoned "B," per Los Angeles 1921 zoning code, a category that allowed all types of multifamily property, including "dwellings, tenements, hotels, lodging houses" as well as churches, public or semipublic institutions, doctor's and dentist's offices and railroad passenger stations (Official Atlas, 1924). This zoning system only governed use, not physical development standards, which were instead set forth in the Los Angeles Department of Building's Dwelling House Requirements (Official Atlas, 1924). The building at 1060 South Cochran would have been classified as an "Apartment House," a building of more than one story used to house three or more families, subject to regulations that defined minimum room sizes, required windows and rear building access.

By 1939, the new, more varied 1930 zoning code was in place and both parcels were transitioned to R4, unlimited residential, though none of the properties on the block were developed as such. The block's development pattern suggests that the R2 zone would have been more appropriate, which by this time allowed up to four-family dwellings on a lot. Although Mrs. Mackey's parcel was zoned for much more intensive development, she looked to the existing development context, rather than the underlying zone, to guide her investment approach.

Density *25 Dwelling Units per Acre vs. 26 to 33 Dwelling Units per Acre*

The case study projects are built to a similar density. 1060 South Cochran is built at 25 dwelling units per acre. The Mackey Apartments are 26 dwelling units per acre if rented as a four-flat and 33 if occupied as a five-flat.

Height/Setbacks

The two-story height limit for both case study projects was the result of state law, enforced locally (Commission on Immigration and Housing of California, 1917). At the time 1060 South Cochran was built, setbacks, or "building lines" were set forth via individual ordinances tied to specific blocks, usually initiated by the property owners (LACPC, 1928, p. 9). The buildings on the block built in the 1920s were all set back approximately 25 feet from the front property line. This is in line with the City's yard ordinance applicable in 1939, where buildings in the R4 zone required a front setback of 15 feet to 25 feet (LACPC, 1938, p. 28).

Parking *Four Cars vs. Five Cars*

Both case study projects provide parking at a rate of one car per unit in garages at the rear of their sites. No parking was required by the City of Los Angeles in 1926, but 1920s was a time of transition from the trolley system to the use of private automobiles and most four-flats provided on-site parking. By the time the Mackey Apartments was built, the City required one parking garage space on-site per unit (LACPC, 1935).

Contributions to the Public Realm *Minimal vs. Minimal*

Neither project provides adequate definition and character to the public realm and both miss opportunities to better contribute to the visual and social aspects of the street.

The front yard and front facade of 1060 South Cochran are visually accessible from the public street and sidewalk. While the facade of the building adds interest with varied window sizes, types and placement, the creation depth with bump-outs and the intersecting gable roof shapes, the lack of landscaping detracts from the streetscape.

The front yard of the Mackey Apartments is fenced off from the public realm with low fences, originally a 3-foot 6-inch "openwork" fence surrounding a lawn. These do provide protected spaces for residents to occupy and potentially participate in the social life of the public realm but essentially allow the building to turn its back to the public realm.

Outcomes

From a planning perspective, the case study projects are essentially the same, even though the local zoning code under which they were approved evolved considerably. Interestingly, both projects followed the cues of the urban context and building type as opposed to underlying zoning. The "unlimited" nature of B/R4 zoning encouraged speculation and the building of large apartment houses, but neither Miller nor Mackey responded to that. They, rather, developed their properties with two different versions of Los Angeles's favorite four-flat.

Conclusion

When Good Market Timing Encourages Both High Design and Profitable Design

The comparative analysis of 1060 South Cochran and the Mackey Apartments underscores how the use of known development models and a favorable market cycle can support meaningful design innovation. Well-known four-flat design practices and a relatively large margin of profitability allowed Mackey and Schindler to improve upon the type given changing regulation, market expectations and design trends. The Mackey's units are aggregated two-up, two-down like most four-flats, but one unit is much more elaborate with an extra story, living room mezzanine and a roof deck. Mackey units have built-in breakfast nooks and bookshelves, not unlike most four-flats, but its furniture is brightly colored and of modern design. Similar to most four-flats, the Mackey units have ample access to daylighting but amplified with transom windows and skylights to bring natural light to interior spaces. Yet, asking rents were comparable to other flats in the neighborhood and the underlying familiarity of the type, for all players, from lenders to building inspectors to tenants, helped hedge the financial risks of design innovation. Sealing the deal was the convertible studio apartment that could be rented independently of the owner's unit for an extra revenue stream, an opportunity few competing four-flats possessed. At the Mackey Apartments, high design was also profitable design.

Case Study Subjects Today

Many four-flats remain desirable to renters and profitable for owners today. 1060 South Cochran is currently privately owned and provides housing on the private market. It is rent-controlled and well-maintained.

The Mackey Apartments was purchased by the Republic of Austria on behalf of the MAK Center for Art and Architecture, an outpost of the Austrian Museum of Applied Arts/Contemporary Art (MAK), in 1995, which was interested to restore and preserve the building for use facilitating architectural and artistic connections between Europe and Los Angeles. The center uses the building to support a 6-month artist and architect in residency program, offered twice a year to two architects and two artists. International applicants are selected by jury to pursue interdisciplinary research and design projects connected to Los Angeles. Each is given lodging in one of the Mackey Apartment units and exhibits work at the end of their residency in a gallery space built over the garage.[11]

Notes

1. The four-flat at 1050 South Cochran Avenue exhibits this type of entry configuration.
2. Ray L. Hommes was new to contracting, having started in 1937 (The Fickett Formula, 1953, p. 132).
3. By this time, Pearl had had enough. The State Association of California Architects wrote to Schindler on May 17, 1940, to let him know that Mrs. Mackey had submitted a complaint against him and hear his side of the story. At a meeting of the Co-ordinating Committee between the architect and the owner on May 24, 1940, the. board found that Schindler's specifications were too vague. Since he often contracted his own projects, his drawings were often inexplicit.
4. The garage at 1060 South Cochran has since been demolished.
5. Schindler was known to have used these types of strategies, for example, labeling what was intended to be a bedroom a study while planning to install an extra kitchen after inspection. On his own house was labeled conventionally on the plans submitted to the Building and Safety Department to camouflage that it was intended for use by two families.
6. This bump out also required a variance (Building and Safety Commissioners Letter dated June 12, 1939).
7. Mrs. Mackey also requested that half the garage roof be used as a roof deck for the second-story flat (Pearl, letter to Schindler July 12, 1939b). It is unclear whether this request was implemented. A gallery space has since been added above the garage.
8. Schindler originally wanted to enclose the front patios with a much higher wall, but since it was to be built in the front setback, LADBS made him reduce the overall height to 3 feet 6 inches and make it 50% open (Niederhofer, 1939).
9. www.bls.gov/data/inflation_calculator.htm
10. www.bls.gov/data/inflation_calculator.htm
11. https://makcenter.org/residency-program/

References

Architectural Resources Group, Inc. (2015, January 23). *Historic Resources Survey Report, Wilshire Community Plan Area, Survey LA, Los Angeles Historic Resources Survey*. Los Angeles, CA: Office of Historic Resources.

Brackman, H. (2007). Making Room for Millions, Housing in Los Angeles. In Hynda L. Rudd and Tom Sitton et al. (Eds.), *The Development of Los Angeles City Government, An Institutional History 1850–2000.* (pp. 371–413). Los Angeles, CA: Los Angeles City Historical Society.

Building Costs Below Peak. (1937, September 26). *Los Angeles Times*, F3. Retrieved from www.proquest.com

Building and Land-Cost Levels Favorable to Investments. (1938, September 11). *Los Angeles Times*, E1. Retrieved from www.proquest.com

City Leads in House Building. (1921, January 9). *Los Angeles Times*, V6. Retrieved from www.proquest.com

City Takes Good Care of Growth. (1923, July 8). *Los Angeles Times*, H12. Retrieved from www.proquest.com

Classified Ad 4. (1940, April 29). *Los Angeles Times*, 16. Retrieved from www.proquest.com

Classified Ad 5. (1940, April 27). *Los Angeles Times*, A13. Retrieved from www.proquest.com

Classified Ad 6. (1926, May 1). *Los Angeles Times*, A12. Retrieved from www.proquest.com

Classified Ad 7. (1926, March 10). *Los Angeles Times*, 23. Retrieved from www.proquest.com

Classified Ad 8. (1926, March 12). *Los Angeles Times*, 21. Retrieved from www.proquest.com

Classified Ad 9. (1940, May 5). *Los Angeles Times*, B8. Retrieved from www.proquest.com

Classified Ad 10. (1940a, April 21). *Los Angeles Times*, B8. Retrieved from www.proquest.com

Classified Ad 10. (1940b, April 28). *Los Angeles Times*, B9. Retrieved from www.proquest.com

Cohan, C. C. (1933, July 9). Fifteen-Year Analysis Shows Local Building Cost Level Lowest in the Nation. *Los Angeles Times*, 19.

Commission of Immigration and Housing of California. (1919). *California State Housing Manual, Containing the State Tenement House Act, State Hotel and Lodging House Act, State Dwelling House Act, Annotated*. San Francisco, CA: State of California.

Display Ad 5. (1939, March 9). *Los Angeles Times*, 8. Retrieved from www.proquest.com

Display Ad 91. (1926, June 27). *Los Angeles Times*, E2. Retrieved from www.proquest.com

Display Ad 204. (1922, July 30). *Los Angeles Times*, V3. Retrieved from www.proquest.com

Eberle, G. J. (1927, December 26). *Eberle Economic Service Weekly Letter*, *4*(52), 311.

Eberle, G. J. (1935a, February 15). *Eberle Economic Service Weekly Letter*, *12*(2), 15.

Eberle, G. J. (1935b, May 1). *Eberle Economic Service Weekly Letter*, *12*(5).

Eberle, G. J., & Riggleman, J. R. (1926, December 17). *Eberle & Riggleman Economic Service Weekly Letter*, *3*(52), 295.

Employers Seek Lumber Strike Peace. (1939, June 19). *Los Angeles Times*, 1. Retrieved from www.proquest.com

Fact and Comment. (1922, October 15). *Los Angeles Times*, V1. Retrieved from www.proquest.com

Family Incomes Show How Los Angeles Prospers. (1925, December 13). *Los Angeles Times*, C23. Retrieved from www.proquest.com

The Fickett Formula: Good Design Works Both Ways. (1953, March). *House + Home*, 132–139.

Find Danger in Housing Bills. (1915, February 13). *Los Angeles Times*, I13.

Findley, J. C. (1958). *The Economic Boom of the Twenties in Los Angeles*. Doctoral Dissertation, Claremont Graduate School. Retrieved from https://search-proquest-com.libproxy1.usc.edu/docview/301877156/37F13EF9832D4A2EPQ/1?accountid=14749

Frank, M. (1924, March 2). Speculative Building vs. Purchases for Homes. *Los Angeles Times*, D10. Retrieved from www.proquest.com

Gebhard, D. (1971). *Schindler*. London: Thames and Hudson Ltd.

Gish, T. (2007). Apartments in Disguise: Small Multi-Family Dwellings in the "City of Homes," 1900–1930. Paper for presentation at the 2007 meeting of the Society for American City and Regional Planning History.

Hammel, L. F., & Cowan, B. D. (Eds.). (1938). *The Los Angeles Blue Book of Land Values*. Los Angeles, CA: Investors Appraisal Service.

Harbor Strike Front Breaks. (1939, July 15). *Los Angeles Times*, A1. Retrieved from www.proquest.com

Holden, T. S. (1927, January 2). New Construction Well Stabilized for 1927. *Los Angeles Times*, 18. Retrieved from www.proquest.com

Home Rentals Here are Low. (1925, December 20). *Los Angeles Times*, E9. Retrieved from www.proquest.com

L.A. Board of Building and Safety Commissioners. (1940, February 1). Letter to R. M. Schindler. (R. M. Schindler papers. 1904–1954).

L.A. Board of Park Commissioners. (1940, February 9). Permit to Plant Street Trees, No. 4189. (R. M. Schindler papers. 1904–1954).

L.A. Building and Safety Commission. (1939a, May 29). Letter to Mr. R. M. Schindler. (R. M. Schindler papers. 1904–1954).

L.A. Building and Safety Commission, Letter to Mr. R. M. Schindler dated June 12, 1939b. (R. M. Schindler papers. 1904–1954).

L.A. Building and Safety Commission. (1940, January 29). Letter to Mr. R. M. Schindler. (R. M. Schindler papers. 1904–1954).

L.A. City Planning Commission. (1928). *Annual Report*. Los Angeles, CA: L.A. City Archive.

L.A. City Planning Commission. (1929). *Annual Report*. Los Angeles, CA: L.A. City Archive.

L.A. City Planning Commission. (1930). *Annual Report*. Los Angeles, CA: L.A. City Archive.

L.A. City Planning Commission. (1931). *Annual Report*. Los Angeles, CA: L.A. City Archive.

L.A. City Planning Commission. (1935). *Annual Report for year ending June 30, 1935*. Los Angeles, CA: L.A. City Archive.

L.A. City Planning Commission. (1952). *Accomplishments 1951*. Los Angeles, CA: L.A. City Archive.

L.A. City Planning Commission. (1953). *Accomplishments 1952*. Los Angeles, CA: L.A. City Archive.

L.A. City Planning Department. (2017). *Miracle Mile Historic Preservation Overlay Zone, LA Ordinance 184334*. Los Angeles, CA: City of Los Angeles.

L.A. County Department of Public Works. (1922a, November 14). Tract No. 4031.

L.A. County Department of Public Works. (1922b, December 13). Tract No. 5070.

L.A. Department of Building and Safety. (1926, March 9). Building Permit No. 7206. Los Angeles, CA: LADBS, Building Records Section.

L.A. Department of Building and Safety (1939a, June 14). Building Permit No. LA23497. Los Angeles, CA: LADBS, Building Records Section.

L.A. Department of Building and Safety. (1939b, June 14). Building Permit No. LA23498. Los Angeles, CA: LADBS, Building Records Section.

L.A. Department of Building and Safety. (1940, February 29). Certificate of Occupancy for Permit No. LA23497. Los Angeles, CA: LADBS, Building Records Section.

Los Angeles Directory Company. (1938). *Los Angeles City Directory 1938*. Los Angeles, CA: Los Angeles Directory Company.

Mackey, P. (1939a, June 17). Letter to R. M. Schindler. (R. M. Schindler papers. 1904–1954).

Mackey, P. (1939b, July 12). Letter to R. M. Schindler. (R. M. Schindler papers. 1904–1954).

Mackey, P. (1940, April 30). Letter to R. M. Schindler. (R. M. Schindler papers. 1904–1954).

McCoy, E. (1960). *Five California Architects*. New York, NY: Reinhold Book Corporation.

New Construction Well Stabilized for 1927. (1927, January 2). *Los Angeles Times*, 18. Retrieved from www.proquest.com

Niederhofer. (1939, November 15). Plan Check Document, Final Inspection (R. M. Schindler papers. 1904–1954).

Official Atlas, District Zoning Maps. (1924). Los Angeles, CA: L.A. City Archive.

Outlook Sound for Realty, State Commissioner Sees Better Market for All Properties. (1939, December 3). *Los Angeles Times*, E2. Retrieved from www.proquest.com

Schindler, R. M. (1939a, January 20). Estimate for the Return on Apartment Bldg for Mrs. Pearl Mackey. (R. M. Schindler papers. 1904–1954)

Schindler, R. M. (1939b, July 5). Letter to Pearl Mackey. (R. M. Schindler papers. 1904–1954).

Schindler, R. M. (1939c, July 14). Letter to Pearl Mackey. (R. M. Schindler papers. 1904–1954).

Schindler, R. M. (1940a, May 1). Letter to Pearl Mackey. (R. M. Schindler papers. 1904–1954).

Schindler, R. M. (1940b). Mrs. Pearl Mackey Plant List. (R. M. Schindler papers. 1904–1954).

Sheine, J. (1998). *R. M. Schindler, Works and Projects*. Barcelona: Editorial Gustavo Gili, SA.

Standard Form of Agreement Between Owner and Architect, November 28, 1938. R. M. Schindler, Architect, Pearl Mackey, Owner (R. M. Schindler papers. 1904–1954).

State of California—The Resources Agency, Department of Parks and Recreation. (2015a, July). Primary Record 1060 S. Cochran.

State of California—The Resources Agency, Department of Parks and Recreation. (2015b, July). Primary Record 1137 S. Cochran.

Subdivision Activity Breaks Past Record. (1922, December 3). *Los Angeles Times*, V1. Retrieved from www.proquest.com

Thornton, R., & Wolicki, D. P. (2004). *California's Kit Homes, A Reprint of the 1925 Pacific Ready-Cut Homes catalog*. Alton, IL: Gentle Beam Publications.

Trend Study Promises Land Valuation Increase. (1939, July 16). *Los Angeles Times*, E2. Retrieved from www.proquest.com

Uptrend of Rents Shown in Extensive Los Angeles Survey. (1937, August 22). *Los Angeles Times*, E2. Retrieved from www.proquest.com

Warn Against Over Building. (1924, March 13). *Los Angeles Times*, 14. Retrieved from www.proquest.com

Weston, R. D. (1922). *Weston's Single and Double Bungalows, An Illustrated Book Devoted to Beautiful and Convenient Homes of One and Two Families*. Los Angeles, CA: R. D. Weston.

Zone Condition Draws Protest. (1928, December 2). *Los Angeles Times*, E1. Retrieved from www.proquest.com

6 Crafting Cost Benefit, Stucco Box/Podium Apartments

1411 N. Hayworth Avenue vs. Hollywood Riviera Apartments

Figure 6.1 Case Study 6: Stucco Box/Podium, 1411 N. Hayworth Avenue vs. Hollywood Riviera Apartments.

Introduction

When Incrementally Innovative Design Supports Real Estate Development Goals

Many factors worked to shape apartment buildings in Los Angeles from the mid-1950s into the 1960s. Rising apartment demand and increasing zoning standards drove the development of denser housing, including the dingbat apartment, a boxy two-story building with tuck-under parking and embellished facade. Trends in apartment lifestyles and rising parking ratios underwrote the stucco box apartment, similar to the dingbat, but usually two or three stories over two lots allowing more room for a central courtyard and, most important, a pool. And, finally, when parking requirements were further increased, stipulating multiple spaces per unit in addition to guest parking, the podium apartment building emerged. This model tucks parking one-half, one or even two levels under a wood or concrete base (i.e., podium), building wood-frame apartments above. These three types of apartment buildings were seemingly driven by a singular focus on yield, ruthlessly efficient with no room for architecture or design except on their extroverted facades. But is maximizing unit count and limiting detail the only way designers can contribute to profitability? A comparative case study of a developer-built apartment building in West Hollywood at 1411 North Hayworth Avenue (1958) and the Hollywood Riviera Apartments (1954), located directly across the street, contrasts two very different design approaches to real estate development and planning regulation (Figure 6.1).

The Stucco Box Apartment

Stucco box apartments are two- and three-story blocky stucco-over-wood-frame buildings with minimal detailing built to maximum lot coverage. They were built with clean lines, smooth surfaces and flat roofs on the sides and rear but had more flamboyant street-facing facades, with scripted font signage, outsized light fixtures and exotic landscaping. Architecture critic and urban designer John Chase observed how the stucco box was simultaneously both more exuberant and more Modern than earlier housing types:

> The stucco-surfaced speculative apartment house is a symbol, for good or for ill, of that golden age of Los Angeles, the 1950s. It was a time when Southern California seemed to come into its own, as a place where social and economic mobility combined with a benign climate to create a mythic good life, accessible, it seemed, to almost everyone. The stucco box apartment house reflected at once the pragmatic and hedonistic character of Southern California.
>
> (Chase, 2000, p. 3)

Built on a single lot, stucco box apartments are usually called dingbats, with a patterned, veneered or festooned front facade maşking 5 to 12 functional apartment units. Larger stucco box apartments were usually built over two lots, included a common courtyard with a pool and have also been called garden courts or garden apartments by preservationists (Architectural Resources Group [ARG], 2008; Treffers, 2012) (Figure 6.2). Stucco boxes with courtyards arguably have more livability than dingbats and certainly promised a more glamorous lifestyle. They may have been less exuberant on their face, but life around the pool was plenty animated. Parking for both dingbats and larger stucco boxes was "tucked under" the building at grade in open carports on the front, side and rear of the building. In West Hollywood, most stucco box buildings replaced either existing single-family homes or smaller apartment buildings in established neighborhoods (Figures 6.2 and 6.3).

Podium Apartments

Less exuberant and more insular, podium apartments emerged in the late 1950s and 1960s, as cities throughout Southern California began to intensify their on-site residential parking requirements in response to increasing car ownership. Parking that had been required at one space per unit was now required at one-and-a-half and even two spaces per unit, depending on unit size, and parking for guests also began to be mandated. Consequently, apartment buildings could no longer be surface parked and built to the maximum underlying density of their

Figure 6.2 A selection of stucco box/podium apartment buildings in West Hollywood.

Figure 6.3 The Hollywood Riviera Apartments and stucco box/podium buildings in West Hollywood, mapped, including 1411 N. Hayworth Avenue (1).

zone. Architects and builders began experimenting with ways to overlap building and parking, initially by placing the building on stilts over ground level surface parking (stucco box apartments, often on hillside sites), building the parking half underground with the building above (many mid-century "minimal traditional" courtyard apartments) and, eventually, fully enclosed underground using a concrete podium, which is a typology still being built today. This strategy elevates the common area for the apartment above the street, further removing it from the public realm.

Architect Edward H. Fickett's West Hollywood apartment buildings express this type of experimentation and transition. At the Sunset Patio Apartments (1127 Horn, 1948) cars are surfaced parked in carports to the left of the building. The Sunset Lanai (1422 North Sweetzer, 1950) parks cars totally underneath the residential building on a very steep hillside site on grade with the lowest point of the lot. And the Fountain Lanai (1285 North Sweetzer, 1953) digs a half level down to park cars underneath the residential buildings, leaving the driveway open to the sky. The Hollywood Riviera combines these solutions, placing parking a half level down over half of the sloping site in a covered carport under the building with the driveway open to the courtyard above. By contrast, 1411 North Hayworth is parked in a concrete podium under the residential building, at grade with the lowest corner of the site.

Development Histories

1411 North Hayworth Avenue was built in West Hollywood in 1958 by developer Nathan Nadal, located between Sunset Boulevard and Fountain Avenue just south of the Sunset Strip (Figure 6.4). The building was designed by architect Jack Chernoff. Its two-story, C-shaped building houses 20 apartment units around a small courtyard and pool above a concrete parking podium. The building's site slopes down dramatically from north to south so that the parking podium is almost fully underground at the northern property line and at grade at the southern property line. The podium houses one parking space per unit plus eight additional spaces with a gated entrance at the center of the front facade. A triangular-shaped stair to the south leads up to the main entrance of the building at podium level. Once inside, a breezeway leads out to the pool deck and two stairways leading to the upper units. The building is single-loaded to the interior of the building so that circulation overlooks the pool. The building's style is low Modern, with minimal detailing, aluminum frame windows and a flagstone skirt

Figure 6.4 By-right case study project: 1411 North Hayworth Avenue in West Hollywood.

on the podium. The building is a vernacular example of a podium building that did not require any discretionary approvals.

The Hollywood Riviera Apartments, located directly across the street at 1400 North Hayworth Avenue, was designed by Fickett and developed by Julian Weinstock and Associates in 1954 (Figures 6.5 and 6.6). Its square building, built over two lots, defines a common courtyard with subtropical landscaping, an irregularly shaped pool and an open parking area. There are a total of 38 units, mostly small one bedrooms, all accessed either directly from the pool deck or from open, single-loaded corridors ringing the courtyard. Similar to 1411 North Hayworth, the building's site drops dramatically from north to south. Parking, one stall per unit plus 13 additional tandem spaces, is located on the southern half of the site, excavated half a level down. The parking is open air but tucked under the building volume so that the building's outdoor corridors bridge over it. An in-ground pool occupies the northern half of the courtyard, on grade with the building entrance. The building's style is Mid-Century Modern characterized by floor-to-ceiling glass, post-and-beam detailing and double-height exterior fins on the front facade. A zone variance was obtained for the double-height third story at the northwest corner of the building. It was designated as a local historical landmark in 2010 (City of West Hollywood, 2010).

Both the case study buildings, like many of the era, are amalgams of former and future typologies. They have features of dingbats, stucco boxes and podium apartments, somewhat chaotically intermixed, before larger scale, higher density buildings built on concrete podiums with underground parking became the norm.

Design

Context

Modernism was flourishing at the time the case study projects were built, perhaps working to transform apartment design more from a

Figure 6.5 By-design case study project: The Hollywood Riviera Apartments located at 1400 North Hayworth Avenue in West Hollywood.

Figure 6.6 Rendering of the Hollywood Riviera Apartments early in the design process before Fickett decided to use a butterfly roof on the front volume of the building.

Credit: Rendering, Hollywood Riviera Apartments, 1953, Edward H. Fickett, FAIA, Collection, USC Special Collections.

low-Modern, rather than high-Modern perspective. By the mid-1950s, the large-scale "Minimal Traditional" and "Vernacular Modern" garden apartment era had waned, in favor of smaller scale stucco box and dingbat apartments that could be built quickly and cheaply:

> Although commercial vernacular architecture often borrows from high architecture, it nonetheless has a life of its own complete with its own vocabulary of forms, design methodology and set of individual designers.
>
> (Chase, 2000, p. 3)

Since the spatial organization and unit layout of these buildings was so formulaic, the conscious "design" of these "glamorously packaged consumer objects" was typically limited to street-facing facades and, if present, interior courtyards (Chase, 2000, p. 3). These often merely signaled "Modern" and a variety of other styles, with paper-thin details that were sometimes just painted on. These details were valued for their graphic, two-dimensional interest as shapes against the backdrop of the building facade, not as three-dimensional forms that shaped space, which effectively disassociated the facade from the volume of the building. The sides and rear of these buildings could also be perceived as "thin" with smooth, abstract volumes and nail-on aluminum windows flush with the building's stucco envelope with little to create shadow or depth. Architects Jack Chernoff, Sam Reisbord, A. J. Arnay Herman Fidler, John Day and Max Starkman were all dingbat and stucco box apartment designers working in the 1950s (Chase, 2000).

Jack Chernoff

Jack Chernoff (whom we met in Chapter 1), architect of 1411 North Hayworth, was known for his high-yield buildings, so much so that his nickname was "Packin' Jack" (Nero, 1972, W24). Chernoff could shoehorn more units onto a site than other architects, even if it meant building at densities and in ways other architects wouldn't advise (Nero, 1972). From the mid-1950s to the early 1970s, Chernoff designed more than 2,000 apartment buildings for small developers, many on single lots like 1411 North Hayworth but also those that were built on two lots with a courtyard in the center like the Hollywood Riviera (Chase, 2000; Nero, 1972). Most were stucco box apartments with flat facades, flat roofs, efficient units and economical detailing. All were maximally dense. The Stardust Apartments at 3838 Gibraltar Street in Baldwin Hills situates 23 units over a 131-foot by 135-foot site, or 57 dwelling units per acre, including a landscaped courtyard, irregularly shaped pool and a bridge over a Japanese garden at the entry (Photo Standalone 18, 1958, F3). A two-story apartment project at 235 South Normandie in what is now Koreatown yielded 14 units on a 50-foot by 160-foot lot, or 76 dwelling units per acre (New Apartment, 1956, E20). The San Pasqual Apartments built at 412 San Pasqual Avenue in Highland Park in 1964 yielded 16 units on a 50-foot by 162-foot site, or 85 dwelling units per acre, also two stories (Ground Broken, 1964, H12). Chernoff also designed many apartments in West Hollywood, including 1411 North Fairfax Avenue, 1350 North Laurel Avenue and 1275 Havenhurst Drive (Architectural Resources Group, 2008, p. 58).

Edward H. Fickett, FAIA

Edward H. Fickett, architect of the Hollywood Riviera Apartments, designed a total of six apartment buildings in West Hollywood, including those discussed in the introduction as well as the Laurel Terrace Apartments at 1245 North Laurel (1949) and the Sunset Capri at 8341 Sunset (1952), but he was a prolific designer who worked on all types of projects. Fickett is known for his close collaborations with merchant builders and the tens of thousands of single-family homes built in Southern California at his direction (The Fickett Formula, 1953). The son, grandson and nephew of builders and developers, he grew up working on construction sites and respected all points of view on the business. Fickett initially worked for architect Sumner Spaulding and became licensed in 1947 (Winship, 2011). He opened his own office in 1949. His single-family homes, both custom and tract, were known for the way they brought the outside in and opened up kitchens, with vaulted ceilings and exposed beams. He often used partial height walls, homemaker-oriented innovations and family rooms and was "a pioneer of the modified modern through decoupling the post-and-beam method of construction from the post-and-beam aesthetic" (Winship, 2011, xiii). Fickett worked for many homebuilders early in his career including Ray Hommes, Coronet Construction Company, Hobart Williams, Ponty-Built Homes and Seacrest Construction Company (Winship, 2011, p. 70). "In all these cases, Fickett was content to incrementally educate developers on the merits of modern design in mass production housing" (Winship, 2001, p. 71).

Most notably given the interests of the case studies in this book, Fickett worked to create opportunities for dialog across housing professions throughout his career and encouraged civic engagement and professional collaboration among architects, builders and regulators. Fickett participated in home design clinics, National Association of Homebuilders conferences and AIA lecture series that brought the industry together. In 1950, for example, Fickett formed a committee of five architects to work with merchant builders and see how architects could be involved in reducing construction costs. In 1955 Fickett was nominated to be part of the seven-man Federal Housing Administration (FHA) Architectural Standards Advisory Committee "to study and make recommendations for revision of the Federal architectural code" (L.A. Architect, 1955, E6). He coordinated entire issues of important journals, including "The Architect and the Homebuilder," a special 1960 issue of the *AIA Journal* exploring architect/builder collaboration. Fickett chaired the AIA National Homebuilding committee beginning in 1959 and was president of the Los Angeles chapter of the AIA in 1962. All in the service of "better buildings for people" (Architect—Client Forum, 1959, p. 14). "Ten years from now," architectural critic and historian Esther McCoy wrote, "Edward H. Fickett believes, practically all houses will be built by architect-builder teams; architects who resist this trend are clinging to the past" (McCoy, 1955, L22). Throughout,

> Fickett effectively acted as a mediator. He built both a network and a reputation for being a pragmatic architect who could speak the language of contractors, builders and bureaucrats alike.
>
> (Winship, 2011, p. 88)

Fickett was honored throughout his career with many National Association of Homebuilders Awards of Merit, a Progressive Architecture

Design Award in 1954 and two AIA Merit Awards in 1956 and 1957. He was named a Fellow of the American Association of Architects in 1969.

To what degree are 1411 North Hayworth Avenue and the Hollywood Riviera Apartments similar or different from a design perspective? Does the Hollywood Riviera's status as a local landmark mean that it is better designed than 1411 North Hayworth? Does the fact that 1411 North Hayworth was built by-right mean that it lacks architectural value?

Parking Strategy *Partially Underground Single Lot vs. Partially Underground Double Lot*

Sites for both case study projects slope down from north to south and are partially excavated for parking, under the full structure for 1411 North Hayworth, and under the southern half of the Hollywood Riviera Apartments (Figure 6.7). Both projects are set 15 feet back from the front property line and minimally set back from the side and rear, about 5 feet. The Hollywood Riviera's double lot is more than twice the size of 1411 North Hayworth Avenue's single lot, 29,888 square feet as compared to 14,838 square feet.

Building Organization and Massing
Two- and Three-Story "C"-Shaped vs.
Two- and Three-Story "O"-Shaped

Both case study buildings are shaped around open space, but the open space at the Hollywood Riviera is larger and more communal than that at

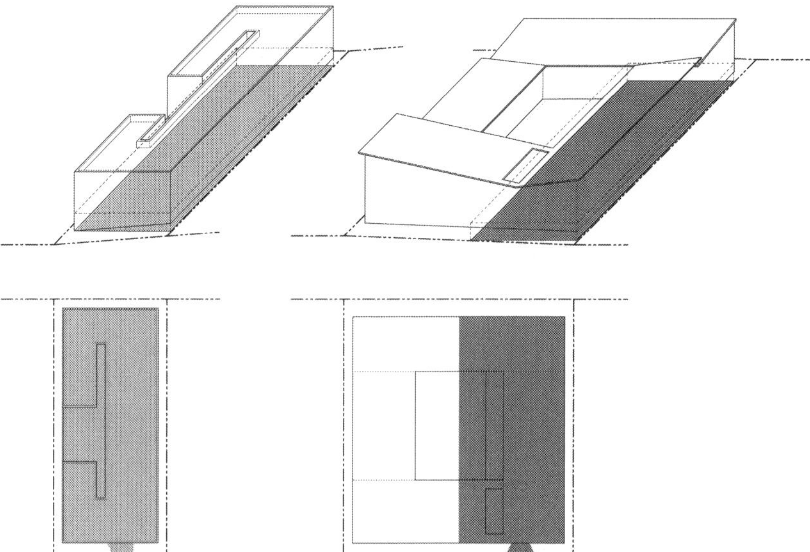

Figure 6.7 Vehicular access and parking diagrams: 1411 North Hayworth Avenue (left) vs. The Hollywood Riviera Apartments (right).

1411 North Hayworth. 1411 North Hayworth's two-story "C"-shaped structure, defines a 50-foot by 33-foot (1,650-square-foot) courtyard at the podium level on the south side of the building, which is mostly taken up by a small oval-shaped pool. The structure has a flat roof.

The Hollywood Riviera Apartments is an "O"-shaped, almost square building, three stories on the northwest corner and two stories everywhere else. Parking is half a story underground under the southern half of the site, making this portion of the structure two-and-a-half stories at the street. The building defines a 70-foot by 75-foot (5,250-square-foot) courtyard in the center of the structure with an irregularly shaped pool on the northern two-thirds. The building has a butterfly roof on the front (i.e., a roof with two opposing wings that meet in a valley) and a shed roof (i.e., a single-angle roof) on the sides and rear.

Unit Types, Sizes and Amenities *Spacious and Compartmentalized vs. Compact and Volumetric*

Units in 1411 North Hayworth Avenue are more spacious than those in the Hollywood Riviera, but the Hollywood Rivera's units have more character. 1411 North Hayworth Avenue houses 20 units, each averaging 926 square feet. There are nine one-bedroom, one-bath units, three one-bedroom two-bath units, six two-bedroom two-bath units and two two-bedroom three-bath units. Units range from 691 to 1,725 square feet and spaces are very enclosed as was typical in the 1950s.

The Hollywood Riviera Apartments contains 38 units, each averaging 670 square feet, smaller than the smallest unit in 1411 North Hayworth. There are 32 one-bedroom one-bath units, three two-bedroom two-bath units and two three-bedroom two-bath units and one two-bedroom three-bath. Units range from 611 to 1,102 square feet. Those on the second level all have vaulted ceilings and modified post-and-beam construction giving them more volume and a greater sense of spaciousness even though they are relatively small. Apartment interiors also made liberal use of floor to ceiling glass, transom windows and partial height walls. Entries, living rooms and some bedrooms overlook the courtyard pool while kitchens and outdoor spaces face out into the surrounding neighborhood. Living spaces are open plan. (Making an apples-to-apples comparison and imagining that the Hollywood Riviera building was a single-lot building, it would have 19 units compared to 20 at 1411 North Hayworth.)

Pedestrian Access, Entry and Circulation *Single-Loaded vs. Single-Loaded*

Both case study buildings use single-loaded circulation systems (Figure 6.8). Pedestrians enter 1411 North Hayworth via a large exterior stair, coupled with the parking entrance at the center of the front facade.

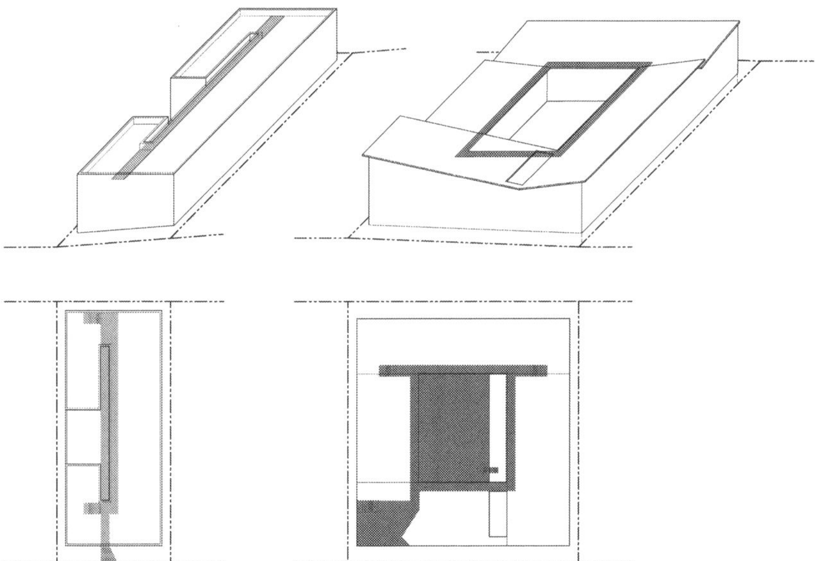

Figure 6.8 Pedestrian circulation diagrams: 1411 North Hayworth Avenue (left) vs. The Hollywood Riviera Apartments (right).

The inset glass entry doors are approximately 8 feet above the street. These lead out to the pool deck from which the stairways and single-loaded corridor are accessible.

Pedestrians enter the Hollywood Riviera Apartments through an open-air, at-grade common entry toward the northern corner of the building. This is now enclosed in floor-to-ceiling glass on two sides but was originally open. The entry leads to a common stair on the left, straight out to the pool deck and to a corridor connecting ground-level units on the right. Second-level apartments are accessed via an exterior corridor ringing the courtyard.

Vehicular Access and Parking *One Car per Unit + 8 vs. One Car per Unit + 13*

The Hollywood Riviera provides a more attractive parking area for its tenants than 1411 North Hayworth at a time when car ownership was increasing. The building at 1411 North Hayworth provides 28 parking spaces in an enclosed concrete parking podium, which is dark and unfriendly. The Hollywood Riviera provides 51 spaces, tucked under the southern half of the building but open to the courtyard, accessed by a driveway under the trough of the butterfly roof. An angled exterior stair leads up from the parking area to the pool deck. The daylighting and strong connection to the common courtyard make it a more inviting space.

Common Open Space *Pool Dominated vs. Pool + Deck + Landscape*

Both case study projects provide common open space with outdoor pools, but the space at 1411 North Hayworth is cramped while that at the Hollywood Riviera is spacious (Figure 6.9). The 1,650-square-foot common open space at 1411 North Hayworth is dominated by a pool, leaving only two small areas for lounging and a narrow corridor along its length.

The Hollywood Riviera's 5,250-square-foot courtyard space is three-quarters pool deck and one-quarter open to the parking area below. The diagonally shaped in-ground pool leaves plenty of deck for lounging plus space for a BBQ, patio tables and landscaping in raised planters. Its common space is over three times as large as 1411 North Hayworth's. (However, evaluating the projects on a more apples-to-apples basis, if we cut the Hollywood Riviera in half and imagine it as a single-lot building, its open space would be 2,625 square feet, 1.6 times larger than 1411 North Hayworth.)

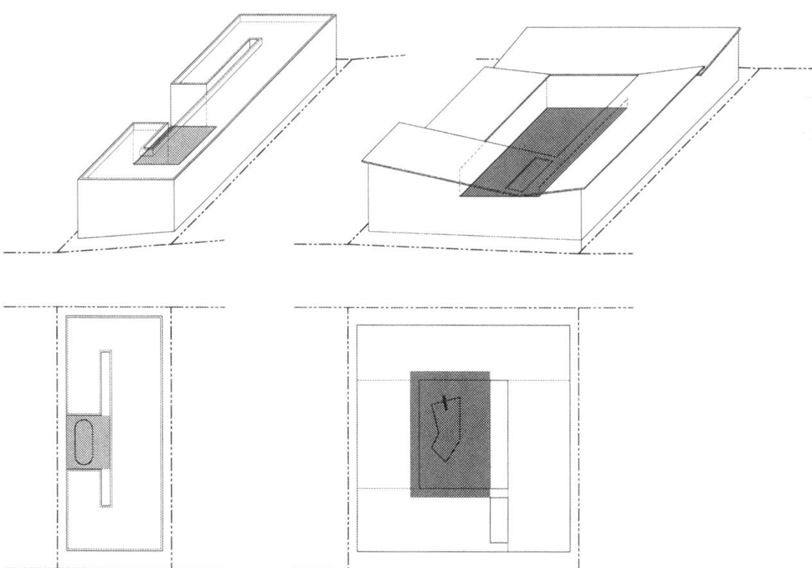

Figure 6.9 Common open space diagrams: 1411 North Hayworth Avenue (left) vs. The Hollywood Riviera Apartments (right).

Private Open Space *Standard vs. Substantial*

Both projects provide private open space for their residents in the form of patios and balconies primarily facing "in" at 1411 North Hayworth and facing "out" at the Hollywood Riviera. At 1411 North Hayworth, all units have small patios on the podium level or slim balconies on the second story. The balconies for units on the sides of the building face in toward the pool while those on the front and back look out into the neighborhood.

Most of the units at the Hollywood Riviera also have patio and balcony spaces. Of the 18 units on the first floor, 16 have patios while 10 of 20 units on the second floor have balconies spanning the full width of the unit facing out into the neighborhood.

Structure and Materials *Wood frame vs. Wood frame + Modified Post-and-Beam*

Both 1411 North Hayworth and the Hollywood Riviera are built of wood frame construction with a stucco exterior, but the Hollywood Riviera's second and third stories are built in a modified post-and-beam construction. This allows the ceilings of the units on these levels to be vaulted, enclosing a greater volume of space making the units feel more spacious. Posts and ceiling beams also give these units more architectural character.

Architectural Style *Vernacular Modern vs. Mid-Century Modern*

Both 1411 North Hayworth and the Hollywood Riviera can be classified as Mid-Century Modern in terms of their architectural style, but the Hollywood Riviera's version of Modern is more detailed and of greater integrity. The architecture of 1411 North Hayworth could perhaps be better characterized as "Vernacular Modern," a low Modern style that takes some characteristics of the high Modern and popularizes or commercializes them. The smooth stucco surfaces, aluminum frame windows and louvered windows of 1411 North Hayworth all characterize this style. The building's only real detailing occurs on the front facade, with a canted balcony and roof overhang that spans the entire front of the building, giving the structure an overall horizontal look. The base of the building is finished with a flagstone skirt. The front facade is dominated by the driveway leading down to the parking level and the front entry stair, which leads up to an inset entry well above the street.

Historical preservationists have called the architecture of the Hollywood Riviera "Googie" Style, architecture with a futurist orientation that reflects the space/atomic age (City of West Hollywood, 2010). *Los Angeles Times* architecture critic Aaron Betsky, who lived in the building in the early 1990s, called the building's style "Swiss Chalet" and argues that "salmon" wasn't its original color (Betsky, 1994). Regardless, the building is definitely Mid-Century Modern and exemplifies many hallmarks of the style, from its double-height fins on the front facade to its louvered jalousie windows to its canted balcony fronts with vertical wood siding. The facade's scripted signage, butterfly roof, fins, bridging balconies and dense front landscaping create animation and interesting detail, while the open entrance makes the second and third floors appear to float. Floating exterior stairs, bridging corridors, combed plywood and pipe railings characterize the courtyard space. The second-floor units have transom windows above what would be the third-floor line. Overall it is considered representative of Fickett's work and a good example of a mid-1950s stucco box apartment (City of West Hollywood, 2010).

Outcomes *Chock-a-Block vs. Small-yet-Spacious*

The design of 1411 North Hayworth Avenue is an exercise in space planning, whereas the Hollywood Riviera makes deliberate decisions around important elements of housing design. 1411 North Hayworth crams together every important housing feature marketable at the time it was built on to a single site. Its amenities, a wide range of unit sizes and types, private open space and a courtyard with a pool, all come at the expense of the building feeling positively overstuffed. The pool takes up most of the courtyard, corridors are narrow and private open space is not large enough to be usable. As a result, everything feels compromised. Chernoff would have been better off forgoing some features in order to make others more impactful. Overall the building doesn't really feel designed, and its "architecture" characterized by blocky overhangs and flagstone veneer.

The design of the Hollywood Riviera clearly trades off unit size and diversity for a larger and more appealing common area and a focus on an outgoing lifestyle. The building's small units encouraged people to participate in the social life of the building and ensured that residents would be singles and couples, but not families, who would enjoy that social scene. The architecture is inventive, consistent and well-detailed.

Real Estate Development

Context

Waning Single-Family Home Development

By the mid-1950s the market for single-family homes in Los Angeles was nearing saturation. The price of land, labor and materials all rose between 1955 and 1957, and single-family development fell by half (NAHB Economist, 1955, E16). Homebuilders began doing more to differentiate their product, offering larger, more luxurious homes with more (and more ridiculous) amenities to compete (Winship, 2011, p. 28). Homes now had three and four bedrooms and occasionally convertible dens, with at least two bathrooms instead of one. "Lanais" (covered porches or verandas), knotty pine kitchens, family rooms, sliding glass doors and intercom systems proliferated, as it became harder and harder for potential homeowners to obtain a loan. By the end of the decade, builders were trying to get homeowners to "trade up" to a larger home. As prices and required down payments escalated, developers introduced no down payment plans as well as rent-to-own packages.

Upswing in Apartments

As the demand for single-family homes stalled, a boom in multifamily housing was taking shape. An upswing in Americans' savings rates, a rise in the population of young people and favorable tax treatment all fueled low-rise apartment development (Smith, 1964). Most of these buildings were built speculatively and were intended to be sold to investors upon completion. Many were dingbats with 10 to 12 units on a single lot, but, increasingly, they were larger stucco box structures over two lots with 20 or more apartments. In contrast to the large-scale garden apartments built in the late 1930s through the early 1950s, these were erected without government subsidy or guarantee and were funded largely by insurance companies, which were building apartments all over the county, not just in individual communities. Investors bought these buildings not for their underlying cash flow but, rather, for their tax benefits (Smith, 1964).

Apartment building, which had been dampened by the Depression, wartime rent controls and a general bias toward single-family homes, boomed in Los Angeles by the beginning of 1957 (Apartment House, 1957, A6). In 1957, permits for multiple dwelling units in the City of Los Angeles outpaced those for single-family homes for the first time since the 1920s, yet the vacancy rate for these buildings remained relatively low at 5.7% in 1960 (Accomplishments, 1960, p. 32).

Cultural Shift

As the baby boomers came of age, a significant cultural shift was also taking place. Boomers were getting married later and planned to live differently than their parents, shedding traditional values and pushing for change. This shift is evident in apartment advertising which touted heated pools, maid service, soundproofing, knotty pine kitchens and even Ping-Pong (Figures 6.10 and 6.11). Decorating advice columns had

Figure 6.10 The pool lifestyle was attractive to young apartment dwellers in the 1950s.

Credit: Young people swimming and playing around a pool, 1940–1950, California Historical Society Collection, 1860–1960, USC Special Collections.

Figure 6.11 The Hollywood Riviera Apartment's irregularly shaped courtyard pool.

Credit: de Gennaro, Photograph, Hollywood Riviera Apartments, 1953, Edward H. Fickett, FAIA, Collection, USC Special Collections.

headlines like "With planning, a new look: Dressing a drab apartment," "The Two-Faced Lounge: A bright solution for the 1-room apartment problem" and "Outdoor living on an apartment balcony" (Lenox, 1959, H8; Richardson, 1958, TW26; With Planning, 1958, J42). Advice on "apartment etiquette" was even offered in the newspaper (Noise Bugs, 1959, A1). West Hollywood, which had more apartment buildings than anywhere else in the county, became associated with a glamorous lifestyle, with celebrities reveling on the Sunset Strip, risqué house parties and a laid-back apartment pool lifestyle. "Lanai" was appended to virtually everything, infusing a resort atmosphere into everyday living.

Nathan E. Nadel

Nathan E. Nadel, developer of 1411 North Hayworth, was a contractor working in Los Angeles by the early 1940s. He was born in St. Petersburg,

Russia, and lived with his wife, Mary, in Angelino Heights, South Los Angeles, Mar Vista and then, finally, West Hills.

Julian Weinstock, Julian Weinstock and Associates

Julian Weinstock, developer of the Hollywood Riviera Apartments, had a long and prolific career in real estate developing a variety of housing types. He began in the late 1940s working as an architect designing custom single-family homes. Once he found that he enjoyed the construction process much more than the design process, however, he left the architecture profession and started his own construction company (Julian Weinstock, 1993). Weinstock moved into development in the early 1950s, and Julian Weinstock and Associates was among the larger scale homebuilders working in postwar Los Angeles, building thousands of homes in the San Fernando Valley by the end of the decade.[1] He often built multiple tracts at the same time at a range of price points. Some, like Granada Hills Estates, were "contemporary" homes, designed by Fickett, with open-beam ceilings, breezeways and breakfast bars, but many more, like homes in Walnut Haven, College Estates and Whitsett Park, were traditionally styled without named architects in their advertising. Weinstock's tracts were often advertised as "Indoor-Outdoor Living at its Best" with "custom construction" and one even featured Mrs. Carole (Robert) Foran, "Mrs. California 1961" at its grand opening (Grand Opening, 1960, M12).

While he was building tracts of single-family homes, Weinstock also constructed and developed many apartment buildings in Beverly Hills, West Hollywood and Los Feliz. Right before the Hollywood Riviera, Weinstock completed the Holiday Apartments at 1263 North Hayworth in late 1953, a two-story courtyard building with a pool and 28 one- and two-bedroom apartments. The building featured private outdoor space for each unit, sliding glass doors, tropical plantings and post lanterns to make it look like a small village at night ($320,000 Building, 1953, E24). He built the Franklin Riviera in Los Feliz in 1959, which rented resort-style one- and two-bedroom apartments from $165 and up (Classified Ad 38, 1959, B31). By the early 1960s, however, Weinstock had changed his focus to high-rise luxury apartments in central locations, capitalizing on the market for people who had "outgrown" their large houses and were tired of the upkeep that a single-family home required. He built Doheny Plaza in Beverly Hills in 1964, the Los Angeles area's first "air-space subdivision," or condominium (New Ownership Plan, 1963, N14).

To what degree are 1411 North Hayworth Avenue and the Hollywood Riviera Apartments similar or different from a real estate development perspective? Does the Hollywood Riviera's status as a local landmark mean that it was less profitable than 1411 North Hayworth? Does the fact that 1411 North Hayworth was built as-of-right mean it was a better investment?

Subdivision *Crescent Heights Tract vs. Crescent Heights Tract*

The town of Sherman, which eventually became West Hollywood, was settled in 1896, established by Moses H. Sherman and Eli P. Clark, who built the Pasadena and Pacific interurban railways connecting the city of Los Angeles to Santa Monica. The town housed rail workers just to the west of San Vincente Boulevard, and the rail line followed what is now Santa Monica Boulevard. Two blocks north, land for both 1411 North Hayworth and the Hollywood Riviera was subdivided in 1905 into 80-foot by 190-foot blocks as part of the Crescent Heights Tract by the Title Insurance Trust Company, partly in the incorporated City of Los Angeles and partly on unincorporated county land. Originally part of Rancho La Brea, the area was agricultural until the late 1890s, growing citrus and winter vegetables at the base of the Hollywood Hills (Masters, 2011). The Pacific Electric Railway ran cars down Santa Monica between 1911 and 1941.

By the 1920s, Sherman's population was booming, and the town began to merge with Hollywood, its neighbor to the east, which was incorporated into the City of Los Angeles in 1910. Already informally known as "West Hollywood," Sherman voted against annexation into Los Angeles in 1924 and voted to officially change its name to West Hollywood in 1925, rejecting East Beverly, Magnetic Springs and Beverly Park (Masters, 2011). Entertainment was an important part of West Hollywood's economy from the early 1900s, home to important movie studios, like the Pickford-Fairbanks Studios, and movie industry workers. The area became a center for nightlife in the 1920s, with glamorous restaurants, hotels and nightclubs on the Sunset Strip including the Trocadero, Ciro's and Mocambo, all fueled by gambling, which was legal in West Hollywood as part of unincorporated Los Angeles County but not in Hollywood, which was part of the city proper. Elegant high-rise apartment buildings were also built at this time, all in exquisitely detailed eclectic styles to house notable entertainers and celebrities. The renter population was, in the main, singles and couples without children. By the 1950s, however, the popularity of the Strip with the rich and famous was waning in favor of Las Vegas, but the street was revitalized in the 1960s as a center for the music industry with clubs like The Roxy and Whisky-a-Go-Go.

Market Timing *Well Timed vs. Better Timed*

The Hollywood Riviera was better timed to market than 1411 North Hayworth since it was built earlier when both land and construction costs were lower, but in place by the time the apartment building boom was accelerating in 1957. By the mid-1950s, rising commute times were making living closer in more attractive and West Hollywood's glamor made it an appealing close-in location for baby boomers just coming of age. Because of rising costs, many single-family developers shifted to speculative apartment development, which was more economical, focusing redeveloping single lots with existing single-family homes (Smith, 1964). Small-scale apartments housing 10 to 16 units in a two-story wood-frame building on a single lot proliferated. By 1958, there was a vacancy scare. The Apartment Association of Los Angeles County, Inc. reported that vacancy rates for furnished apartments were 10.18% and unfurnished 8.15%, the highest experienced since 1929–1930 (Walsh, 1958, C8). By 1960, however, demand had increased again, and Keith Gordon reported that "Reconversion [was] Spurring a West Hollywood Boom," encouraging the large-scale redevelopment of existing residential properties, made more appealing to the apartment set because of their adjacency to luxurious Beverly Hills, Hollywood and the Hollywood Hills (Gordon, 1960, M11).

Building Cost *$233,600 vs. $210,300*

The Hollywood Riviera cost less overall and less per unit to build than 1411 North Hayworth Avenue. Permit records show that 1411 North Hayworth's building was built for $230,000 and its pool for $3,600 for a total of $233,600 or $11,680 per unit (State of California, Department of Parks and Recreation, 2007). The Hollywood Riviera was reported to cost $207,300 on its building permit plus $3,000 for the pool for a total of $210,300, or $5,534 per unit, 52% less. (State of California).[2] The building at 1411 North Hayworth Avenue cost $12.62 per rentable square foot (18,508 sq ft) while the Hollywood Rivera cost only $8.02, 36% less. (26,210 sq ft). Building small units allowed the Hollywood Riviera to build nearly twice as many units for a similar overall construction cost.[3]

Funding

Private banks, savings and loans and insurance companies all loaned funds for apartment development in the 1950s, and this is likely how Nathan Nadel funded 1411 North Hayworth Avenue. Presumably, Julian Weinstock funded his apartment investments with proceeds from sales in his single-family subdivisions, but if not, lenders were actively shifting their residential lending into apartments rather than single-family homes. Either way, the speculative apartment had such great tax advantages that low-rise dingbats and stucco boxes were valued less for their cash flow and more as a tax shelter. Indeed, net cash flow was often minimal, and most developers did not do any real market analysis (Smith, 1964). Land was typically not financed and was an equity investment.

The Internal Revenue Service (IRS) also gave favorable capital gains treatment to investors who intended to keep the apartment building as a long-term investment. This encouraged professional developers, whose gains would typically be taxed as ordinary income, to partner with "amateurs" who become developers "in name only" (Smith, 1964). This could potentially be how 1411 North Hayworth Avenue was built since Nadel is not known to have been involved in any other development projects. The IRS also allowed accelerated depreciation at double the straight line rate for "first users," applied to a declining balance (Smith, 1964). This meant apartments quickly built equity, and investors had losses they could apply to other income. In addition, since mortgage proceeds were not taxable, many developers held onto the apartments they built and simply "mortgaged out" of them (Smith, 1964). Mortgage funds were often almost as much as they might have gotten from a buyer.

Marketing and Absorption Resort Lifestyle vs. Resort Lifestyle

Marketing for both case study projects emphasized a carefree lifestyle filled with relaxed luxury and celebrity-like glamor. Unlike the Hollywood Riviera, 1411 North Hayworth, did not have an aspirational name, but it did advertise "Resort Living" with game rooms, a heated pool, garden and outdoor barbeques (Classified Ad 29, 1959, B22). Asking rent in 1959 was $165 and up. Assuming this rate for the smallest available apartment, a one-bedroom, one-bath of 691 square feet, translates to a rate of $0.24 cents per square foot. Based on this rate, rents at 1411 North Hayworth would have ranged from $165 to $268 (the largest unit is 1,118 sq ft), and gross monthly income would be about $4,441.

When first advertised in 1954, the Hollywood Riviera claimed to be the "finest modern apartment building in Southern California" with resort-style living that included private patios, mountain views, a heated swimming pool, expansive glass and beamed ceilings (Display Ad 115, 1954, E13). Rent for the project's smallest units, ranging from 611-square-foot to 739-square-foot studios (called a "living room and bedroom suite") was initially $125 and up. Assuming $125 for the smallest one-bedroom unit, the unit type's asking rent would range up to $155 per month, $0.20 a square foot. Asking rent for the project's largest unit, a penthouse with two bedrooms and two baths of 1,102 square feet, was $265, or $0.24 a square foot.

By 1957 rents for one-bedroom/one-bath apartments at the Hollywood Riviera had increased to $135 and up (Classified Ad 36, 1957, I35). The owners began to emphasize its tropical living amenities to compete with a growing number of new resort-style apartments, including the Hollywood Hawaiian and the Tahitian Apartments, many of which had hotel service and were rented month-to-month, daily or weekly, addressing the growing celebrity culture attracted to the Sunset Strip. By 1959, the area had no fewer than five apartments oriented around "Lanais," including the Sunset Lanai (also designed by Fickett), the Havenhurst Lanai, the Los Feliz Lanai, the Hollywood Lanai and the Sycamore Lanai. By 1959, the year 1411 North Hayworth came to market, units at the Hollywood Riviera were still renting for $135 and up, or $0.22 per square foot, generating about $5,766 in gross monthly income. At this time, advertising for the building emphasized its "Tropical Atmosphere" with furniture available, as well as a "Deluxe Quiet Dignified Atmosphere" for discriminating residents (Classified Ad 33, 1959, B27; Classified Ad 52, 1959, I47).

***Outcomes** Higher Construction Costs and Lower Gross Rents vs. Lower Construction Costs and Higher Gross Rents*

1411 North Hayworth spent 11% more on construction than the Hollywood Riviera to generate 23% less gross income, not accounting for land cost which would have increased the Hollywood Riviera's overall comparative cost. At least initially, however, both case study projects were reasonable investments that achieved profitability in different ways, though the Hollywood Riviera was better targeted to the population and culture of West Hollywood. Weinstock sold the Hollywood Riviera in the fall of 1955 to Mr. and Mrs. Joseph Cameo for $500,000, with two unimproved Beverly Hills parcels as part of the exchange (Article 41, 1955, F22).

Planning

Context

West Hollywood's development pattern in the first half of the twentieth century did not align with that of the rest of Los Angeles, city or county. The area's role as a hub of the entertainment industry; the fact that its industries, entertainment, oil and aviation, experienced less of a downturn and an earlier recovery from the Depression; along with more relaxed zoning standards; all encouraged intensive apartment development (ARG, 2008). West Hollywood was always denser than its surrounding communities, but really began to build up dramatically in the 1920s and 1930s in response to the need for housing for people who worked in the movie industry, cameramen and famous stars alike. Unlike most parts of Los Angeles, West Hollywood has whole blocks of tall luxury apartment buildings in elegant period styles dating from the 1920s and 1930s, mainly between Sweetzer and Fairfax and Sunset and Fountain (ARG, 2008). The county also allowed the building of multiple units in single-family zones so West Hollywood had an intermixture of dwelling types throughout its residential areas. By the 1940s, the West Hollywood was largely built out, so it did not see the kind of FHA-insured large-scale garden apartment development or vast tracts of single-family homes seen in many parts of Los Angeles. At this time, West Hollywood developers focused mostly on infill sites, developing familiar Los Angeles housing types, duplexes, house courts and flats (ARG, 2008).

By the time 1411 North Hayworth Avenue and the Hollywood Riviera were built, West Hollywood was 1.9 square miles of unincorporated county surrounded by the City of Los Angeles to the north, south and east and Beverly Hills to the west. New multifamily housing types, the dingbat, stucco box and podium apartments, were introduced in the 1950s and 1960s, which destroyed some single-family neighborhoods. Lax zoning had meant that West Hollywood integrated multifamily housing with single-family on mixed blocks rather than ringing multifamily housing on commercial streets around protected enclaves of R1 like the City of Los Angeles. But then many in these same neighborhoods requested a zone change from R1 to R3 in the 1950s (ARG, 2008, p. 37). This, coupled with the need for increased parking capacity, ensured that areas that were once a mix of single-family homes and small-scale apartments now had larger, boxier, more modern housing. By the end of the 1950s, apartment buildings dominated the West Hollywood residential landscape.

The 1400 block of North Hayworth Avenue is a microcosm of this development history, and its development timeline tracks the evolution of parking's impact upon housing design. While West Hollywood had been served by the trolley system, by the early 1940s living in West Hollywood required a car. There are no single-family homes left on the block, but there is a series of three duplexes on the northwest corner of North Hayworth and Fountain, as well as three bungalow courts built in the 1920s, all in a row just north of the Hollywood Riviera's site, with parking garages on the back property line. Hayworth Tower, also built in the 1920s at 1314 North Hayworth, is a classy seven-story apartment building built in the Churriguresque style with a parking structure at the rear. Opposite, there is a courtyard building of the same era, with lush landscaping and a high degree of architectural detail and another bungalow court at 1313 Hayworth, two stories with a driveway down the center, both surface parked at the rear. Minimal Traditional courtyard apartments built in the 1940s with driveways down the side and parking garages at the rear are also common. There is one other single-lot stucco box building with a pool at 1433 North Hayworth, with parking tucked under the side of the building in open carports. On the southwest corner of North Hayworth and Sunset Boulevard is a large 1990s-era podium apartment building with five levels of housing over a two-story concrete parking podium. The most recent building on the block, built in 2016 to much opposition, is the Hayworth Townhomes, 16 units in a four-story building over a fully subterranean garage with parking for 36 cars, essentially the same parking strategy as 1411 North Hayworth, 58 years later.

How do 1411 North Hayworth and the Hollywood Rivera compare from a planning perspective? Does one meet planning goals better than the other?

Needed Housing Types

The industries and amenities in West Hollywood increased the demand for rental housing relative to the rest of the county, and skewed demographics toward singles and couples without children. The area was also a center for nightlife, meaning lots of newcomers and tourists who also needed to be housed. Rental housing was appropriate for all of these demographics.

Development Standards

Planning in the county of Los Angeles was less robust than that in the City of Los Angeles, somewhat understandably given the county's size and diversity of planning environments. In general, regulations and processes were much looser. From 1954 to 1958, Los Angeles County's Regional Planning Commission made close studies of specific regional areas like the Antelope Valley and the East San Gabriel Valley, instituted a county beautification committee, studied prospective school and recreational area site locations, evaluated planned Civic Center facilities and stipulated increased development standards for off-street parking (LARPC, 1955, 1956, 1958, 1959). They also developed a riding and hiking trails plan, planned harbor development for small watercraft and studied hillside development standards (LARPC, 1955, 1956, 1958, 1959) All in addition to administering the regional master plan, managing subdivision applications, preparing zone maps and adjudicating zone changes, and providing planning services to contract cities (LARPC, 1955, 1956, 1958, 1959).

Zoning R3 vs. R3

Both case study projects were zoned R3 at the time they were built and both sites had been previously improved with a single-family home, which was razed. In Los Angeles County, the R3, or Limited Multiple Residence Zone, allowed single-family dwellings, duplexes, bungalow courts and apartment units. (Land Use Survey Co., 1952) The zone had a two-story height limit, required a 15-foot front setback and parking for one car per dwelling unit (Land Use Survey Co., 1952). Unlike zoning in the City of Los Angeles at the time, no side or rear setbacks were required, nor was there a required amount of lot area per dwelling unit that would restrict density. And, as mentioned earlier, the county did not use a system to organize how land was zoned, as Los Angeles did, so residential areas were intermixed using heterogeneous physical standards.

Density *58 Dwelling Units per Acre vs. 55 Dwelling Units per Acre*

Both case study projects are similar in terms of density. The building at 1411 North Hayworth is built at 58 dwelling units per acres and has 741 square feet of lot area per dwelling unit. The Hollywood Riviera is built at 55 dwelling units per acres and has 786 square feet of lot area per dwelling unit. The zoning code had no restrictions on density at the time the case study projects were built.

Parking *One per Unit + Eight Guest Spaces vs. One per Unit + Thirteen Guest Spaces*

Los Angeles County required one parking space per unit in an onsite garage at the time both case study projects were built (Zoning Atlas, 1953). The building at 1411 North Hayworth is parked one per unit plus eight additional spaces in a semi-subterranean concrete garage. The Hollywood Riviera is parked one per unit plus thirteen additional spaces in a semi-subterranean open carport.

Outcomes

More relaxed planning regulations lead to a great degree of housing diversity, but also left more room for bad acting. Lax zoning relative to housing type encouraged redevelopment in existing neighborhoods, ensuring that neighborhoods had a range of housing types and a commensurate range of residents. But the lack of a density requirement allowed 1411 North Hayworth to jam-pack units on the site, with the additional parking requirements facilitated by the building's full-site parking podium.

Conclusion

When Incrementally Innovative Design Supports Real Estate Development Goals

Evolving parking regulations challenged architects to develop new housing types that could profitably meet planning guidelines. Jack Chernoff and Edward Fickett took opposing strategies as architects working for developer clients. Chernoff's practice assumed that design only adds value from the perspective of yield, that is, how many units can be crammed onto a lot while still meeting regulatory standards, especially those for parking. Yield is important, but there are many other ways for designers to contribute to profitability, on both the revenue and cost sides of the proforma. Fickett's apartments are designed so that unit count is relatively high but in ways that ensure that decisions about unit type, size and aggregation do not compromise a building's important common elements: entries, circulation systems and open space. Fickett also worked to find ways to use design to simultaneously reduce construction costs while boosting marketability. At the Hollywood Riviera he used modified post-and-beam construction to add volume and character to small units, making them both cheaper to build and more desirable to tenants (The Fickett Formula, 1953). He traded off smaller units that were cheaper to construct for a generous and well-appointed common courtyard just as the apartment lifestyle was becoming an important social trend. And he sourced jalousie windows, a desirable feature in the 1950s, from a company in Australia that could provide them more cheaply than U.S. manufacturers (The Fickett Formula, 1953).

In the end, Chernoff just gave developers what they wanted while Fickett gave his clients real design value. Chernoff's buildings relegate actual design to the front facade and imply that innovative design is not valuable to the developer. By contrast, Fickett used design to enhance his developer client's vision and ensure that it was financially feasible. His incremental advances improved design and development simultaneously, proving that wholesale avant-gardism or complete rolling over, patron or patsy, aren't the only two models of successful architect/developer collaboration. Architects have ideas that can be profitable, not just costly. Yield has its limits. Developers should hire architects who will enhance their vision, not just deliver it.

Lessons Learned

Incrementally Innovative Design Can Shape Profitable Development Models

In this case, incremental design innovation supported real estate development and urban planning goals. Fickett was well known for his work with production homebuilders, interest in developing collaborative models for building professionals and cost-effective construction methods for modern architectural elements. We see this same perspective at work in the Hollywood Riviera, where he both adapted mid-century stylistic elements such as an open plan, beamed ceilings, custom light fixtures and floor-to-ceiling glass so that they could be built profitably and innovated in the fundamental building typology, which is a hybrid courtyard apartment on a half podium. Podium became a successful housing strategy in Los Angeles because it could be profitably adjusted to meet increasing zoning demands but was stylistically and organizationally flexible.

In the end,

> [b]y taking a leadership role on the local and national level, Fickett fostered healthy dialogue between the architects, contractors, planners, lenders, and policy makers with the net result that quality architectural ideas and innovations were absorbed into the large-scale production of single- and multi-family residential housing in the latter part of the twentieth century.
>
> (Winship, 2011, p. 92)

Case Study Projects Today

Both 1411 North Hayworth and the Hollywood Riviera were converted to condominiums in 1982 (Tract # 37872; Tract #38894). The City of West Hollywood incorporated in 1984. The Hollywood Riviera was designated as a local Cultural Resource by the City of West Hollywood on October 18, 2010 (Resolution 10–4099).

Notes

1. Weinstock, who was Jewish, was among a number of top Los Angeles homebuilders who refused to sell homes to African Americans, believing that white people would not buy homes in integrated subdivisions (Sides, 2006).
2. Builders and developers are incentivized to underestimate building costs on permit applications since fees are based on valuations. While these permit valuations for 1411 North Hayworth Avenue and the Hollywood Riviera are likely low, the comparison is still apples-to-apples since both use the costs reported by their developers to the Los Angeles County Building and Safety Department.
3. We know now that the construction quality of the Hollywood Riviera was relatively poor. The homeowners' association is struggling with building maintenance and systems upgrades.

References

$320,000 Building Newly Completed. (1953, October 19). *Los Angeles Times*, E24. Retrieved from www.proquest.com

Apartment House Building Spurts: Multiple Structures Erected Here in First Seven Months at New All-Time High. (1957, August 25). *Los Angeles Times*, A6. Retrieved from www.proquest.com

Architectural Resources Group. (2008, November). *City of West Hollywood, R2, R3, R4 Multi-Family Survey Report*. West Hollywood, CA: City of West Hollywood, Community Development Department.

Article 41. (1955, October 2). *Los Angeles Times*, F22. Retrieved from www.proquest.com

Betsky, A. (1994, January 6). Look at the Critic's Own Environment Gives Rise to Musings. *Los Angeles Times*. Retrieved from http://articles.latimes.com/1994-01-06/news/we-8971_1_living-spaces

Chase, J. (2000). *Glitter Stucco and Dumpster Diving, Reflections on Building Production in the Vernacular City*. New York, NY: Verso.

City of West Hollywood, Resolution No. 10–4099 designating 1400 North Hayworth Avenue as a Local Cultural Resource. October 18, 2010.

Classified Ad 29. (1959, February 27). *Los Angeles Times*, B22. Retrieved from www.proquest.com

Classified Ad 33. (1959, June 1). *Los Angeles Times*, B27. Retrieved from www.proquest.com

Classified Ad 36. (1957, September 15). *Los Angeles Times*, I35. Retrieved from www.proquest.com

Classified Ad 38. (1959, May 7). *Los Angeles Times*, B31. Retrieved from www.proquest.com

Classified Ad 52. (1959, May 17). *Los Angeles Times*, I47. Retrieved from www.proquest.com

Display Ad 115. (1954, November 28). *Los Angeles Times*, E13. Retrieved from www.proquest.com

The Fickett Formula: Good Design Works Both Ways. (1953, March). *House + Home*, 132–139.

Gordon, K. (1960, May 1). Reconversion Spurring West Hollywood Boom. *Los Angeles Times*, M11. Retrieved from www.proquest.com

Grand Opening of New Tract Set for Today. (1960, May 22). *Los Angeles Times*, M12. Retrieved from www.proquest.com

Ground Broken for Highland Park Project. (1964, November 29). *Los Angeles Times*, H12. Retrieved from www.proquest.com

Julian Weinstock; Built Thousands of Homes. (1993, January 13). *Los Angeles Times*. Retrieved from http://articles.latimes.com/1993-01-13/news/mn-1149_1_julian-weinstock

L.A. Architect Member of FHA Committee. (1955, April 10). *Los Angeles Times*, E6. Retrieved from www.proquest.com

Land Use Survey Co. (1952). *Property zoning Atlas of central and West Los Angeles*. Los Angeles, CA: Brewster Enterprise.

Lenox, B. (1959, December 27). Outdoor living on an apartment balcony. *Los Angeles Times*, H8. Retrieved from www.proquest.com

Los Angeles City Planning Commission. (1960). *Accomplishments 1960*.

Los Angeles County Regional Planning Commission. (1955). *Annual Report*, Fiscal Year July 1, 1954—June 30, 1955. Los Angeles, CA: L.A. County.

Los Angeles County Regional Planning Commission. (1956). *Annual Report*, Fiscal Year July 1, 1955—June 30, 1956. Los Angeles, CA: L.A. County.

Los Angeles County Regional Planning Commission. (1958). *Annual Report*, Fiscal Year July 1, 1957—June 30, 1958. Los Angeles, CA: L.A. County.

Los Angeles County Regional Planning Commission. (1959). *Annual Report*, Fiscal Year July 1, 1958—June 30, 1959. Los Angeles, CA: L.A. County.

Masters, N. (2011, December 1). *How the Town of Sherman Became the City of West Hollywood*, Lost L.A., KCET. Retrieved from https://www.kcet.org/shows/lost-la/how-the-town-of-sherman-became-the-city-of-west-hollywood

McCoy, E. (1955, March 12). What I Believe. . . *Los Angeles Times*, L22. Retrieved from www.proquest.com

NAHB Economist Sees Uptrend in Home Cost. (1955, July 10). *Los Angeles Times*, E16. Retrieved from www.proquest.com

Nero, B. (1972, February 13). The Blooming of the Plastic Hibiscus, Hollywood apartments come in two styles: gaudy and depressing. *Los Angeles Times*, W24. Retrieved from www.proquest.com

New Apartment. (1956, August 12). *Los Angeles Times*, E20. Retrieved from www.proquest.com

New Ownership Plan Offered at Apartment. (1963, June 30). *Los Angeles Times*, N14. Retrieved from www.proquest.com

Noise Bugs Them. (1959, November 2). *Los Angeles Times*, A1. Retrieved from www.proquest.com

Photo Standalone 18. (1958, July 27). *Los Angeles Times*, F3. Retrieved from www.proquest.com

Rapaport, R. (2014). *California Moderne and the Mid-Century Dream, The Architecture of Edward H. Fickett*. New York, NY: Rizzoli.

Richardson, A. (1958, June 29). The Two-Faced Lounge: A Bright Solution for the 1-Room Apartment Problem. *Los Angeles Times*, TW26. Retrieved from www.proquest.com

Sides, J. (2006). *L.A. City Limits: African American Los Angeles from the Great Depression to the Present*. Berkeley, CA: University of California Press.

Smith, W. F. (1964). *The Low-Rise Speculative Apartment Building*. Berkeley, CA: University of California Printing Department.

State of California, Department of Parks and Recreation. (2007). Primary Record, 1411 North Hayworth Avenue.

Treffers, S. A. (2012). *The Dingbat Apartment: The Low-Rise Urbanization of Post World War II Los Angeles*, 1957–1964 (Master's Thesis), University of Southern California. Retrieved from https://search-proquest-com.libproxy1.usc.edu/docview/1027918285/7C9868F23157440DPQ/1?accountid=14749

Walsh, H. (1958, August 28). March of Finance: Apartment House Surplus Reported. *Los Angeles Times*, C8. Retrieved from www.proquest.com

Winship, S. (2011). *Quantity and Quality: Architects Working for Developers in Southern California, 1960–1973* (Master's Thesis), University of Southern California. Retrieved from https://search-proquest-com.libproxy1.usc.edu/docview/914208994/18F02F8B93984EF1PQ/2?accountid=14749

With planning, a new look: dressing a drab apartment. (1958, March 30). *Los Angeles Times*, J42. Retrieved from www.proquest.com

Conclusion

Collaborative Prospects

Individually, each by-right, by-design case study illustrates important trade-offs among housing disciplines and foregrounds opportunities for their group effort. Taken together as a whole, they suggest that projects that balance design, real estate development and urban planning interests at their inception do better over time by all measures.

Negative Disciplinary Trade-Offs

Taking a siloed perspective, many of the case study projects seem to only uphold negative stereotypes and entrench uncharitable beliefs: Innovative architects design housing that is too costly to build. More commercially oriented architects design housing that is derivative. Enlightened developers take risks that leave money on the table. Conventional developers' ruthless pursuit of profit creates neighborhoods that are focused on individual gain and not community building. Urban planners' weak regulation of the built environment gives too much away to developers and encourages unimaginative design. Onerous regulation from all levels of government slows development and dampens design innovation. These attitudes are commonplace among housing professionals, and while they might be correct in certain instances, they don't lead to solutions that produce better housing. Taken as a whole, these negative trade-offs foreground just how much each housing profession matters for the production of good housing.

Design vs. Development

Too Much Focus on Development Over Design

The Chesapeake Rodeo Apartments did the minimum from the perspective of design in favor of streamlining development, with small units, few unit types, no significant private open space and inarticulate common open spaces. This lack of design attention compromised marketability as the housing market shifted and became more competitive. Design features that could have helped the project compete were not included and difficult to retrofit: a diversity of unit types, good storage, ample private open, extra parking and more development-wide amenities.

Too Much Focus on Design Over Development

The Modernique Homes sacrificed development performance for design goals, so much so that the developer could not remain a going concern. The efficiencies and benefits the project's design purported to achieve for the developer were not realized. The Modernique Homes were more expensive to insure, construct and market, the costs of which were all transferred to future buyers. Few consumers were ready to accept the houses' Modern design, convertible features and communal landscape at the asking price point, which was out of sync with the surrounding neighborhood.

Development vs. Planning

Too Much Focus on Development Over Planning

The Chesapeake Rodeo Apartments chose an expedient approach to planning regulation rather than actively using best planning practices. This strategy aided profitability from a time-value-of-money standpoint but did not boost the project's long-term marketability or value. Just playing by the rules (as far as anyone knew at the time) wasn't enough to create a sustainable housing project. Not pursuing the planning strategies successfully demonstrated at Baldwin Hills Village, even if they required more time-consuming discretionary approvals, ensured that the Chesapeake Rodeo is now less valuable than its notable neighbor.

Too Much Focus on Planning Over Development

The Hirsh Tract's singular attention to subdivision guidelines created an irrational development pattern rather than a cohesive neighborhood. Houses on the northern and southern edges of the tract and on May Street face out onto streets with no corresponding houses facing back to them. The two cul-de-sacs create small neighborhood units, but they are marooned off from the rest of the neighborhood with little articulation of the public realm. These situations do not seem to have detracted from the project's marketability, but they create a disjointed neighborhood with little relation or connection to the development surrounding it. Though the project followed the rules in force at the time, those rules did not add up to what planners were trying to achieve, an interconnected neighborhood that operates a variety of scales, from house to block to tract.

Planning vs. Design

Too Much Focus on Planning Over Design

Dingbat apartments employed minimum planning standards as their sole design parameters, neglecting important housing design goals, types and rules of thumb. The typical dingbat used underlying zoning density and parking requirements to determine the number of units that could fit on a site, ignoring past housing types, issues of family composition and building-wide social relationships. The dingbat is built to maximum lot coverage, creating a stark box on the setback line, indifferent to surrounding context, past neighborhood identity and a well-functioning public realm. And since there were no planning regulations mandating common or individual open space, most dingbats didn't have any beyond their exterior motel-style corridors. This focus on planning minimums may have maximized yield but maligned the dingbat as a housing type.

Too Much Focus on Design Over Planning

Since Horatio West Court was built before the advent of much urban planning regulation in Santa Monica, it was free to focus on its singular design rather than addressing the neighborhood at large. The project is inwardly focused, walled off from the rest of the structures on its block with its only connection to the public realm a narrow driveway. The houses themselves are similarly insular with little space for communal activities.

Positive Models for Collaboration

However, if we take a broader perspective and look at the interactions among disciplines evident in these cases, specifically at the collaborative models that were used to get them built, we gain a much more nuanced picture, one that instead of validating one disciplinary perspective, encourages us to look beyond singular points of view. This stance reveals more balanced housing models that can be used to generate "triple-win" projects, those which perform well from the point of view of all three disciplines.

Design and Development

Uses Design to Support Profitable Development Outcomes

Clark Court uses a basic but dependable design to ensure profitability. A tried-and-true house court design, with built-in furniture, efficient but functional planning, good street presence and a just a little style, all enhanced by a desirable location, added up to a profitable development project. Its design is not innovative, but it is solid and familiar and provides real quality of life.

Uses Development to Support Innovative Design Outcomes

Architect Edward Fickett knew how to use design to support profitable development outcomes, but he also used development to support innovative apartment design. Fickett-designed tract homes kept the ceilings high, the plan open and the roof line visible, all characteristics that developer Ray Hommes attributed to the fast sales of the contemporary homes in his tracts. Fickett applied many of these techniques at the Hollywood Riviera, using semi-modular post and beam construction, for example, to open up and add character to small units and a dramatically shaped butterfly roof, rarely seen on single-family homes let alone stucco box apartments, to create a distinctive front façade and high ceilings for second-story units.

Development and Planning

Uses Development to Support Equitable Planning Outcomes

The social values held by the Modernique Home's designer and developer made for a more communal subdivision that sought to bring both individual identity and collective identity into balance. The urban planning profession shared these goals ostensibly, at the time, though the development and site-planning strategies of the Modernique Homes met these goals better than Los Angeles's planning regulations.

Uses Planning to Support Good Development Outcomes

The Cheviot Manor Apartments uses a good understanding of housing type and adherence to changing urban planning requirements to support a profitable development project. Its overall plan looks to the courtyard garden apartment type, familiar to architects and planners, and makes good use of newly allowable planning strategies, that is, the redefinition of *story* to allow for semi-subterranean parking, to create a familiar and marketable housing on a formerly uneconomical site.

Planning and Design

Uses Planning to Support Innovative Design Outcomes

The fact that the Mackey Apartments directly builds on the familiar fourflat housing type made it easier for Zoning Engineer Huber Smutz to approve its design innovations. From a planning perspective, the building was different, but not that different, and its differences all had both design and development value. The double-height owner's unit for Mrs. Mackey creates the distinctive interlocking "Ls" on the facade but also made for a marketable and valuable unit that had features no other four-flat could boast. Brightly colored built-in furniture made the project easier for tenants to occupy just like other four-flats, but with more character and style. Ample private open space, something few four-flats had, helped the building compete with the open space provided by single-family homes.

Uses Design to Support Positive Planning Outcomes

At Baldwin Hills Village, money that would have otherwise been spent on unremarkable street infrastructure was spent on high-quality landscape and open space instead: Something in the "background" was brought into the "foreground" so it could be actively used to market the project, setting it apart from its competitors. The project team put energy into what architects would call planning and planners would call urban design, instead of costly stylistic details. Good planning can essentially cost nothing. At Baldwin Hills Village, its superblock spatial organization ensures access to protected green space that is truly unavailable anywhere else in Los Angeles, something that was highly marketable at the time the project was built and continues to be highly desirable today. Pushing regulatory boundaries allowed Baldwin Hills Village to implement development strategies that improved investment performance over time.

Triple-Win Projects

Ultimately, of the 12 projects studied, three stand out as ones that perform well from the point of view of all three professions and can be considered "triple-win" projects. Clark Court is as desirable, valuable and appropriate given contemporary lifestyles as it was when it was built. It speaks to not only today's small house and micro-unit movement but also our current desire for more community connection. The only way it could be improved, in the author's estimation, is with more articulate landscaping and the provision of private open space, both of which are well within reach. Baldwin Hills Village has only improved with age. The quality, size and level of access of its open space are truly unparalleled in Los Angeles today. Its wide range of unit types and generous unit size have ensured their marketability as household demographics changed. Though it was notable for its accommodation of the car when it was first built, with the opening of the Exposition Line, it is now transit-oriented and livable without a personal vehicle. And the Mackey Apartments with its flexible fifth unit speaks to our desire to make our housing do more for us, both financially and to accommodate varying life stages and styles. One could easily imagine occupying this extra unit in different permutations, housing an elderly parent with a caregiver, an adult child returning home or an extended family, but available to generate extra cash flow should the need arise.

Conclusions for New Housing

Move From Biased to Balanced Housing

If housing is approached as a zero-sum game, it will be a zero-sum outcome. If one discipline's "win" detracts from the ability of others to meet their own goals, opportunities to collaborate and find mutually beneficial housing strategies are shut down. Taken together, the by-right, by-design case studies demonstrate that projects that balance these three interests at their inception do better over time, by all measures. Studying triple-win projects, like Baldwin Hills Village, the Mackey Apartments and Clark Court, from a cross-disciplinary perspective illuminates housing strategies that support the goals and values of multiple housing disciplines. Better performance from the point of view of development, planning and design at the beginning made these projects more resilient over time, worthy of continued investment as demographics, lifestyles and markets evolved. But also, experimental projects deserve support in interdisciplinary ways—not just financial support but policy and regulatory support as well.

Draw the Right Line Between By-Right and By-Design

An increasing need for by-design or by-variance solutions can indicate a disconnect between the facts on the ground and idealized or generic code requirements. Be on the lookout for positive by-design approaches that could be made by-right to better mesh with development realities. Taken together, the by-right, by-design case studies demonstrate how the line between as of right and by-variance processes can either incentivize quality housing production or make it markedly more difficult. The dingbat and house court case studies show clearly how the location of this line can either intensify or skew both the quality and quantity of housing produced.

Leverage Housing Types and Typologies

Planning policy and development practice can create barriers to specific housing types, making historic or known types out of compliance and restricting the emergence of new typologies as demographics, lifestyles and expectations change. Taken together, the by-right, by-design case studies show that by-right works best when linked to type, not to floor area ratio, density, building envelopes or parking requirements. The four-flat and stucco box/podium case studies demonstrate how amplifying and hybridizing types can lead to meaningful innovations while keeping known knowns.

Design for Diverse Values

Good design is not as monolithic as architects would like people to think. Design interests do not have to be maximized in every project, but we do need to make sure to get the basics right since poor design can hurt value to a greater degree than good design can boost it. Taken together, the by-right, by-design case studies demonstrate that by-right development types are often well-designed, just not necessarily innovatively designed. The four-flat and house court development types show how good design ideas can be found in unexpected places and can be generated by values that extend beyond design itself.

Invest in Open Rather Than Closed Systems

Housing is a long-lived asset. A singular focus on profit without understanding how design and planning efforts contribute to the bottom line ensures short-term success over long-term investment potential. Taken together, the by-right, by-design case studies demonstrate how encoding flexibility can create housing that is desirable for longer. Baldwin Hills Village, the Hollywood Riviera and the four-flat and bungalow court development types all demonstrate how housing can transform over time to accommodate new tenure types, lifestyles and family types.

Make Plans Responsive to Fluctuating Demand and Real Estate Cycles

The United States has a market-based system of housing production. Policy and planning mechanisms can reshape value and engender development opportunities but not necessarily incentivize development when underlying fundamentals are poor. Taken together, the by-right, by-design case studies show how the time lag between planning efforts and actual development can hamper response to market signals. The four-flat and stucco box/podium case studies show how the shifting relationship between land use and economic cycles can be advantageous or detrimental.

Index

Note: Page numbers in *italics* indicate a figure on the corresponding page.

1060 South Cochran Avenue 167; architectural style 179; common open space 176, 178; density 190; development context 180, 181; development history 168, 169; funding 184, 185; height and setbacks 190; land and construction costs 184; landscape 179; market timing 182, 183, 184; marketing and absorption 185, 186; massing 175; parking 190; pedestrian access and circulation 176; planning, context for 186, 187, 188, 189; private open space 178; public realm 190, 191; real estate development, context for 180, 181; subdivision 181, 182; unit types and aggregation 175, 176; vehicular access and parking 176; vernacular design of 179, 180; zoning and development standards 189, 190

1411 North Hayworth Avenue 192n8, 202; architectural style 210, 211; building costs 217; building organization and massing 206, 207; common open space 209; density 222; design context 202, 203, 204; development context 212, 213, 214; development history 201, 202; funding 217, 218; Jack Chernoff 204; market timing 216, 217; marketing and absorption 218, 219; Nathan E. Nadel 214, 215; parking 206, 208, 209, 222; pedestrian access and entry 207, 208; planning, context for 219, 220, 221; private open space 210; structure and materials 210; subdivision 216; unit types and amenities 207; zoning and development standards 221, 222

Abbott, Wyllys S. 147, 152

actors in the housing profession 3

Ain, Gregory 12, 56, 60, 70, 71

Alexander, Robert 5, 84n7, 90, 105, 107

approval of by-design projects 8

architectural style: comparing between 1060 South Cochran Avenue and Mackey Apartments 179; comparing between 1411 North Hayworth Avenue and Hollywood Riviera Apartments 210, 211; comparing between Chesapeake Rodeo Apartments and Baldwin Hills Village 103; comparing between Cheviot Manor Apartments and National Apartments 43; comparing between Clark Court and Horatio West Court 143; comparing between Mar Vista Tract and Hirst Tract 75; Early Modern 179; "Googie Style" 211; of house courts 129, 130; Mid-Century Modern 55; "Minimal Traditional" 55; Period Revival 173; Spanish Colonial Revival 179

as-of-right projects 7; *see also* by-right projects

Baldwin, Anita 105

Baldwin, Baldwin M. 113

Baldwin Hills Village 12, 93; architects 96; architectural style 103; building organization and

massing 98; common open space 101; community life 118, 119; conditions of approval 95; density 116; design 95, 96, 97; design performance 103; development of 104, 105; development standards 115, 116; funding 106, 107; honors and awards for its architecture 103; and housing needs 114, 115; innovativeness of 93; investment performance 112, 113; land acquisition 105; land and construction costs 106; landscape 102; market timing 107; marketing 107, 108; massing 98; "modern vernacular" style of 93; operating costs 110, 112; parking 116, 117; pedestrian access and entry 99, 100; planning performance 119; private open space 102; public realm 118; "Radburn Plan" 97; rents and absorption 108; site strategy 97, 98; unit types and amenities 98, 99; urban planning context 113, 114; vehicular access and parking 100, 101; *see also* "Lost in Translation" case study
Bella Vista Terrace 133
Berg, Theo W. 22
Berry, Richard 104
Betsky, Aaron 211
Bogardus, Emory 151
building organization and massing: comparing between 1411 North Hayworth Avenue and Hollywood Riviera Apartments 206, 207; comparing between Chesapeake Rodeo Apartments and Baldwin Hills Village 98; comparing between Cheviot Manor Apartments and National Apartments 39
building permit fees 84n2
bungalow courts 13, 158n2; plans for 152; St. Francis Court 133, 138; *see also* Clark Court; Horatio West Court; "Proliferating a Product Type" case study
Burns, Fritz 76
by-design projects 1, 3, 7; approval of 8; National Apartments 26; *see also* Baldwin Hills Village; Hollywood Riviera Apartments; Mackey Apartments; Mar Vista Tract; Modernique Homes; National Apartments
Byers, Charles Alma 152
Byers, John 138
by-right, by design framework 7, 8; cross-disciplinary comparative case method 8, 9, 10; overview of comparative cases 10
by-right projects 1, 3, 7; *see also* 1060 South Cochran Avenue; 1411 North Hayworth Avenue; Chesapeake Rodeo Apartments; Cheviot Manor Apartments; Hirsh Tract
by-variance projects *see* by-design projects

Campbell, Wilbur W. 174
Carmona, Matthew 4
case studies: "Crafting Cost Benefit" 14; by-design projects 3; "Design Well-Timed" 14; "Lost in Translation" 12, 13; "Proliferating a Product Type" 13; "Type in Transition" 11, 12; "Value Out of Balance" 12
Case Study Program 69
challenges, of "good" housing production 3
Chase, John 198
Chernoff, Jack 37, 38, 204
Chesapeake Rodeo Apartments 12, 13, 90, 92, 93, 96; architectural style 103; building organization and massing 98; common open space 101; community life 118, 119; density 116; design 95, 96, 97; design performance 103; development of 104, 105; development standards 115, 116; focus on development over design 227, 228; funding 106, 107; Herbert Kronish 90; and housing needs 114, 115; investment performance 112, 113; land acquisition 105; land and construction costs 106; landscape 102; market timing 107; marketing 107, 108; massing 98; operating costs 110, 112; parking 116, 117; pedestrian access and entry 99, 100; planning performance 119; private open space 102; public realm 118; rents and absorption 108; site strategy 97, 98; unit types and

amenities 98, 99; urban planning context 113, 114; vehicular access and parking 100, 101; *see also* "Lost in Translation" case study
Cheviot Manor Apartments 22, *23*, 27; architectural style 43; building organization and massing 39; common open space 41, 42; construction costs 30, 31, 32; density 36; height and setbacks 36; market timing 30; parking 36; pedestrian access and entry 40, 41; planning performance 37; private financing 33; private open space 42, 43; public realm 36; site strategy 39; structure and materials 43; style of 24; subdivision 29, 30; unit types and amenities 39, 40; vehicular access and parking 41; zoning 35, 36
Clark, Eli P. 216
Clark, John N. 135
Clark Court 135, 157; architectural style 143; construction costs 147; density 156; design context 138, 139; development standards 153, 154; funding 147, 148; investment performance 149, 150; market timing 146, 147; marketing and absorption 148, 149; massing 139, 140; open space 141; outcomes 150; parking 141, 156; pedestrian access and entry 141; real estate development, context for 144; site and building organization 139; structure and materials 141, 142; subdivision 145, 146; unit types and amenities 140, 141; urban planning, context for 150, 151; zoning 155, 156
close-in neighborhoods, rezoning of 44
Coate, Roland 138, 173
code-switching 2
Commission on Immigration and Housing of California 154, 155, 158n1; State Housing Manual 155
common open space: comparing between 1060 South Cochran Avenue and Mackey Apartments 176, 178; comparing between 1411 North Hayworth Avenue and Hollywood Riviera Apartments 209; comparing between Chesapeake Rodeo Apartments and Baldwin Hills Village 101; comparing between Cheviot Manor Apartments and National Apartments 41, 42
Community Homes 71
comparative cases 9, 10; case study project map *11*; "Crafting Cost Benefit" 14; "Design Well-Timed" 14; "Lost in Translation" 12, 13; "Proliferating a Product Type" 13; "Type in Transition" 11, 12; "Value Out of Balance" 12
construction costs: comparing between 1060 South Cochran Avenue and Mackey Apartments 184; comparing between 1411 North Hayworth Avenue and Hollywood Riviera Apartments 217; comparing between Cheviot Manor Apartments and National Apartments 30, 31, 32; comparing between Clark Court and Horatio West Court 147; comparing between Mar Vista Tract and Hirst Tract 78, 79
"Crafting Cost Benefit" case study 14; architectural style, comparing between projects 210, 211; building costs, comparing between projects 217; building organization and massing, comparing between projects 206, 207; common open space, comparing between projects 209; density, comparing between projects 222; design context 202, 203, 204; funding, comparing between projects 217, 218; lessons learned from 223, 224; market timing, comparing between projects 216, 217; marketing and absorption, comparing between projects 218, 219; parking, comparing between projects 206, 208, 209, 222; pedestrian access and entry, comparing between projects 207, 208; planning, context for 219, 220, 221; private open space, comparing between projects 210; real estate development, context for 212, 213, 214; structure and materials, comparing

between projects 210; subdivision, comparing between projects 216; unit types and amenities, comparing between projects 207; zoning, comparing between projects 221, 222; *see also* Hollywood Riviera Apartments
Creviston, Russel G. 181
cross-disciplinary comparative case method 8, 9, 10

Day, Alfred 56, 71
density: comparing between 1060 South Cochran Avenue and Mackey Apartments 190; comparing between 1411 North Hayworth Avenue and Hollywood Riviera Apartments 222; comparing between Chesapeake Rodeo Apartments and Baldwin Hills Village 116; comparing between Clark Court and Horatio West Court 156; comparing between Mar Vista Tract and Hirst Tract 68
Denzer, Anthony 79
design: in the post-World War II era 69; using to support positive planning outcomes 231; using to support profitable development outcomes 229, 230; *see also* building organization and massing; common open space; pedestrian access and entry; private open space; site strategy; structure and materials; style; unit types and amenities; vehicular access and parking
"Design Well-Timed" case study 14; architectural style, comparing between projects 179; common open space, comparing between projects 176, 178; density, comparing between projects 190; design context 173, 174, 175; funding, comparing between projects 184, 185; height and setbacks, comparing between projects 190; land and construction costs, comparing between projects 184; landscape, comparing between projects 179; market timing, comparing between projects 182, 183, 184; marketing and absorption, comparing between projects 185, 186; parking, comparing between projects 190; pedestrian access and circulation, comparing between projects 176; planning, context for 186, 187, 188, 189; private open space, comparing between projects 178; public realm, comparing between projects 190, 191; real estate development, context for 180, 181; site strategy and massing 175; subdivision, comparing between projects 181, 182; unit types and aggregation, comparing between projects 175, 176; vehicular access and parking, comparing between projects 176; zoning, comparing between projects 189, 190; *see also* Mackey Apartments
development standards: comparing between Chesapeake Rodeo Apartments and Baldwin Hills Village 115, 116; comparing between Clark Court and Horatio West Court 153, 154
Dingbat 2.0 competition 20
dingbat apartments 12, 19, *21*, 27, 47n2, 197, 198; Cheviot Manor Apartments 22, 24; demise of, reasons for 44, 45, 46, 47; emergence of 20, 21; modern style of 37; National Apartments 24, 25, 26; "proto-dingbats" 22, 24, 26; style of 20; *see also* "Type in Transition" case study
Driveway Approach and Curb Space Control Ordinance 45

Eames, Charles 37
Eames, Ray 37, 69
Early Modern style 179
Eckbo, Garrett 71, 74
"economy house plan" 70
Edelman, B.M. 12, 54, 60, 77, 78
Eichler, Joseph 70
Ellwood, Craig 37

FHA (Federal Housing Administration) 60, 106; *Land Planning* and *Technical Bulletins* 66; mortgage insurance 79; *Principles of Planning Small Houses*

72; promotion of rental housing 104; Regulation X 71; underwriting criteria 62, 63, 65, 66
Fickett, Edward H. 14, 70, 200, 204, 205, 206
financing, comparing between Cheviot Manor Apartments and National Apartments 33
fixed house plans 72
flexible house plans 72
fostering balanced outcomes in housing production 7
four-flats 14, 164, 165; architectural styles 173; characteristics of 165; evolution as housing type 166; plans for 168, 169; popularity of 167; *see also* 1060 South Cochran Avenue; "Design Well-Timed" case study; Mackey Apartments
funding: comparing between 1060 South Cochran Avenue and Mackey Apartments 184, 185; comparing between 1411 North Hayworth Avenue and Hollywood Riviera Apartments 217, 218; comparing between Chesapeake Rodeo Apartments and Baldwin Hills Village 106, 107; comparing between Clark Court and Horatio West Court 147, 148

garden apartments 89, 90; characteristics 92; design context 95, 96, 97; *see also* Baldwin Hills Village; Chesapeake Rodeo Apartments
Gault, Charles A. 174
Gibbs, Hugh 56, 70, 84n10
Gill, Irving 13, 15n3, 133, 136, 137, 138, 139, 174
Gish, Todd 132
"good design," Hommes on 6
"good" housing 1; architects' role in 4, 5; production challenges 3; real estate developers' role in 5; urban planners' role in 5
"Googie Style" architecture 211
Greene, Charles 138
Greene, Henry 138, 139
Gruen, Victor 96

height and setbacks: comparing between 1060 South Cochran Avenue and Mackey Apartments 190; comparing between Cheviot Manor Apartments and National Apartments; comparing between Mar Vista Tract and Hirst Tract 68
Hirsh, Harold 54, 56, 77
Hirsh, Sylvia 56
Hirsh-Edmunds Building Company 56
Hirsh Tract 54, *54*, 70; architectural style 75; construction 73; construction costs 78, 79; density 68; development 56; development outcomes 82; height and setbacks 68; house plans 72; investment performance 81, 82; market timing 80; marketing and absorption 79, 80; massing 72; mortgage insurance 79; pedestrian access and entry 73; planning outcomes 68, 69; public realm 75; spatial organization 67, 68; subdivision 56, 78; yards and landscape 73, 74, 75; zoning 68
Hollywood Riviera Apartments 14; architectural style 210, 211; building costs 217; building organization and massing 206, 207; common open space 209; density 222; design context 202, 203, 204; development context 212, 213, 214; development history 201, 202; Edward H. Fickett 204, 205; funding 217, 218; "Googie Style" 211; Julian Weinstock 215, 216; market timing 216, 217; marketing and absorption 218, 219; Mid-Century Modern style 202; parking 206, 208, 209, 222; pedestrian access and entry 207, 208; planning, context for 219, 220, 221; private open space 210; structure and materials 210; subdivision 216; unit types and amenities 207; zoning and development standards 221, 222; *see also* "Crafting Cost Benefit" case study
Home Builders Institute Los Angeles 70
Hommes, Ray 169, 205; on "good design" 6
Horatio West Court 13, 15n3, 136, 137, 139, 157; as "affordable" housing 158n8; architectural style 143; construction costs 147; density 156; design context 138, 139; development standards 153,

154; funding 147, 148; investment performance 149, 150; market timing 146, 147; marketing and absorption 148, 149; massing 139, 140; open space 141; outcomes 143, 150; parking 141, 156; pedestrian access and entry 141; real estate development, context for 144; site and building organization 139; structure and materials 141, 143; subdivision 145, 146; unit types and amenities 140, 141; urban planning, context for 150, 151; zoning 155, 156; *see also* "Proliferating a Product Type" case study
house courts 130, 131, 132, 152; architect-designed 133; architects 138, 139; Bella Vista Terrace 133; bungalow courts 132; Clark Court 135; discussion of in trade publications 138; Horatio West Court 136, 137, 139; "Model Village Movement" 152; promotion of by the Los Angeles Housing Commission 152; social and community advantages of 151; St. Francis Court 133; styles 131; vernacular 132; *see also* Clark Court; Horatio West Court; "Proliferating a Product Type" case study
house plans, comparing between Mar Vista Tract and Hirst Tract 72
house tracts 53
Housing Institutes 154, 155
housing production, fostering balanced outcomes in 6, 7
housing regulation 2; Commission on Immigration and Housing of California 154, 155; State Dwelling House Act 155
Howard, Ebenezer 89, 90
HPOZ (Historic Preservation Overlay Zone) 84
Hunt, Myron 138

innovation: in the Mackey Apartment's design 180; in the Mar Vista Tract 60
investment performance: comparing between Clark Court and Horatio West Court 149, 150; comparing between Mar Vista Tract and Hirst Tract 81, 82

Johnson, Joseph 56, 71, 84n3
Johnson, Reginald D. 90, 96, 97, 138, 173
Jones, A. Quincy 70

Kahan, Robert 71
Kaplin, Shy 71
Kappe, Phineas 24, 28, 29, 48n8
Kappe, Raymond 11, 24, 26, 28, 29, 34, 38, 48n8
Kauffman, Gordon 138
Kinney, Abbot 144
Kinsey, Ray 105
Koenig, Pierre 37
Krisel, William 70
Kronish, Herbert 90, 105, 122n15

landscape: comparing between 1060 South Cochran Avenue and Mackey Apartments 179; comparing between Chesapeake Rodeo Apartments and Baldwin Hills Village 102
Lewis, F. B. 133
Lincoln, Harry H. 174
Llano del Rio 71
Loring, R. S. 174
Los Angeles 2; "Blight Study Committee" 44; Driveway Approach and Curb Space Control Ordinance 45; first comprehensive zoning plan 21, 22; garden apartments 90; housing inequity in 2, 3; "post-war minimal house" 54, 55; single-family house tracts 53
Los Angeles City Planning Department, subdivision regulation 61, 62
Los Angeles Forum for Architecture and Urban Design, Dingbat 2.0 competition 20
Los Angeles Housing Commission 159n14; promotion of house court development 152
Los Angeles Times 10
"Lost in Translation" case study 12, 13; architectural style, comparing between projects 103; Chesapeake Rodeo Apartments 90; common open space, comparing between projects 101; community life, comparing between projects 118, 119; density, comparing between projects 116; design context 95, 96, 97; design outcomes 103, 104;

design performance, comparing between projects 103; development standards, comparing between projects 115, 116; funding, comparing between projects 106, 107; garden apartments 89, 90; housing needs, comparing between projects 114, 115; investment performance, comparing between projects 112, 113; land acquisition, comparing between projects 105; land and construction costs, comparing between projects 106; landscape, comparing between projects 102; lessons learned from 120, 121; market timing, comparing between projects 107; marketing, comparing between projects 107, 108; massing, comparing between projects 98; operating costs, comparing between projects 110, 112; outcomes 119, 120; parking, comparing between projects 116, 117; pedestrian access and entry, comparing between projects 99, 100; planning performance, comparing between projects 119; private open space, comparing between projects 102; public realm, comparing between projects 118; real estate development, context for 104, 105; rents and absorption, comparing between projects 108; site strategy, comparing between projects 97, 98; unit types and amenities, comparing between projects 98, 99; urban planning context 113, 114; vehicular access and parking, comparing between projects 100, 101; *see also* Chesapeake Rodeo Apartments; Village Green

Mackey, Pearl 169, 170, 179, 185

Mackey Apartments 14, 167; architectural style 167, 179; building permit approval 170; common open space 176, 178; construction of 170, 171, 173; density 190; as "by-design" project 173; development context 180, 181; funding 184, 185; height and setbacks 190; land and construction costs 184; landscape 179; market timing 182, 183, 184; marketing and absorption 185, 186; massing 175; parking 190; pedestrian access and circulation 176; planning, context for 186, 187, 188, 189; private open space 178; public realm 190, 191; real estate development, context for 180, 181; subdivision 181, 182; unit types and aggregation 175, 176; vehicular access and parking 176; zoning and development standards 189, 190; *see also* "Design Well-Timed" case study

Maltzman, Max 90, 96, 103

Mar Vista Tract 53, 70; architectural style 75; construction 73; construction costs 78, 79; density 68; development outcomes 82; goal of 59, 60; gridiron subdivision pattern 60; height and setbacks 68; house plans 72; innovations 60; investment performance 81, 82; market timing 80; marketability of 60; marketing and absorption 79, 80; massing 72; mortgage insurance 79; pedestrian access and entry 73; planning outcomes 68, 69; public realm 75; spatial organization 67, 68; subdivision 56, 78; yards and landscape 73, 74, 75; zoning 68; *see also* Modernique Homes

market timing: comparing between 1060 South Cochran Avenue and Mackey Apartments 182, 183, 184; comparing between 1411 North Hayworth Avenue and Hollywood Riviera Apartments 216, 217; comparing between Chesapeake Rodeo Apartments and Baldwin Hills Village 107; comparing between Cheviot Manor Apartments and National Apartments 30; comparing between Clark Court and Horatio West Court 146, 147; comparing between Mar Vista Tract and Hirst Tract 80

marketability, of the Mar Vista Tract 60

marketing and absorption: comparing between 1060 South Cochran

Avenue and Mackey Apartments 185, 186; comparing between 1411 North Hayworth Avenue and Hollywood Riviera Apartments 218, 219; comparing between Clark Court and Horatio West Court 148, 149
Marlow, Fred 76
Marston, Sylvanus 133, 138
Martin, A. C. 138
massing: comparing between 1060 South Cochran Avenue and Mackey Apartments 175; comparing between Chesapeake Rodeo Apartments and Baldwin Hills Village 98; comparing between Clark Court and Horatio West Court 139, 140
Maston, Carl 24, 48n8
May, Cliff 70
McCoy, Esther 205
merchant builders 53
Merrill, Edwin E. 90
methodology: analysis of comparative cases 9, 10; comparative case pairings 9; data collection 9; interviews 9
Mid-Century Modern style 55, 202
Miller, William B. 168
minimal modern style 43
"Minimal Traditional" style 55
"modern vernacular" style: Baldwin Hills Village 93
Modernique Homes 12, 53, 54, 55, 56; interior layout 59; *see also* "Value Out of Balance" case study
Modernism 37, 82
modernist houses 69, 70
mortgage insurance, comparing between Mar Vista Tract and Hirst Tract 79
multifamily housing development: dingbat apartments 27; in the mid-1950s 26, 27

Nadel, Nathan E. 214, 215
National Apartments 22, 24, *25*, 26; architectural style 43; building organization and massing 39; common open space 41, 42; construction costs 30, 31, 32; density 36; height and setbacks 36; market timing 30; parking 36; pedestrian access and entry 41; planning performance 37; private financing 33; private open space 42, 43; public realm 36; Section 608 112; site strategy 39; structure and materials 43; style of 24; subdivision 29, 30; unit types and amenities 39, 40; vehicular access and parking 41; zoning 35, 36
National Boulevard Apartments 11; *see also* "Type in Transition" case study
National Housing Act 90; Section 207 106, 107; Section 608 104, 105
Neff, Wallace 138, 173
negative disciplinary trade-offs: design vs. development 227, 228; development vs. planning 228; planning vs. design 229
Neutra, Richard 37, 69, 71, 96, 122n15
"New Neighborhoods for Old" program 44

Ocean Park 144, 145, 146

Park Planned Homes 71
parking: comparing between 1060 South Cochran Avenue and Mackey Apartments 190; comparing between 1411 North Hayworth Avenue and Hollywood Riviera Apartments 206, 222; comparing between Chesapeake Rodeo Apartments and Baldwin Hills Village 116, 117; comparing between Clark Court and Horatio West Court 141, 156
pedestrian access and entry: comparing between 1060 South Cochran Avenue and Mackey Apartments 176; comparing between 1411 North Hayworth Avenue and Hollywood Riviera Apartments 207, 208; comparing between Chesapeake Rodeo Apartments and Baldwin Hills Village 99, 100; comparing between Cheviot Manor Apartments and National Apartments 40, 41; comparing between Clark Court and Horatio West Court 141; comparing between Mar Vista Tract and Hirsh Tract 73

Period Revival era 173
players in the housing profession 3
podium apartment buildings 198, 199, 200, 201
Poles, Barnett B. 56
post and beam construction 73
"post-war minimal house" 54, 55
prefabricated housing 71
private financing, comparing between Cheviot Manor Apartments and National Apartments 33
private open space: comparing between 1060 South Cochran Avenue and Mackey Apartments 178; comparing between 1411 North Hayworth Avenue and Hollywood Riviera Apartments 210; comparing between Cheviot Manor Apartments and National Apartments 42, 43
"product types" 93
"Proliferating a Product Type" case study 13, 140; architectural style, comparing between projects 143; Clark Court 135; construction costs, comparing between projects 147; density, comparing between projects 156; development standards, comparing between projects 153, 154; funding, comparing between projects 147, 148; Horatio West Court 136; investment performance, comparing between projects 149, 150; lessons learned from 157; market timing, comparing between projects 146, 147; marketing and absorption, comparing between projects 148, 149; open space, comparing between projects 141; outcomes, comparing between projects 143, 150; parking, comparing between projects 141, 156; pedestrian access and entry, comparing between projects 141; real estate development, context for 144; site and building organization, comparing between projects 139; structure and materials, comparing between projects 141, 143; subdivision, comparing between projects 145, 146; unit types and amenities, comparing between projects 140, 141; zoning, comparing between projects 155, 156; *see also* Clark Court; Horatio West Court
"proto-dingbats" 22, 24, 26
public realm: comparing between 1060 South Cochran Avenue and Mackey Apartments 190, 191; comparing between Chesapeake Rodeo Apartments and Baldwin Hills Village 118; comparing between Mar Vista Tract and Hirst Tract 75

real estate development 2, 7; 1411 North Hayworth Avenue and Hollywood Riviera Apartments 212, 213, 214; biased outcomes 4; building permit fees 84n2; challenges faced in "good" housing production 3; Clark Court and Horatio West Court 144; Community Homes 71; definition of "good" housing 5; Julian Weinstock 215, 216; performance analysis 10; Samuel Sheff 27; using to support innovative design outcomes 230; *see also* construction costs; funding; market timing; marketing and absorption; subdivision; "Value Out of Balance" case study
recommendations for new housing 232, 233
Regional Planning Association of America 90
rental housing, FHA's promotion of 104
Riis, Jacob 151
Rubin, Barbara 46, 47

Schindler, Rudolph 71, 169, 170, 171, 173, 174, 192n5, 192n8
Section 608 projects, "mortgaging out" 112, 113
servantless homes 84n9
Sheff, Samuel 22, 24, 27, 33
Sherman, Moses H. 216
single-family house tracts 52, 53
site strategy: comparing between 1060 South Cochran Avenue and Mackey Apartments 175; comparing between Chesapeake Rodeo

Apartments and Baldwin Hills Village 97, 98; comparing between Cheviot Manor Apartments and National Apartments 39
Smiley, David 37, 69
Smith, Ira J. 181
Smutz, Huber 6
Soriano, Raphael 70
Spanish Colonial Revival style 179
Spaulding, Sumner 37, 69, 205
State Dwelling House Act 155
State Housing Manual 155
Stein, Clarence 90; "Radburn Plan" 97
stereotypes 2
St. Francis Court 133, 138
structure and materials: comparing between 1411 North Hayworth Avenue and Hollywood Riviera Apartments 210; comparing between Cheviot Manor Apartments and National Apartments 43; comparing between Clark Court and Horatio West Court 141, 143
stucco box apartments 198, 199
subdivision: comparing between 1060 South Cochran Avenue and Mackey Apartments 181, 182; comparing between 1411 North Hayworth Avenue and Hollywood Riviera Apartments 216; comparing between Cheviot Manor Apartments and National Apartments 29, 30; comparing between Clark Court and Horatio West Court 145, 146; comparing between Mar Vista Tract and Hirst Tract 56, 78

traditional styles, "Minimal Traditional" 55
"Type in Transition" case study 11, 12; Chernoff, Jack 37, 38; Cheviot Manor Apartments 22; construction costs 30, 31, 32; design, comparing between the National Apartments and the Cheviot Manor Apartments 39, 40, 41, 42, 43, 44; dingbat apartments 19, 20; emergence of dingbat apartments 20, 21; investment performance 34; land 29, 30; lessons learned from 47; market timing 30; marketing and absorption 33, 34; National Apartments 22; outcomes 43, 44; Phineas Kappe 28, 29; private financing 33; "proto-dingbats" 22, 24, 26; Raymond Kappe 28, 29; real estate development 26, 27; Samuel Sheff 27; style of dingbat apartments 20; zoning and development standards 35, 36, 37; *see also* Cheviot Manor Apartments; National Apartments

ULI (Urban Land Institute), *Community Builders Handbook* 76, 77
unit types and amenities: comparing between 1060 South Cochran Avenue and Mackey Apartments 175, 176; comparing between 1411 North Hayworth Avenue and Hollywood Riviera Apartments 207; comparing between Chesapeake Rodeo Apartments and Baldwin Hills Village 98, 99; comparing between Cheviot Manor Apartments and National Apartments 39, 40; comparing between Clark Court and Horatio West Court 140, 141
Urban, Clarence 183
urban planning 7, 34, 60; approval of by-design projects 8; biased outcomes 3, 4; challenges faced in "good" housing production 3; "Crafting Cost Benefit" case study, context for 219, 220, 221; definition of "good" housing 5; "Design Well-Timed" case study, context for 186, 187, 188, 189; "Lost in Translation" case study, context for 113, 114; performance analysis 10; "Proliferating a Product Type" case study, context for 150, 151; stereotypes 2; using to support innovative design outcomes 230, 231; using to support positive development outcomes 230; "Value Out of Balance" case study, context for 60, 61; *see also* "Lost in Translation" case study; needed housing types; zoning and development standards

"Value Out of Balance" case study 12; architectural style, comparing between projects 75; B. M. Edelman 77, 78; construction, comparing between projects 73; construction costs, comparing between projects 78, 79; density, comparing between projects 68; design, context for 69, 70, 71; design outcomes 75, 76; development outcomes 82; FHA underwriting criteria 62, 63, 65, 66; Harold Hirsh 77; height and setbacks, comparing between projects 68; house plans, comparing between projects 72; investment performance, comparing between projects 81, 82; lessons learned from 83; Los Angeles City Planning Department subdivision regulation 61, 62; market timing, comparing between projects 80; marketing and absorption, comparing between projects 79, 80; massing, comparing between projects 71, 72; mortgage insurance, comparing between projects 79; pedestrian access and entry, comparing between projects 73; planning outcomes 68, 69; public realm, comparing between projects 75; real estate development, context for 76, 77; spatial organization, comparing between projects 66, 67, 68; subdivision, comparing between projects 78; urban planning, context for 60, 61; yards and landscape, comparing between projects 73, 74, 75; zoning, comparing between projects 68; *see also* Mar Vista Tract; Hirsh Tract
vehicular access and parking: comparing between 1060 South Cochran Avenue and Mackey Apartments 176; comparing between 1411 North Hayworth Avenue and Hollywood Riviera Apartments 208, 209; comparing between Chesapeake Rodeo Apartments and Baldwin Hills Village 100, 101; comparing between Cheviot Manor Apartments and National Apartments 41
vernacular 139
vernacular modern style 43, 210
Village Green 12; *see also* "Lost in Translation" case study

Walters, William 33
Watson, Loyall F. 95
Weinstock, Julian 215, 216, 224n2
West, Horatio D. 136
West Hollywood apartment buildings 200, 201
Weston's Single and Double Bungalows 135, 168, 169
Williams, Paul R. 96, 173
Wilson, Lewis E. 90
Witmer, David J. 95
wood frame construction 73
Wright, Frank Lloyd 174
Wurster, William 69

yards and landscape, comparing between Mar Vista Tract and Hirst Tract 73, 74, 75

Zeiger, Mimi 20
zoning and development standards: comparing between 1060 South Cochran Avenue and Mackey Apartments 189, 190; comparing between 1411 North Hayworth Avenue and Hollywood Riviera Apartments 221, 222; comparing between Cheviot Manor Apartments and National Apartments 35, 36, 37; comparing between Clark Court and Horatio West Court 155, 156; comparing between Mar Vista Tract and Hirsh Tract 68; effect on dingbat apartment development 44, 45, 46, 47; Los Angeles' first comprehensive plan 21, 22

Made in the USA
Coppell, TX
23 June 2021

57918873R10144